Meal Prep Cookbook

by Wendy Jo Peterson MS, RDN

Meal Prep Cookbook For Dummies®

Published by: **John Wiley & Sons, Inc.,** 111 River Street, Hoboken, NJ 07030-5774, www.wiley.com

Copyright © 2021 by John Wiley & Sons, Inc., Hoboken, New Jersey

Published simultaneously in Canada

For general information on our other products and services, please contact our Customer Care Department within the U.S. at 877-762-2974, outside the U.S. at 317-572-3993, or fax 317-572-4002. For technical support, please visit https://hub.wiley.com/community/support/dummies.

Wiley publishes in a variety of print and electronic formats and by print-on-demand. Some material included with standard print versions of this book may not be included in e-books or in print-on-demand. If this book refers to media such as a CD or DVD that is not included in the version you purchased, you may download this material at http://booksupport.wiley.com. For more information about Wiley products, visit www.wiley.com.

Library of Congress Control Number: 2021942680

ISBN 978-1-119-81498-6 (pbk); ISBN 978-1-119-81499-3 (ebk); ISBN 978-1-119-81508-2 (ebk)

SKY10028560_072821

Contents at a Glance

Recipes at a Glance

Bowls

Main Dishes

Sides

Snacks

Desserts

Table of Contents

Introduction

When I was a kid, my mom was a pro at meal planning and meal prep. She worked full-time and had three kids to hustle around to activities. Plus, she was on a tight budget. I remember going to a big grocery store once a month with a long list and helping her find the matching coupons. Then we would go home and she would pre-portion out meats for the freezer and wash all her vegetables for easy use during the week. She always had lasagne, spaghetti sauce, or stuffed peppers in her freezer for those nights where life was busy and she needed ready-to-heat-and-eat meals. As I grew up and began my own family, I leaned on those meal-prep principles my mom shared with me, modifying them to meet the changing demands of my own busy family. As a dietitian who has worked with hundreds of families, I've listened to what works and what doesn't. We live in a busy society, and meal prep is one way to help us slow down and capture the importance of sitting down and enjoying a meal with less stress on our plates.

Maybe you manage a busy family, work long hours, or just want to eat out less. Whatever your reason, meal prep is appealing. By prepping for a couple days or a week, you take control of mealtime instead of allowing mealtime to take control of you. Consider this book as a gentle guide to encourage you to take your meal planning and meal prep to the next level, and stick with it!

This book offers a plethora of new and exciting recipes you can create in advance. You can do so much more than frozen pizzas and takeout — though both have their place! Meal prep can give you back time, add in valuable nutrient-dense foods, and take the guessing game out of weeknight meals. Meal prep can transform your busy weeknight schedule and give you back the time you crave.

All you need is the courage to plan for a week. Whether it's a sheet-pan meal, a quick salad, or a roast, your taste buds and wallet will thank you.

About This Book

Think of this book as your own personal coach to meal prep! It offers the tools you need to make meals that fit your lifestyle, your family, your dietary needs, and your schedule. In these pages, I get you ready to successfully meal-prep, whether for one week or eight.

Each recipe in this book is designed to meet you where you are today, both in terms of your confidence with cooking and your nutritional needs. I offer time-saving tips and notes throughout the book to ensure that you feel confident in making delicious meals for you and your family.

As you get ready to make the recipes in this book, sit down and plan for two, three, four, or more days to help make your life easier. Keep a grocery list, like the one in Appendix B, so you know what you have on hand and what you need to purchase to complete a meal. Read every recipe from beginning to end to ensure you have all the ingredients before you start your meal prep.

When it comes to the recipes, keep in mind the following:

>> Herbs may be fresh or dried — whatever you have on hand. Just remember that you should use three times as much fresh as you would use dry, because fresh herbs aren't as potent or concentrated. So, 1 teaspoon of dried herbs is equivalent to 1 tablespoon of fresh.

>> All temperatures are Fahrenheit. For conversion to Celsius, see Appendix A.

>> Vegetarian recipes are marked with the tomato icon (🍅) in the Recipes In This Chapter and Recipes in This Book lists.

Finally, within this book, you may note that some web addresses break across two lines of text. If you're reading this book in print and you want to visit one of these web pages, simply key in the web address exactly as it's noted in the text, pretending as though the line break doesn't exist. If you're reading this as an e-book, you've got it easy — just click the web address to be taken directly to the web page.

Foolish Assumptions

In writing this book, I made a few assumptions about you, the reader:

>> Your time is important to you, and you want to spend less time in the kitchen, from meal prepping to executing a meal.

>> You may be an experienced cook or a beginner. Whichever end of the spectrum you fall on (or somewhere in between), this book is for you!

>> Healthy, delicious meals are important to you and your family, and you don't have a ton of time on your hands to make them.

If this sounds like you, you've come to the right place!

Icons Used in This Book

Throughout this book, you'll see the following icons in the margin. Here's a guide to what the icons mean:

The Tip icon marks information that can save you time and money as you're planning, shopping for, and prepping meals in advance.

I use the Warning icon when I'm filling you in on important safety tips or tricks.

When I have an important message or reminder, I use the Remember icon.

Beyond the Book

In addition to the book you have in your hands, you can access some helpful extra content online. Check out the free Cheat Sheet for tips on keeping vegetables fresh, tips on freezing foods, and meal-prep hacks by going to www.dummies.com and entering **Meal Prep Cookbook For Dummies** in the Search box.

Where to Go from Here

If you're brand-new to meal planning and meal prep, spend some time getting to know the process in Part 1. If you're ready to start coming up with a meal plan, head to Part 2. Ready to start cooking? Parts 3, 4, and 5 are for you. Short on time? Part 6 sets you up with ten sauces to make meals pop, ten recipes for meal kits you can make at home, and more.

I hope you find family favorites, recipes you come back to again and again in this book and that it's the first book you pick up when life gets crazy and you need to focus on meal prep to get some sanity. Enjoy!

1

Getting Started with Meal Prep

IN THIS PART . . .

Discover what meal prep means to you.

Stock your kitchen and pantry with the right tools for meal prep.

Shop for groceries for the weeks ahead.

» **Figuring out which method is best for you**

Chapter **1**

Finding the Meal-Prep Method That's Right for You

In this chapter, I introduce you to a variety of styles of meal prep, from prepping all on one day to partial prep to freezing meals and batch cooking. There's no right way to do meal prep — it's more about figuring out what works best for you and your family. You can do all your meal prep on one day, or you can prep parts of a meal, or a combination of both.

REMEMBER

As you embark on the journey of meal planning and into meal prep, be sure to give yourself a little time, patience, and grace. Changing habits takes time, but the more you do it, the faster and easier it'll become.

MEAL PREP VERSUS MEAL PLANNING

Meal planning is planning which meals you want to make in the week ahead — lasagne on Monday, tacos on Tuesday, and so on. You can use your meal plan to create a grocery list so you have all the ingredients to make those meals.

Meal prep is actually preparing the meals. You can do meal prep in stages or all at once.

Meal planning and meal prep don't have to be complicated. You don't have to cook every day, and they aren't strictly set in stone. Instead, think of them as useful tools to help you create budget-friendly, healthy meals at home, instead of stressing about what you'll eat for every meal.

Prepping One Day, Eating for the Week

Whether it's just prepping breakfast, lunch, or even all your meals, some people enjoy cranking out meal prep in one day, so they only have to do minimal cooking throughout the week.

How to do it

With this approach, you start by planning however many meals you need for the week. Then you create a grocery list and go shopping. Finally, you prep as many of the components as you can for each meal. This may mean combining spices in advance, premeasuring and prechopping ingredients, labeling the items for the meal, and refrigerating together.

With this form of meal prep, consider prepping for three or four days at a time. This will give you room for leftovers or a change in plans that may prevent you from eating at home. Besides, most ingredients are best prepped only a couple days ahead of time in order to retain the freshness and integrity of the food.

Who it's for

If you have the mental bandwidth to plan and prep for the week, the time to prep one day a week, and little time for cooking during the week, this method is for you. I use this method of meal prep when I know I'll have very little time in the coming week, but I want to make sure we're eating at home. You can also use a variety of meal preps to help execute the full week of meals — from freezer meals to ready-to-eat meals.

TIP

If this style of meal prep makes you happy, consider checking out my dear friend and fellow chef and dietitian, Allison Schaaf, over at PrepDish.com (`https://prepdish.com`). She specializes in gluten-free meal prep, prepped one day and enjoyed for the week.

MEALS THAT GUIDE YOUR YEAR

On average, most Americans have about a dozen meals that they routinely make all year long. For instance, my mom would make spaghetti, sloppy joes, hamburgers, cream of turkey over biscuits, shake-and-bake chicken, stuffed peppers, tacos, chicken noodle soup, macaroni and cheese, pizza, grilled chicken, and fried chicken regularly — and I'm recounting this after 30 years of not living in her house! Humans like to eat what we're comfortable with and what's familiar. A great way to expand on this menu pattern is to create subtle changes in the menu. Take a moment and write down 12 meals you frequently make in your home.

Then work on revamping and revitalizing these meals with subtle changes. For instance, using my mom's meals as an example, here's how I would morph her standard meals and create new ones:

Instead of . . .	Try . . .
Spaghetti	Beef, mushroom, and kidney bean spaghetti
Sloppy joes	Southwestern turkey sloppy joes
Hamburgers	Greek lamb burgers
Cream of turkey over biscuits	Cream of turkey with peas over whole-grain biscuits
Shake-and-bake chicken	Shake-and-bake Mexican chicken
Stuffed peppers	Quinoa-stuffed peppers
Tacos	Fish tacos
Chicken noodle soup	Chicken and sweet potato soup
Macaroni and cheese	Butternut squash macaroni and cheese
Pizza	Whole-grain pizza
Grilled chicken	Grilled chicken with chimichurri sauce
Fried chicken	Fried chicken salad

Using a different spice blend, protein, or more vegetables can really transform a meal. Now you have 24 meals in your routine, instead of just 12!

Preportioning Meals

Another popular style of meal prep is where you prep meals in advance. Generally, people make one set meal and then place it in a container for the week, to be reheated or enjoyed cold.

How to do it

Make a stew, roast, or sheet-pan meal on one day. Then take that meal and preportion it into containers to eat for the week. You can also do this with breakfasts, salads, or bowls (see Part 3).

Who it's for

If you're okay with eating the same thing all week, if you prefer cooking only one day and reheating for a meal, or if you're really tight on time for the week, this approach is for you.

TIP

Be sure to get some variety. Eating the same thing for every dinner doesn't provide a variety of nutrients, so consider mixing up the proteins and vegetables each week to ensure you're getting enough nutrients.

WARNING

One potential downside to this approach is boredom. By day 3, the drive-thru may be more tempting than microwaving the same meal again or eating the same salad.

Batch Cooking

Batch cooking is a budget-friendly way to cook large portions of meat or vegetables and then create different meals with them for the week. Chapters 9–13 highlight ways to make popular large cuts of meat and ways the meats can be used in different meals to keep it fun and new.

How to do it

Batch cooking requires buying meat in bulk and spending a good amount of time to roast or pressure-cook the meat in advance. While the meat is cooking, you can utilize the time to prep meals you want to make with the meat for the week.

Who it's for

If you prefer to buy meat in bulk, if you have the time to slow-roast or cook the meat on one day, and if you don't mind eating the same meat all week, this method is for you. (You could also freeze the cooked meat and use it another week, if you don't want to eat the same meat all week.)

Prepping and Freezing

If you love your Instant Pot or slow cooker this may be the style of meal prep for you! You just need the freezer space to store the meals.

How to do it

Plan freezer-friendly, slow-cooker, or multicooker meals. Prep and place the meals in freezer bags, label the bags, and freeze them for another day within the next month.

Who it's for

If you don't have much time to meal-prep every week and you prefer to knock meals out for the month; if you have ample freezer space (like a deep freezer); or if you absolutely love stews, soups, and pot roasts, this method is for you. During cold months, this approach may be especially appealing; perhaps less so in the summer. Check out Chapters 7 and 15 if this method appeals to you. I like having these meals on hand; I work them in throughout the week to mix things up!

Making Sheet-Pan Meals

Sheet-pan meals have become incredibly popular and are super simple. The concept is that you have your protein, vegetables, and starch all on one sheet pan that roasts for the same time and yields a complete meal when it's done cooking. The trick is having each element cook at the same temperature and time, but the bonus is less cleanup!

How to do it

Plan a starch, protein, and vegetable that can cook at the same time and temperature (or head to Chapter 14 where I've done the work for you!). Prep each element in advance and store them together. (For example, marinate your vegetables, create a spice mix for your protein, and cut up potatoes and store them in water prior to cooking.) Then, when it's time to execute, place each element on a parchment-lined sheet pan, roast, and serve.

Who it's for

If you have the oven space, you're cooking for fewer than four people, if you have the time and refrigerator space to prep and store, and if you don't mind heating up your home with the oven, this method is for you.

TIP

If you have a larger family, you can use more sheet pans and oven racks.

Following a Formula

No, this method isn't about breaking out a scale and doing math equations! Instead, the formula is more about planning a protein, a starch, and a vegetable, and keeping it simple. Honestly, this is about 50 percent of how I do meal prep. Every week, I harvest vegetables or pick up something from my local farmer's market that inspires a meal. I keep meat stocked in my freezer that I pull out for the week. Then I find a yummy starch (rice, couscous, pasta, or potatoes) to pair with the meal. This is where sauces come in handy. Head to Chapter 20 where I highlight sauces just for these occasions.

How to do it

Get inspired by your local, in-season produce or protein deals at your favorite market. Create a meal plan that accounts for a protein, vegetables, and add a starch. From here, you can do partial prep for the week and pull together a quick meal. Having a well-stocked pantry is essential with this type of meal prep!

Who it's for

If you like to create meals from bargain buys or seasonal produce, if you get a community supported agriculture (CSA) box or you have a vegetable garden, if you buy meat in bulk and need to work through it in your freezer, or if the idea of this simple formula (protein + veggies + starch) appeals to you, this method is for you. Head to Chapters 16, 17, and 20 for recipes to start with.

Hammering Out "Build-Your-Own" Bars

Salad bars, potato bars, pizza bars, taco bars, sandwich bars . . . maybe meal prep in your house needs to speak to many different taste buds. If this is the case, creating a "bar" is a great approach.

How to do it

Let your family members build their own meals. Plan out your favorite toppings, prep them in separate containers for the meal, store them, and pull them out to serve. This can be the ultimate family-style dining experience. Taco bars, salad bars, and potato bars are my family's favorites for the week. Roasting potatoes in advance or using the microwave can make this bar come together quickly.

Who it's for

Creating bars can help win the war with picky eaters. As a dietitian and a parent, I encourage you to let go of the dinnertime battles and empower your kids to serve themselves what they want to eat. We follow Ellyn Satter's (www.ellynsatterin stitute.org) Division of Responsibility, which means parents get to decide what will be served, when, and where, and the kid gets to decide if they eat and how much. I recommend always serving something they like on the "bar" but letting go of any other battles around the food after that. There's a lot of sound research out there supporting the Division of Responsibility. If you have a picky eater, head to Ellyn's website for added support! Now, "bars" don't require recipes, but if this sounds like you, head to Chapters 16 and 17 for baked potato and seasonal salads inspiration!

HANDLING PICKY EATERS

When meal planning, consider everyone who eats with you. If you have a picky eater in the house, consider offering at least one to two food items that you know they'll eat, but continue to serve other options, as well. For example, if your picky eater likes apples, peanut butter, and yogurt, make sure you have two of those offered at the table for each meal. When you take the time to plan and prep for the week, make sure that meals fit the tastes of your family. You can also remove a lot of unwanted arguments and pressure around the table and mealtimes.

Get kids involved in the meal planning and preparation for the week. Even if a picky eater won't eat the food, it's okay for them to help prep it. Kids are far more capable than we realize. Have them help with making yogurt parfaits or overnight oats. Let them build their own salad in a jar — even if it's nothing but bacon and ranch! The more they're exposed to new foods, even by touching the foods, the better!

Chapter **2**

Knowing Which Supplies You Need

Having the right tool for the job can really help save time and energy when meal prepping. You may already have on hand some tools; others you may need to buy. Assess your kitchen and see if you have the storage space for some fancier items. A cluttered kitchen will leave you less inspired to cook, so skip any unnecessary tools and stick to the basics.

Must-Haves: Tools You Need for Meal Prep

When you're committed to meal prep, certain tools are just a requirement. The following sections cover those tools you need to meal-prep with ease.

Chef's knife

A chef's knife is an all-purpose knife, perfect for slicing and dicing vegetables, chopping meats, or chopping nuts. A 6- or 8-inch version is a great tool to have on hand, especially as your knife skills improve (see the nearby sidebar). For most home kitchens, a mid-priced knife is good enough. Many great brands are out there, from Wüsthof (www.wusthof.com) to Henckels (www.zwilling.com/us/henckels-international/cutlery).

SHARPENING YOUR KNIFE SKILLS

Learning how to hold and work a knife can make you much more efficient in the kitchen. In culinary school, knife skills are always taught within the first week and emphasized throughout all courses. The following photo shows how to hold a knife. In order to have a stable grip on a chef knife, grip the handle and inch your hand up toward the blade. Your thumb should be on the metal part of the blade, and your index finger should be gripped over the top of the knife. If you just hold the handle, the knife isn't as stable and can slip.

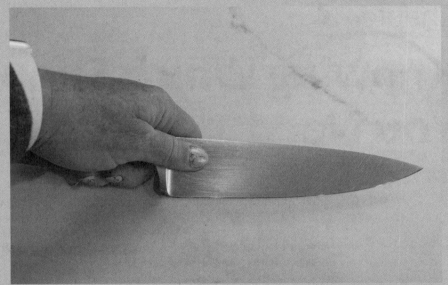

Photograph by Wendy Jo Peterson and Geri Goodale

Learning how to cut foods evenly helps with aesthetics but also with improved cooking times. Here are some popular cuts referred to in cookbooks, including this one (see the following photograph for what the cuts look like):

- **Julienne (top left):** Also referred to as matchsticks, these are narrow strips that are the same length and width. A thicker julienne cut could be referred to as a *bâtonnet*.

- **Chiffonade (top right):** This is when you roll up greens, like basil or kale or spinach, and do thin cuts to give a shredded appearance.

- **Brunoise (bottom left):** This is a tiny dice. Typically, you start with the julienne cut and then do a small dice from the narrow strips. These create uniformity in salads or soups.

- **Dice (bottom right):** Small, medium, or large diced items are squared pieces that are of equal size.

- **Rounds (bottom middle):** From carrots to cucumbers, slicing rounds is keeping the round shape, but slicing of equal thickness.

Photograph by Wendy Jo Peterson and Geri Goodale

Be sure to keep your knives sharp. A sharp knife is less likely to cause an accident than a dull blade. A dull blade can slip with pressure, possibly causing injury.

TIP

A knife that has the metal blade extend throughout the handle is more stable and less likely to break over time. Be sure to hand-wash a good knife and dry it immediately to extend the life of your knife.

Cutting board

Wooden cutting boards are my absolute favorite for cutting all foods. Using a good mineral oil on your clean cutting boards will help extend their life and prevent bacteria from inching its way into the grooves of the board. Wooden cutting boards are also friendly on your knives, unlike stone varieties.

If food contamination is an issue or concern, pick up colored plastic cutting boards and label them for the use (for example, green for vegetables and fruits, red for meats, yellow for poultry, blue for fish, and white for all other foods). A bonus to plastic cutting boards is that many are dishwasher safe!

Measuring spoons and cups

Pick up a set of volumetric measuring spoons and cups. The recipes in this book use the standard American tool for volumetric measuring.

Sheet pans

Having one good, heavy-duty aluminum sheet pan is especially useful if you enjoy sheet-pan meals! Nordic Ware (www.nordicware.com) is my top pick for sheet pans.

Baking dishes

Ideally, have a 9-x-13-inch casserole dish and either a 9-x-9-inch or an 8-x-8-inch casserole dish. Baking dishes are essential for meal prep and executing a fast meal.

TIP

Metal casserole dishes conduct heat better than tempered glass or stoneware, so depending on the pan you use, you may need to alter the bake time.

Muffin pans

Muffin pans aren't just for baking muffins. They're great for baking mini meat loaves, frittatas, or portioned-out items. If you're short on storage space, consider picking up silicone individual muffin holders — they're sturdy and they can be baked on a sheet pan instead.

Parchment paper

When it comes to easy clean up, parchment paper is a must-have kitchen buy. It's safe at high oven temperatures, and it helps keep foods from sticking to sheet pans while baking. Just make sure you don't mistake wax paper for parchment paper — they aren't the same thing!

Digital thermometer

Blame it on my culinary training, but I'm a firm believer that every kitchen needs a digital thermometer, particularly the instant-read variety. Whether you're checking to see if your meat loaf is fully cooked or whether your steak is cooked to perfection, having a thermometer on hand can save you from cutting into food to check for doneness and losing precious juices and drying out your food. Pick up a simple one by OXO (www.oxo.com) or a more expensive one by ThermoWorks (www.thermoworks.com); they range in price from $20 to $100.

Storage containers

When it comes to storage containers, you need two types:

TIP

>> **Silicone:** Reusable silicone storage containers are dishwasher, microwave, and often oven safe. They're also free of the harmful chemicals found in plastic products that can leach into your foods.

Some of my favorite products are Souper Cubes (www.soupercubes.com) for portioning out pasta sauce, soups, or stews and freezing to enjoy later. (re)zip (https://rezip.com) storage bags are leakproof and stand up for easy storage organization in the refrigerator. Net Zero Company (www.netzerocompany.com) makes stretchable silicone storage lids, which helps minimize the use of plastic wrap.

>> **Glass:** Glass storage containers are heat and cold safe. Glass is incredibly useful for storing prepped items and can be stacked neatly in the refrigerator for clean storage and food identification.

TIP

If you enjoy meal-prepping lunches, consider bento-box-style food storage containers like the ones from Bentgo (https://bentgo.com).

Mason jars

Mason jars are great for food storage and as a cooking vessel in both the oven and microwave. You can also save glass jars, such as pickle jars or jam jars, and use them for food storage, but don't assume you can heat them in the microwave or oven. Wide-mouthed Mason jars are great for soups and salads in a jar!

WARNING

Never heat or cook in jars that aren't tempered and oven safe. If you aren't sure whether your jar is oven safe, just use it for food storage.

Nice-to-Haves: Tools to Add to Your Wish List

Some kitchen tools make your life easier, but they aren't absolutely essential for meal prep. On the other hand, it's always nice to get a shiny new kitchen gadget. . . . So, if your family is asking for suggestions for your birthday, or you're just looking to treat yourself, read on.

Mandoline

A mini mandoline is useful for quickly slicing fruits and vegetables. The OXO V-Blade Mandoline Slicer (www.oxo.com/oxo-good-grips-v-blade-mandoline-slicer.html) is a time-saving tool for fast meal prep.

Spiralizer

Spiralized hard fruits and vegetables are fun and popular in the meal-prep world. This tool is fun, but not necessary, especially if space is limited. Don't fret if you don't have the space; you can find many pre-spiralized vegetables at grocery stores.

Silicone baking mats

The silicone version of parchment paper is easy to use, easy to clean, and good for about two years of regular use. It's best to only heat up to 450 degrees when using a silicone baking mat. Silicone is a nontoxic polymer made from sand. Silpat (www.silpat.com), a popular brand of silicone mats, can run from $15 to $30 per mat.

Food processor, blender, or immersion blender

This can be a splurge for many households, both in terms of price and space. But a high-powered blender or food processor is a time-saving tool for making salsas, soups, sauces, and smoothies. If space is limited, consider a handheld immersion blender (also referred to as a stick blender). Find one that fits your budget. Good brands to consider are Black & Decker (www.blackanddecker.com), Cuisinart (www.cuisinart.com), KitchenAid (www.kitchenaid.com), Ninja (www.ninjakitchen.com), and Vitamix (www.vitamix.com).

Food vacuum sealer

A food vacuum sealer removes air and vacuum seals food in plastic bags for long-term storage, whether freezing or in the pantry. Vacuum sealers are also useful for resealing cereal bags or cracker bags to keep them from going stale. My family buys our meats in bulk, and we use a vacuum sealer to help store them in our deep freezer.

If you have the space, a vacuum sealer can be useful. You can find a good one for less than $100.

Beeswax wraps

If you love to take sandwiches to go, pick up beeswax wraps or make your own! This is a great way to ditch single-use plastics.

TIP

To make your own beeswax wraps, you need 100 percent cotton fabric, scissors, beeswax pellets, a baking sheet, parchment paper, and a spatula. Then follow these steps:

1. **Cut the fabric to your preferred size.**

2. **Place a piece of parchment paper on a baking sheet and preheat the oven to 180 degrees.**

3. **Place the fabric on the parchment paper, and sprinkle with 2 to 3 tablespoons beeswax pellets.**

4. **Place another piece of parchment paper on top of the beeswax pellets.**

5. **Place the baking sheet into the oven for 3 to 4 minutes or until the pellets have melted.**

6. **Remove the baking sheet from the oven and, with the parchment paper still on top, use a spatula to spread the beeswax.**

7. **After the beeswax has cooled, remove it from the parchment paper.**

You can wash the towels in cold water up to 50 times before you need to toss them.

Multicooker

A multicooker utilizes pressure to quickly cook food. It's a useful tool to get your typical slow-cooked foods on the table in a fraction of the time. If you're cooking for two people, a mini 3-quart pot can be sufficient; if you're cooking for a larger family, you may want to invest in an 8-quart multicooker.

TIP

For most of the recipes in this book, I used a 6-quart Instant Pot. Even if budget isn't an issue, I still recommend the basic Duo Instant Pot over the newer, more expensive models.

REMEMBER

When using a multicooker be sure to read the user manual that comes with your appliance. Pressure cookers take time to come to pressure and time for the pot to depressurize after cooking. This time varies based on the temperature of the food you're cooking and your altitude.

Chapter **3**

Going Shopping

Navigating a grocery store has changed a lot over the past couple decades, and even more during the pandemic. In this chapter, you explore different avenues for shopping. I also give you tips for shopping on a budget. After you've figured out where to shop, you're ready to stock your kitchen!

Navigating the Grocery Store

In this section, I dive into the variety of grocery stores available in the United States. Of course, this information will vary if you live in a more a rural setting versus a major metropolitan area, so keep those differences in mind.

Standard grocery stores

Your neighborhood market is close and ready to serve you. Standard grocery chains often highlight their deals with bins, placement in the markets, or with weekly ads. You can also save a lot of money by becoming a free member, if it's offered. Taking the time to compare prices and plan meals based on what's on sale is a great way to keep your grocery budget in check.

SHOPPING FOR BARGAINS

You can bargain-shop at almost any grocery store, as long as you pay attention. If you happen to have a bargain grocery store near you, such as a warehouse market or a discount grocery chain, be sure to watch their weekly advertisements for the best buys. These markets may require you to become a member.

Be sure to check the unit price of an item. Sometimes those big cans can look like they're a better price, but if you check the unit price, it could be more expensive. Most markets list unit price under the price of the item on the shelf.

The unit price is often printed on the price tag on the store shelf, but if it isn't, you can calculate it yourself. To do so, divide the total price by the quantity. For example, if a 28-ounce jar is $1.29 the unit price would be $1.69 ÷ 28 = $0.06 per ounce. If the 14.5-ounce jar is $1.19, then the unit price would be $1.19 ÷ 14.5 = $0.08 per ounce. So, in this example, the larger can is the better price.

Store brands are often a great way to get a bargain buy, but check the nutrition labels to make sure the product has the same ingredients as your favorite brand.

Be sure to check expiration dates! If you overlook the expiration date, you may get home and realize your package of meat needs to be frozen or used by tomorrow.

Bulk food stores

Some major retailers, such as Costco, are known for bulk buying. Shopping at these stores is a great way to save money if you have the space to store bulk items and you have a lot of hungry mouths to feed. Look for store brands for the best deals and the greatest savings.

Costco's much-loved rotisserie chicken deal is actually a loss financially for the chain, but they know it gets you in the door and that you're (most likely) going to shop for other items while you're there.

These chains have really stepped up their quality and offerings in the past decade, with more organic items and expanded frozen and packaged goods. From a bargain perspective, they can save you a ton of money.

WARNING

If you don't have the space to store all that food, bulk buying isn't a good idea. A cluttered home or kitchen will most likely hinder you from wanting to meal-prep or cook. Plus, if you bulk buy a lot of food, you may not have the room in your refrigerator or freezer to store prepped meals. Consider your space before bulk buying.

Grocery delivery services

With the pandemic, many people wanted to avoid grocery stores entirely. Meal delivery services — such as from Amazon and Instacart — may be limited to bigger cities and may include an annual fee. Although they're handy, they aren't for the savvy bargain shopper.

I've used Instacart when I needed to get groceries and didn't have the time to make it to a grocery store, or when I didn't want to drag my young child into the market and have her hands everywhere (and then in her mouth).

A pitfall to grocery delivery services is that you don't know who's selecting your groceries, so if you're highly selective about your tomatoes and how to pick a watermelon, this may frustrate you. Overall, I like delivery services, and I think they'll only expand and improve in the years to come.

Community supported agriculture and farmer's markets

Find out if your area has a farmer's market, selling locally sourced produce, meat, dairy, or baked goods. Often, local products can be fresher, more nutrient-dense (due to reduced travel time), and less expensive. Plus, you can meet the local farmers and get to know their practices, which can connect you more to your food and community.

If driving to a farmer's market is tough, consider checking out a community supported agriculture (CSA). CSAs can work in a few ways. For instance, some CSAs require you to buy into an annual or biannual share, where you receive various goods throughout the year. Some CSAs have a weekly box, where it's whatever is grown seasonally and harvested that week, often delivered to your home or a nearby drop spot where you can pick up your box on a set day. If you're in a larger agricultural area, you may even have CSA boxes that allow you to pick which items you get each week. Our local CSA allows me to add on baked goods, meats, and even prepared foods. During the pandemic, our CSA has been a great way to minimize person-to-person contact and still support our local farmers.

TIP

If you're interested in learning more about CSAs in your area, check out www.localharvest.org.

Building a Well-Stocked Kitchen

Keeping a well-stocked kitchen helps not only during a pandemic, but with meal planning and prep. The pantry, the refrigerator, and the freezer all have useful food items that are useful to keep on hand, from condiments to grains.

Pantry essentials

Don't mistake a pantry that's bursting with food for a well-stocked pantry. If you can't see it, you may forget you have it. Take time to organize your pantry and keep in mind the rule of FIFO: First In, First Out (meaning, using the items you purchased first before using your new items). Check the expiration dates to decide which product you'll use first and to further avoid food waste.

Here are the items you need for a well-stocked pantry:

>> **Bread:** Flat breads, sandwich breads, tortillas, buns, and so on (**Note:** These may need to be stored in the freezer for longer storage times.)

>> **Beans:** Canned or dried, your favorite varieties

>> **Pastas:** Dried shapes of choice

>> **Rice:** White, brown, jasmine, or basmati

>> **Grains:** Farro, couscous, bulgur, quinoa, and so on

>> **Flours:** All-purpose, whole-wheat pastry flour, almond flour, and so on

>> **Broths or stocks:** Beef, chicken, or vegetable

>> **Baking essentials:** Baking soda, baking powder, and sugars

>> **Cereals:** Hot or cold varieties

>> **Oils:** Avocado, extra-virgin olive oil, grapeseed oil, canola oil

>> **Vinegars:** Red wine, white wine, balsamic, and so on

>> **Canned goods:** Tomatoes, olives, artichokes, capers, red peppers, corn, beans, and so on

>> **Canned meats:** Tuna, sardines, anchovies, chicken, and so on

>> **Nuts or nut butters:** Peanut butter, almonds, walnuts, pistachios, hazelnuts, and so on

>> **Sauces or marinades:** Barbecue, Italian dressing, marinade packets, low-sodium soy sauce, and so on

>> **Spices:** Salt, pepper, cinnamon, cumin, coriander, cayenne, garlic powder, and so on (see the nearby sidebar for tips on making your own spice mixes)

MAKING YOUR OWN SPICE MIXES

Upcycle glass jars to create your own spice mixes. Here are some favorites to keep on hand:

- **Taco seasoning:** 2 tablespoons chili powder, 2 teaspoons garlic powder, 1 teaspoon paprika, 2 teaspoons cumin, 1 teaspoon onion powder, 1 tablespoon oregano, ½ teaspoon ground pepper, and 1 teaspoon salt

- **Ranch seasoning:** 2 tablespoons dried parsley, 1 tablespoon dried chives, 1 tablespoon dried dill weed, 2 teaspoons garlic powder, 2 teaspoons onion powder, 1 teaspoon salt, and ½ teaspoon ground pepper

- **Chili seasoning:** 3 tablespoons chili powder, 2 teaspoons garlic powder, 2 teaspoons cumin, 2 teaspoons oregano, 1 teaspoon ground coriander, and 1 teaspoon onion powder

- **Barbecue seasoning:** 1 tablespoon ground pepper, 2 tablespoons chili powder, 1 tablespoon garlic powder, 1 tablespoon paprika, 1 tablespoon onion powder, 2 tablespoons brown sugar, and 1 tablespoon salt

- **Italian seasoning:** 1 tablespoon dried oregano, 1 tablespoon dried parsley, 1 tablespoon dried thyme, 2 teaspoons dried basil, 1 teaspoon garlic powder, 1 teaspoon ground pepper, and 1 teaspoon salt

Remember: You can change an entire meal, just by shifting the spices!

Fridge-friendly staples

Use bowls, baskets, or shelf organizers to help group similar items together, from fruits and vegetables to snacks. Using glass or clear storage containers can help you identify items quickly.

WARNING

Keeping a refrigerator door open too long can increase the temperature and spoil food faster. Be sure to keep the doors securely closed to keep the foods in a safe temperature zone. The ideal temperature range for a refrigerator is 34 to 37 degrees.

Here are products to keep stocked in the refrigerator:

- **Dairy products:** Milks, yogurts, butters, cheeses.
- **Fresh fruit:** Apples, citrus, precut fruit.
- **Fresh vegetables:** Boxed lettuce, onions, celery, carrots, cucumbers, pre-chopped vegetables

>> **Condiments:** Dressings, ketchup, mustard, mayonnaise, soy sauce, Worcestershire sauce, hot sauce, Sriracha, and so on.

>> **Jams or jellies.**

>> **Fresh herbs:** Place cut herbs in a glass of water and cover with a plastic bag to prolong shelf life.

>> **Beverages.**

>> **Eggs.**

>> **Lunch meat.**

Freezer wise buys

Keeping your freezer well stocked can make meal planning a breeze. Here are items to keep on hand:

>> **Meats**
- Chicken (whole, breasts, and thighs)
- Beef (steaks, ground, and roasts)
- Pork (chops, tenderloins, and ground)
- Sausage (kielbasa and breakfast)
- Bacon

>> **Seafood**
- Shrimp
- Fish sticks

>> **Vegetables**
- Mirepoix (mix of onions, carrots, and celery)
- Broccoli
- Green beans
- Soup mix
- Peas
- Edamame
- Spinach

» **Starches**

- Rice

- Potatoes (hash browns or chopped)

- Breads

- Tortillas

- Pie crusts

» **Fruits**

- Berries

- Smoothie blends

- Bananas

- Wild blueberries

» **Premixed soups**

» **Pizza**

» **Sweets**

SAVING TIME WITH CONVENIENCE FOODS

While stocking your kitchen with meal prep in mind, consider these convenience items to help shave time in the kitchen:

- **Fruit and veggie trays:** If you're having trouble eating more fruits and vegetables, consider keeping a tray of precut fruits and vegetables. This can be store-bought or made by you!

- **Boxed greens:** Lettuce, kale, spinach, and mixed greens make for simple salads or bowls.

- **Hummus:** Great as a dip for vegetables or add to a sandwich.

- **Pizza dough:** Turn it into a flatbread side dish or create a main dish pizza loaded with veggies any night of the week.

- **Boxed broth:** Great for making sauces or simple soups.

- **Marinades or sauces:** From barbecue sauce to Italian dressing, find your favorites to keep on hand.

- **Rotisserie chicken:** Check out Chapter 12 for delicious ways to use a roasted chicken.

Shopping with the Seasons

Berries may sound delicious in the winter, but they really aren't in season in the Unitec States during the colder months. You may opt to buy berries in the winter, but they'll be a lot pricier and, honestly, probably not as nutrient-dense as you may think. For produce to get to our markets off season, they're most likely grown in Mexico or South America. Then they're shipped long distances to get to our tables. During this process, vegetables and fruits succumb to oxidation and lose some nutritional density along the way.

There are many positive aspects to shopping local and in-season produce. The less distance the food has to travel, the better the price and nutrient density.

Here's a condensed version of seasonal produce around the United States. If you're in the southern or western states, this list may vary. Check with your local farmer's market to know what and when produce grows best for your area.

» **Spring:** Apricots, artichokes, arugula, asparagus, butter lettuce, cabbage, citrus, fava beans, fennel, green beans, peas, pineapple, rhubarb, spinach, Swiss chard, watercress

» **Summer:** Avocados, beets, bell peppers, berries, cherries, corn, cucumber, eggplant, grapes, green beans, melons, okra, peppers, stone fruit, summer squash, tomatoes, watermelon

» **Fall:** Apples, broccoli, Brussels sprouts, cauliflower, cabbage, grapes, lettuce, pears, plums, winter squashes, turnips

» **Winter:** Citrus, collard greens, kale, kiwi, leeks, sweet potatoes, rutabaga, winter squash, turnips

2

Jumping into Meal Planning

Create a meal plan right for you and your family.

Discover ways to accommodate allergies and other special meal-planning needs.

Chapter **4**

Meeting the Meal Plans

Meal prep is simply batch cooking or preparing foods in advance for the week. In this chapter, I offer more than 40 meals ideas — eight weeks of five meals per week. You can choose how much prep you do in advance, but for consistency, I suggest the meal prep you can do, in most cases, in less than two hours. The idea behind these menus is to prepare for a couple hours in advance to significantly cut the time you spend on meal prep throughout the week. (The only exceptions are the days when you roast meat or poultry for the week.)

I also include one week focused on families. In reality, kids can eat the same foods as the rest of the family, but we all know most kids love to eat certain kinds of foods, so I offer a plan focused on those recipes. Feel free to modify the plan to meet your child's unique demands, er, needs.

REMEMBER

Most prepped foods are good for three to five days in the refrigerator. The fifth day can really push the limits of quality for many foods. Taking this into considera-tion, I provide a lot of frozen options on the fifth day.

These weeks are not meant to be eaten consecutively. You can pick and choose each week, as you like. You can easily make adjustments based on the season or what's on sale. Turn to Chapter 3 for seasonal considerations to help you pick the right produce for seasonal meal planning!

TIP

Week 1: Plant Forward

Plant-forward eating emphasizes fruits and vegetables, with an accent of meat. When serving up a plant-based meal, consider meat as a side dish. The stars of the plate are the plants — including beans, grains, seeds, nuts, fruits, and vegetables. Plant-forward eating can be high in fiber, heart-healthy, and nutrient-dense. To discover more of the benefits of plant-forward eating, check out `https://fruitsandveggies.org/plant-forward-eating-guide` from the Produce for Better Health Foundation.

Here's what the week looks like:

>> **Monday:** Serve Mediterranean Quinoa Bowls (Chapter 8).

>> **Tuesday:** Serve Lemony Salmon and Asparagus (Chapter 14) and tomato bread. Also, transfer the Creamy Peanut Chicken from the freezer to the refrigerator for Wednesday.

>> **Wednesday:** Serve Creamy Peanut Chicken (Chapter 15), Lemony Broccoli (Chapter 17), and rice.

>> **Thursday:** Serve Skewer-Free Chicken Kabobs (Chapter 14) and flatbread. Also, transfer the Springtime Pea Soup from the freezer to the refrigerator for Friday.

>> **Friday:** Serve Springtime Pea Soup (Chapter 7) and either crusty French bread or grilled-cheese sandwiches.

To prep for this week, do the following on Sunday:

TIP

>> Cook the quinoa and refrigerate for Monday.

>> Place the salmon on ice in the refrigerator for Tuesday.

>> Clean the asparagus and refrigerate for Tuesday.

>> Prepare the Creamy Peanut Chicken and freeze for Wednesday.

>> Prechop and wash the broccoli and refrigerate for Wednesday.

>> Marinate the chicken and vegetables for Thursday.

>> Prepare and freeze the Springtime Pea Soup for Friday.

>> Ready the cheese and herb topping and refrigerate for Friday.

Week 2: Meat Eater's Delight

If you consider a meal without meat just a snack, this meal plan is for you! Just because meat takes center stage, doesn't mean that it's lacking in nutrient-dense vegetables. It's all about how you pair the plate. Meat lovers are sure to love this menu, which kicks off with Roasted Brisket (Chapter 10).

Here's what the week looks like:

>> **Monday:** Serve Street Tacos (Chapter 10) and Zesty Cabbage Slaw (Chapter 17).

>> **Tuesday:** Serve Peachy Pork Tenderloin with Green Beans and Carrots (Chapter 14) and rice.

>> **Wednesday:** Serve French Dip Sandwiches (Chapter 10) and Garlicky Greens (Chapter 17). Also, transfer the Beef Paprikash from the freezer to the refrigerator for Thursday.

>> **Thursday:** Serve Beef Paprikash (Chapter 15), Braised Cabbage (Chapter 17), and French bread.

>> **Friday:** Serve Loaded Baked Potatoes (Chapter 16) and a side salad.

TIP

To prep for this week, do the following on Sunday:

>> Make Roasted Brisket (Chapter 10).

>> Prepare the Zesty Cabbage Slaw and refrigerate for Monday.

>> Prep the Peachy Pork Tenderloin for Tuesday.

>> Precut and wash the carrots and green beans for Tuesday.

>> Prewash the kale greens for Wednesday and store wrapped in a paper towel in a plastic bag.

>> Prepare and freeze the Beef Paprikash for Thursday.

>> Prepare your favorite baked potato toppings and refrigerate for Friday.

Week 3: Bring on the Bowls

Bowls consist of a grain base, topped with protein foods and loaded with vegetables. Bowls are great for families because everyone can decide which items they want to add to their bowl. They're also great for grab-and-go lunches because you can pre-assemble heat-safe items and then keep the fresh toppings on the side for assembly at lunchtime.

Here's what the week looks like:

>> **Monday:** Serve Southwestern Bowls (Chapter 8).

>> **Tuesday:** Serve Korean Spiced Bowls (Chapter 8).

>> **Wednesday:** Serve Chinese Chicken Slaw Bowls (Chapter 8).

>> **Thursday:** Serve Thai Steak Salad (Chapter 8). Also, transfer the Hearty Bean Chili from the freezer to the refrigerator for Friday.

>> **Friday:** Serve Hearty Chili with Beans (Chapter 7).

TIP

To prep for this week, do the following on Sunday:

>> Roast a chicken or purchase a rotisserie chicken, shred the meat, and place it in two separate containers for Monday and Wednesday.

>> Cook the rice for Monday and Tuesday.

>> Prepare the peanut dressing for Thursday.

>> Prepare and freeze the Hearty Chili with Beans for Friday.

Week 4: Savoring the Southwest

Beans, spiced meats, and fresh elements like corn, carrots, cilantro, and tomatoes are stars of the Southwest. These meals are packed with bold, smoky flavors. Skip the Mexican restaurants and make this meal plan instead!

Here's what the week looks like:

>> **Monday:** Serve Carnitas (Chapter 11) and Carrot and Cilantro Salad (Chapter 17).

>> **Tuesday:** Serve Fiesta Taco Salad (Chapter 8). Also, defrost the empanada wrappers.

>> **Wednesday:** Serve Pork and Beans Empanadas (Chapter 11) and a side salad.

>> **Thursday:** Serve Tortilla Soup (Chapter 12). Also, transfer the Chicken and Roasted Poblano Soup from the freezer to the refrigerator for Friday.

>> **Friday:** Serve Chicken and Roasted Poblano Soup (Chapter 7) and either quesadillas or grilled-cheese sandwiches.

TIP

To prep for this week, do the following on Sunday:

>> Roast a chicken or purchase a rotisserie chicken, shred the meat, place into two separate containers for Thursday and Friday, and refrigerate.

>> Cook the Braised Pork Butt (Chapter 11). Divide the meat into two separate containers for Monday and Wednesday, and refrigerate.

>> Cook the meat, drain and rinse the beans, and ready the ingredients for the bowls for Tuesday.

>> Prep the empanada filling for Wednesday.

>> Prepare and freeze the Chicken and Roasted Poblano Soup for Friday.

Week 5: Globe Trotting

Explore the flavors of the world with this menu plan, which has touches of the Mediterranean as well as India. These meals can transport you to different places in the world with each bite. This meal plan uses the freezer and is perfect for those who have a busy week ahead.

Here's what the week looks like:

>> **Monday:** Serve Moroccan Mini Meatloaves with Cauliflower (Chapter 14). Also, transfer the Chicken Cacciatore from the freezer to the refrigerator for Tuesday.

>> **Tuesday:** Serve Chicken Cacciatore (Chapter 15) and Parmesan Spiralized Zucchini Noodles (Chapter 17). Also, transfer the Butter Chicken from the freezer to the refrigerator for Wednesday.

>> **Wednesday:** Serve Butter Chicken (Chapter 15), rice, and steamed cauliflower, broccoli, or green beans. Transfer the Tuscan Kale and Potato Soup from the freezer to the refrigerator for Thursday.

>> **Thursday:** Serve Tuscan Kale and Potato Soup (Chapter 7) and French bread. Transfer the Mediterranean White Bean Soup from the freezer to the refrigerator for Friday.

>> **Friday:** Serve Mediterranean White Bean Soup (Chapter 7) and cheesy garlic bread.

TIP

To prep for this week, do the following on Sunday:

>> Mix together the meat loaf ingredients and refrigerate for Monday.

>> Wash and cut the cauliflower for Monday.

>> Spiralize or purchase spiralized zucchini for Tuesday.

>> Prep and freeze the Chicken Cacciatore for Tuesday.

>> Wash and cut the vegetables for Wednesday.

>> Prep and freeze the Butter Chicken for Wednesday.

>> Prep and freeze the Tuscan Kale and Potato Soup for Thursday.

>> Prep and freeze the Mediterranean White Bean Soup for Friday.

Week 6: Simply Sheet Pan

Sheet-pan meals are fast with minimal cleanup. Prepping ahead saves you even more time, but if you find yourself unable to prep ahead, this meal plan is still quick to pull together with minimal prep work needed to complete the meals.

Here's what the week looks like:

>> **Monday:** Serve Baked Salmon with Capers and Zucchini (Chapter 14).

>> **Tuesday:** Serve Sage-Spiced Chicken and Butternut Squash (Chapter 14) and Nutty Herbed Couscous (Chapter 17).

>> **Wednesday:** Serve Meatballs and Caramelized Onion Green Beans (Chapter 14).

>> **Thursday:** Serve Sausage and Bell Peppers (Chapter 14) and Tropical Fruit Salad (Chapter 17).

>> **Friday:** Serve Sheet-Pan Mediterranean Pasta (Chapter 14).

TIP

To prep for this week, do the following on Sunday:

>> Place the salmon on ice in the refrigerator for Monday.

>> Prep the zucchini for Monday.

>> Wash and cut the butternut squash and refrigerate for Tuesday.

>> Prep the spices for Tuesday.

>> Mix together the meatball ingredients and refrigerate for Wednesday.

>> Wash and cut the bell peppers for Thursday. Place in an airtight container with a piece of paper towel and refrigerate.

>> Place the ingredients for the Sheet-Pan Mediterranean Pasta (except the pasta) into the roasting dish and cover with plastic wrap. Refrigerate for Friday.

Week 7: 20-Minute Meals

If you have no time to prep meals, this meal plan is for you! Each meal takes 20 minutes from start to finish! If you prep ahead just a little you can shave off more valuable minutes during the week.

Here's what the week looks like:

>> **Monday:** Serve Zesty Bean and Cheese Tostadas (Chapter 16) and Tropical Fruit Salad (Chapter 17).

>> **Tuesday:** Serve Pan-Fried Burgers with Creamy Feta Green Salad (Chapter 16).

>> **Wednesday:** Serve Cilantro Shrimp with Spicy Guacamole (Chapter 16) and Carrot and Cilantro Salad (Chapter 17).

>> **Thursday:** Serve Smoked Salmon Pasta with Greens (Chapter 16).

>> **Friday:** Serve Dinner Charcuterie Board (Chapter 16).

TIP

To prep for this week, do the following on Sunday:

>> Drain and rinse beans and set aside for Monday.

>> Prepare Tropical Fruit Salad for Monday.

>> Prepare raw burger patties for Tuesday. Place on a plate with parchment paper and cover with plastic wrap. Prepare the dressing for the salad.

>> Pull items together for the Dinner Charcuterie Board on Friday and place in the refrigerator.

Week 8: Family Focused

All foods are fit for a family, and kids can eat what you eat. However, I understand that there are foods that kids absolutely love. This meal plan consists of some of my daughter's favorites, like pot pie and Turkey and Noodles. It also consists of foods where kids have the power to choose what goes on top of their salad or on their tostada. Empowering kids to get involved with meal preparation and building their own plate encourages them to try new foods. If you have a child who is excited about meal prep, have them help you with the Zesty Bean and Cheese Tostadas. It's a great beginner meal for dashing young cooks!

Here's what the week looks like:

>> **Monday:** Serve Turkey and Broccoli Pot Pie (Chapter 9).

>> **Tuesday:** Serve Beefy Chop House Salad (Chapter 8).

>> **Wednesday:** Serve Turkey and Noodles (Chapter 9) and raw veggies with ranch dip.

>> **Thursday:** Serve Zesty Bean and Cheese Tostadas (Chapter 16).

>> **Friday:** Serve Caprese Pasta (Chapter 16) with cheesy garlic bread.

To prep for this week, do the following on Sunday:

>> Prep the Turkey and Broccoli Pot Pie and refrigerate to be baked on Monday.

>> Roast a turkey, shred the meat, and refrigerate for Wednesday.

>> Prepare the ingredients for the Beefy Chop House Salad on Tuesday. (Leave deconstructed and let the kids create their own salad bowls with the ingredients they choose.)

>> Wash and prep your child's favorite raw vegetables and fruits to be enjoyed all throughout the week. If they're hungry while you pull together a meal, you can pull this tray out and they can snack while you prepare the meal.

Always serve at least one thing you know your kids will enjoy at every meal. This strategy will help them feel comfortable to enjoy the meal. Consider serving cut raw vegetables with dip, fresh fruit, and/or yogurt with every meal.

IN THIS CHAPTER

» Following the Mediterranean Diet

» Going gluten-free

» Choosing low-carb options

» Skipping dairy

» Planning meals the vegetarian way

Chapter **5**

Planning Meals When You Follow a Special Diet

When you or someone you love has dietary restrictions, you may feel especially stressed about prepping meals. Never fear! In this chapter, I offer meal plans that can help you meet a variety of dietary needs and keep everyone happy. As a dietitian, I work with clients who have varying dietary needs, and the recipes in this book can satisfy their dining requests or preferences.

Mediterranean Diet

The Mediterranean Diet is a plant-forward or plant-focused way of eating. If someone in your family is on a heart-healthy meal plan, these menu options are a great starting point. As one of the authors of the *Mediterranean Diet Cookbook For Dummies* (Wiley), I naturally gravitate toward creating recipes with Mediterranean flair! If this style of eating speaks to your heart, you'll find ample recipes with a focus on fruits, vegetables, legumes, extra-virgin olive oil, and seafood here.

Here's what the week looks like:

>> **Monday:** Serve Mediterranean Quinoa Bowls (Chapter 8).

>> **Tuesday:** Serve Baked Salmon with Capers and Zucchini (Chapter 14) and French bread. Also, transfer the Greek Meatballs in Tomato Sauce from the freezer to the refrigerator for Wednesday.

>> **Wednesday:** Serve Greek Meatballs in Tomato Sauce (Chapter 15) with Simple Salads for All Four Seasons (Chapter 17). Also, transfer the Chicken Cacciatore from the freezer to the refrigerator for Thursday.

>> **Thursday:** Serve Chicken Cacciatore (Chapter 15) with a side dish of pasta.

>> **Friday:** Serve Canned Tuna Niçoise Salad (Chapter 8) and either crusty French bread or grilled-cheese sandwiches (call them panini if you want to feel Mediterranean).

TIP

To prep for this week, do the following on Sunday:

>> Cook the quinoa and refrigerate for Monday.

>> Place the salmon on ice in the refrigerator for Tuesday.

>> Clean and prep the zucchini and refrigerate for Tuesday.

>> Prepare the Greek Meatballs in Tomato Sauce for Wednesday.

>> Prepare the Cacciatore for Thursday.

>> Prep one of the Simple Salads for All Four Seasons for Wednesday.

>> Prep the salad ingredients for Friday.

TIP

If you're looking for ideas for breakfast, lunch, or dessert, check out the following:

>> **Breakfast:** Yogurt Parfaits (Chapter 6), Breakfast Quinoa Porridge (Chapter 6), and Greek Yogurt Deviled Eggs (Chapter 6)

>> **Lunch:** Mediterranean White Bean Soup (Chapter 7) and Mediterranean Quinoa Bowls (Chapter 8)

>> **Dessert:** Chocolate Avocado Mousse (Chapter 19), Strawberries with Mascarpone, Basil, and Balsamic (Chapter 19), and Grilled Peaches with Amaretti Cookies (Chapter 19)

Gluten-Free Considerations

If you're creating a menu that's strictly gluten-free, familiarize yourself with the ingredients label. Look for packages that state "gluten free," which is a labeling term monitored by the Food and Drug Administration (FDA). Areas where gluten can "sneak" into foods include broths, anything with malt or malt extracts, packaged goods, and many other foods.

WARNING

Watch out for cross-contamination. Cross-contamination can occur when a food with gluten is prepped, served, or stored and accidently contaminates a gluten-free food. An example would be cutting bread on a cutting board, and then cutting vegetables on that same cutting board without thoroughly washing it first. Even the smallest amounts of gluten can make some people very sick. When preparing the following meals, be sure to check the nutrition labels yourself, just in case. For more help, check out the Celiac Disease Foundation and their meal plan ideas at https://celiac.org/eat-gluten-free/meal-plans/7-day-meal-plan or pick up *Gluten-Free Cooking For Dummies* by Danna Korn and Connie Sarros (Wiley).

Here's what the week looks like:

>> **Monday:** Serve Carnitas (Chapter 11) and Zesty Cabbage Slaw (Chapter 17).

>> **Tuesday:** Serve Sage-Spiced Chicken and Butternut Squash (Chapter 14) with quinoa.

>> **Wednesday:** Serve Cilantro Shrimp with Spicy Guacamole and Chips (Chapter 16). Also, transfer Hearty Chili with Beans from the freezer to the refrigerator for Thursday.

>> **Thursday:** Serve Hearty Chili with Beans (Chapter 7) and corn chips. Also, transfer the Butter Chicken from the freezer to the refrigerator for Friday.

>> **Friday:** Serve Butter Chicken (Chapter 15), Cilantro Lime Rice (Chapter 17), and Lemony Broccoli (Chapter 17).

TIP

To prep for this week, do the following on Sunday:

>> Bake the pork for Carnitas and refrigerate for Monday.

>> Prepare Zesty Cabbage Slaw and refrigerate for Monday.

>> Cut up the butternut squash (or buy previously chopped butternut squash) and refrigerate with the defrosted chicken for Tuesday.

>> Prepare and freeze Hearty Chili with Beans for Thursday.

>> Prepare and freeze Butter Chicken for Friday.

>> Prepare and freeze rice for Friday.

>> Wash and chop broccoli for Friday.

TIP

If you're looking for ideas for breakfast, lunch, or dessert, check out the following:

>> **Breakfast:** Apple Cinnamon Steel-Cut Oats, made with gluten-free oats (Chapter 6); Overnight Oats, made with gluten-free oats (Chapter 6); Wild Blueberry Smoothie Bowls, made with gluten-free granola or omitted (Chapter 6); and Greek Yogurt Deviled Eggs (Chapter 6)

>> **Lunch:** Mediterranean Quinoa Bowls (Chapter 8); and Korean Spiced Bowls, made with tamari in place of soy sauce (Chapter 8)

>> **Dessert:** Chocolate Avocado Mousse (Chapter 19); and Peanut Butter Cereal Bars, made with gluten-free cereal (Chapter 19)

WARNING

When preparing foods for a gluten-free diet, always read labels.

Lower-Carb Meal Ideas

Carbohydrates are an important component of a well-balanced eating plan, but some people want or need to focus on higher-fiber options, like legumes and whole grains. The meal plan in this section is meant to support a person living with diabetes or following a lower-carb diet, while encouraging more vegetables at a meal and a higher-fiber diet. To jumpstart planning meals, consider combining protein foods with loads of fresh vegetables and a sprinkling of whole grains.

Here's what the week looks like:

>> **Monday:** Serve Tortilla Soup (Chapter 12).

>> **Tuesday:** Serve Chicken Korma (Chapter 15), Garlicky Greens (Chapter 17), and Asian Pickled Cucumbers (Chapter 17).

>> **Wednesday:** Serve Shredded Buffalo-Style Chicken Wraps (Chapter 12) with fresh berries and almonds. Also, transfer the Chicken Cacciatore from the freezer to the refrigerator for Thursday.

>> **Thursday:** Serve Chicken Cacciatore (Chapter 15) with Grilled Balsamic Asparagus (Chapter 17). Also, place the ground beef in the refrigerator to defrost for Friday.

>> **Friday:** Serve Pan-Fried Burgers with Creamy Feta Green Salad (Chapter 16).

TIP

To prep for this week, do the following on Sunday:

>> Roast or purchase one or two rotisserie chickens, shred the meat, and refrigerate for Monday and Wednesday.

>> Place the ingredients for the Chicken Korma in a dish and refrigerate for Tuesday.

>> Wash the kale for Tuesday.

>> Prepare the Chicken Cacciatore and freeze for Thursday.

>> Wash and prep the asparagus for Thursday.

TIP

If you're looking for ideas for breakfast, lunch, or dessert, check out the following:

>> **Breakfast:** Chimichangas (Chapter 6) with blackberries and Greek Yogurt Deviled Eggs (Chapter 6) and avocado toast

>> **Lunch:** Beefy Chop House Salad (Chapter 8) and Canned Tuna Niçoise Salad (Chapter 8)

>> **Dessert:** Chocolate Avocado Mousse (Chapter 19) and Grilled Peaches with Amaretti Cookies (Chapter 19)

Swapping Out Dairy

Much like living with gluten intolerance, living with a dairy allergy can be challenging and scary. Dairy can sneak into foods as milk solids, whey, casein, or any packaged goods labeled "contains milk." Meal planning for a dairy-free week can be as simple as taking a favorite dish and removing the cheese, butter, or milk. The recipes in this section are made without dairy, but you should still look for any labels that say "contains milk" if you have a food allergy.

Here's what the week looks like:

>> **Monday:** Serve Turkey and Vegetable Soup (Chapter 9) with flatbread or crackers.

>> **Tuesday:** Serve Sausage and Bell Peppers (Chapter 14) with French bread and olive oil for dipping.

>> **Wednesday:** Serve Turkey and Noodles (Chapter 9). Also, defrost the pork tenderloin for Thursday.

>> **Thursday:** Serve Cherry Balsamic Pork Tenderloin with Brussels Sprouts (Chapter 14). Also, defrost the Sloppy Joes for Friday.

>> **Friday:** Serve Sloppy Joes (Chapter 15) serve with dairy-free hamburger buns and Carrot and Cilantro Salad (Chapter 17).

To prep for this week, do the following on Sunday:

>> Roast a turkey for Monday and Wednesday (or buy precooked turkey meat).

>> Wash and prep the Brussels sprouts for Thursday.

>> Wash the carrots for Friday.

>> Prep and freeze sloppy joes for Friday.

If you're looking for ideas for breakfast, lunch, or dessert, check out the following:

>> **Breakfast:** Overnight Oats, made with a dairy alternative (Chapter 6); Wild Blueberry Smoothie Bowls (Chapter 6)

>> **Lunch:** Spicy Sweet Potato Soup, made with a dairy-free broth (Chapter 7); Chinese Chicken Slaw Bowls (Chapter 8)

>> **Dessert:** Caramelized Bananas with Walnuts, replacing the butter with vegan butter or increasing the oil, and serving with dairy-free ice cream (Chapter 19); Jam Bars, made with vegan butter (Chapter 19)

A Week of Vegetarian Dining

A vegetarian way of eating can be nutrient-dense and balanced. You can choose to omit any dairy, eggs, or honey to fit a vegan meal plan, or you can grill up meat and serve it on the side for your meat-loving friends. Be sure to use vegetable broth when making soups or sauces. The focus of this meal plan is on legumes to provide ample protein.

Here's what the week looks like:

>> **Monday:** Serve Indian Spiced Cauliflower and Garbanzo Beans (Chapter 14) with flatbread.

>> **Tuesday:** Serve Sheet-Pan Tofu Buddha Bowls (Chapter 14).

>> **Wednesday:** Serve Loaded Baked Potatoes (Chapter 16).

>> **Thursday:** Serve Veggie Power Bowls (Chapter 8).

>> **Friday:** Serve Sheet-Pan Mediterranean Pasta (Chapter 14).

TIP

To prep for this week, do the following on Sunday:

>> Wash and cut the cauliflower for Monday.

>> Wash and prep the vegetables for the Sheet-Pan Tofu Buddha Bowls on Tuesday.

>> Ready vegetarian-friendly toppings (such as salsa, beans, cheese, broccoli, and so on) for the Loaded Baked Potatoes on Wednesday.

>> Cook the quinoa and prep the vegetables for the Veggie Power Bowls on Thursday.

>> Mix together the ingredients for Sheet-Pan Mediterranean Pasta, cover with plastic wrap, and refrigerate until baking on Friday.

TIP

If you're looking for ideas for breakfast, lunch, or dessert, check out the following:

>> **Breakfast:** Pumpkin Pancakes (Chapter 6) and Hearty Berry Muffins (Chapter 6)

>> **Lunch:** Springtime Pea Soup, using vegetarian broth (Chapter 7) and Lebanese Spiced Veggie Bowls (Chapter 8)

>> **Dessert:** Caramelized Bananas with Walnuts, replacing the butter with vegan butter or increasing the oil and served with dairy-free ice cream (Chapter 19); Jam Bars, made with vegan butter (Chapter 19)

REMEMBER

Vegetarian dining can include milk products and eggs. If you're following a vegan menu, omit all dairy products, honey, gelatin, and eggs, in addition to meat and fish.

3

Starting with Breakfast, Soups, and Salads

IN THIS PART . . .

Discover ways to prep in advance for breakfast and lunch.

Consider new ways to cook soups straight from the freezer.

Find creative ways to take your salads on the go.

Chapter **6**

Breakfasts

Wait! Before you head out the door, don't forget breakfast! Many people consider breakfast the most important meal of the day. In fact, research has shown that a high-quality breakfast can improve health and result in a higher quality of life. Inversely, skipping breakfast has been linked to eating less fruits and vegetables, depression, worsened sleep, and poor academic performance.

Especially on busy weekdays, finding the time to make breakfast can be difficult, but you can prep breakfasts in advance and place them in the freezer or store them in the refrigerator for up to five days, depending on the recipe.

Protein is important at breakfast, so each recipe in this chapter centers around high-quality protein. If you prefer vegetarian options, check out the variations included at the bottom of each recipe. Another key component of breakfast is fiber. Breakfast is a great time to boost your fiber intake, whether from whole grains, fruits and vegetables, or beans.

Get your taste buds ready! In this chapter, I offer quick and easy breakfast choices, from protein- and fiber-packed Wild Blueberry Smoothie Bowls to freezer-friendly Chimichangas. My family's favorite is the Pumpkin Pancakes.

Chimichangas

INGREDIENTS

½ pound center-cut bacon

10 large eggs, whisked

Ten 8-inch flour tortillas

½ cup canned refried beans

1½ cups shredded cheddar cheese

Salt to taste

Freshly ground black pepper to taste

DIRECTIONS

1 Preheat the oven to 400 degrees.

2 Place a piece of parchment paper onto a sheet pan. Lay the bacon strips side-by-side across the parchment paper. Bake for 20 minutes, or until desired doneness.

3 Remove the cooked bacon onto a paper towel to remove excess grease. Then transfer to a cutting board and coarsely chop the bacon.

4 Spray cooking spray into a nonstick skillet, and heat the pan over medium heat. Pour the whisked eggs into the skillet. Using a heat-safe rubber spatula, gently stir the eggs occasionally until fully cooked, about 5 minutes for a soft scramble.

5 On a clean work surface, lay out the tortillas in an assembly line. Spread the refried beans onto the center of each tortilla, about 2½ teaspoons per tortilla. Next, divide the eggs, bacon, and cheese equally among the tortillas.

6 Working with 1 tortilla at a time, fold in the left edge, fold in the bottom and top edges, and roll the folded edges onto the right edge. Spray the tops of the chimichangas with cooking spray.

7 Heat a nonstick skillet over medium-high heat. Heat the chimichangas for 1 to 2 minutes on each side (you may be able to make 2 chimichangas at a time, depending on the size of your skillet), until they have a lightly golden crust. If you prefer, you can use an air fryer at 380 degrees for 3 to 4 minutes.

8 Place a piece of parchment paper on a baking sheet or plate that can fit easily in the freezer. Place the chimichangas onto the parchment paper and freeze for 2 hours. Transfer to a freezer-safe bag or container and store for up to 1 month.

9 To reheat, wrap each chimichanga in paper towel and microwave 45 seconds on one side; then flip over and continue cooking for another 45 seconds to 1 minute, or until heated through. (If you prefer, you can cook them in an air fryer at 330 degrees for 10 minutes or in an oven at 350 degrees for 15 minutes.)

PER SERVING: *Calories 421 (From Fat 229); Fat 25g (Saturated 10g); Cholesterol 245mg; Sodium 724mg; Carbohydrate 29g (Dietary Fiber 2g); Protein 18g.*

TIP: If you know you'll be eating the chimichangas this week, you can prep them and store them in the refrigerator for up to 5 days (instead of freezing them). Just pan-fry to heat them up.

Mini Breakfast Quiche

INGREDIENTS

One 8-ounce tube refrigerated crescent rolls

½ cup chopped broccoli

½ cup shredded cheddar cheese

2 large eggs

½ teaspoon salt

¼ teaspoon freshly ground black pepper

DIRECTIONS

1 Preheat the oven to 375 degrees. Spray a muffin pan with cooking spray or use a nonstick muffin pan.

2 Open the can of crescent rolls and divide the 8 triangles. Place each crescent roll triangle into a muffin cup. Using your fingers, work the dough up the sides of the muffin cups. Then place 1 tablespoon of chopped broccoli and 1 tablespoon of shredded cheese into each muffin cup.

3 In a medium bowl, whisk together the eggs, salt, and pepper. Using a spoon, equally divide the mixture among the 8 muffin cups.

4 Bake for 20 to 22 minutes or until the quiches are no longer soft in the center. Cool completely. If using a convection oven, start checking for doneness after 14 minutes.

5 Then place a piece of parchment paper onto a freezer-safe plate and transfer the cooled quiches onto the plate. Freeze for 2 to 8 hours, and then transfer to a freezer-safe bag. Store in the freezer up to 1 month.

6 To reheat, cover with a lightly dampened paper towel and microwave for 1 minute or until heated through. (If you prefer, you can heat them in the oven at 350 degrees for 8 to 10 minutes.)

PER SERVING: *Calories 294 (From Fat 92); Fat 10g (Saturated 5g); Cholesterol 121mg; Sodium 757mg; Carbohydrate 36g (Dietary Fiber 2g); Protein 14g.*

NOTE: This recipe can be doubled if you have enough muffin tins.

VARY IT! Try replacing the frozen broccoli with cooked and squeezed-dry spinach or frozen, shredded potatoes.

Nutty Breakfast Cookies

| PREP TIME: ABOUT 10 MIN | COOK TIME: 10 MIN | YIELD: 8 SERVINGS |

INGREDIENTS

1 cup pitted dates

1 cup boiling water

1 cup natural peanut butter

2 large eggs

1 cup rolled oats

1 teaspoon vanilla extract

½ cup dark chocolate chips

½ cup dried cherries

DIRECTIONS

1 Preheat the oven to 325 degrees.

2 In a small heat-safe bowl, mix together the dates and boiling water. Allow the dates to reconstitute for 5 minutes; then drain off the excess water.

3 In a food processor, mix together the dates, peanut butter, eggs, oats, and vanilla. Process for 1 to 2 minutes or until combined. Remove the blade and stir in the chocolate chips and cherries.

4 Place a piece of parchment paper onto a baking sheet. Make 16 dough balls and place them on the baking sheet. Gently press the dough to flatten it slightly. Bake for 10 to 12 minutes or until slightly golden. Cool completely before transferring for storage.

5 Wrap in plastic wrap or store in an airtight container at room temperature for up to 2 days or freeze up to 1 month. The cookies can be enjoyed straight from the freezer or let them defrost at room temperature.

PER SERVING: *Calories 384 (From Fat 193); Fat 21g (Saturated 6g); Cholesterol 54mg; Sodium 168mg; Carbohydrate 44g (Dietary Fiber 6g); Protein 12g.*

VARY IT! You can replace the peanut butter with your favorite creamy nut butter. If nut allergies are a concern, go for sunflower butter instead.

Ham and Egg Sandwiches

PREP TIME: ABOUT 20 MIN	COOK TIME: 18 MIN	YIELD: 12 SERVINGS

INGREDIENTS

12 large eggs

½ teaspoon salt

½ teaspoon freshly ground black pepper

3 tablespoons whole milk

12 English muffins

12 teaspoons salted butter, softened to room temperature

Twelve 1-ounce slices Canadian bacon or ham

Twelve 1-ounce slices cheddar cheese

DIRECTIONS

1 Preheat the oven to 350 degrees. Spray a 9-x-13-inch casserole dish with cooking spray.

2 In a medium bowl, whisk together the eggs, salt, pepper, and milk. Pour the eggs into the casserole dish and bake for 18 minutes.

3 Meanwhile, split open the English muffins and slightly brown them in the toaster. Spread 1 teaspoon butter onto 12 of the toasted English muffin halves.

4 After the eggs are baked, remove them from the oven and let cool for 10 minutes. Slice the eggs into 12 equal egg squares.

5 To assemble, place 1 egg square on the butter side of each English muffin; top with a slice of Canadian bacon or ham and then a slice cheese. Top with the remaining English muffin half. Cool completely.

6 To freeze, wrap each sandwich in parchment paper. Then place in a freezer-safe bag and freeze up to 1 month.

7 To reheat, defrost overnight; then heat a parchment-wrapped egg sandwich in the microwave for 45 seconds on one side, flip over, and heat for an additional 30 to 45 seconds or until heated through.

PER SERVING: Calories 406 (From Fat 195); Fat 22g (Saturated 11g); Cholesterol 268mg; Sodium 975mg; Carbohydrate 28g (Dietary Fiber 0g); Protein 25g.

NOTE: If you prefer to eat the sandwiches throughout the week, you can store wrapped sandwiches in the refrigerator up to 5 days and reheat in the microwave.

NOTE: You can also broil the English muffins on a baking sheet for 3 to 5 minutes instead of heating in a toaster.

VARY IT! You can use cooked bacon, sausage patties, or vegetarian sausage patties in place of the Canadian bacon or ham, if you like.

Waffles

PREP TIME: ABOUT 10 MIN | **COOK TIME: 30 MIN** | **YIELD: 8 SERVINGS**

INGREDIENTS

3 large eggs

1 cup 4% fat cottage cheese

1 cup rolled oats

1 cup whole-wheat flour

1 teaspoon vanilla extract

½ teaspoon salt

2 tablespoons coconut oil

¼ cup natural peanut butter

¼ cup whole milk (optional)

DIRECTIONS

1 Place the eggs, cottage cheese, oats, flour, vanilla, salt, coconut oil, and peanut butter in the blender and process until smooth, about 2 minutes. If the batter is very thick, add the milk until slightly thinned. The batter will be thicker than pancake batter, but should not be stiff.

2 Spray a waffle iron with cooking spray and heat and cook the waffles according to the machine's instructions.

3 After they're cooked, cool the waffles completely.

4 To freeze, line a baking sheet with a piece of parchment paper and place the waffles flat on the paper. Freeze for 1 to 8 hours or until frozen. Then place individually frozen waffles in a freezer-safe bag and freeze up to 1 month.

5 To reheat, place individual waffles in a toaster and heat until crisp and warmed, about 1 to 2 minutes. To serve, drizzle with maple syrup or pureed berries.

PER SERVING: *Calories 238 (From Fat 112); Fat 12g (Saturated 6g); Cholesterol 88mg; Sodium 320mg; Carbohydrate 22g (Dietary Fiber 3g); Protein 12g.*

Pumpkin Pancakes

| PREP TIME: ABOUT 10 MIN | COOK TIME: 30 MIN | YIELD: 8 SERVINGS |

INGREDIENTS

1 cup whole-wheat flour

1 cup all-purpose flour

1 tablespoon baking powder

1 teaspoon cinnamon

1 cup canned pumpkin

2 large eggs

1¾ cups whole milk

2 tablespoons melted coconut oil

1 teaspoon vanilla extract

DIRECTIONS

1 In a medium bowl, stir together the whole-wheat flour, all-purpose flour, baking powder, and cinnamon.

2 In a separate bowl, whisk together the pumpkin, eggs, milk, coconut oil, and vanilla.

3 Make a well in the center of the dry ingredients and pour the wet ingredients into the center of the dry ingredients. Stir for 1 minute; the batter may still be slightly lumpy.

4 Heat a heavy skillet or griddle over medium-high heat. Spray with cooking spray. Using a ¼ cup measuring cup, scoop the batter onto the skillet and cook in batches, 2 to 3 minutes per side. The pancakes should form bubbles to indicate when they're ready to flip. Adjust the temperature lower if they start to brown too quickly. Cool completely. Batter should make about 16 pancakes.

5 To freeze, line a baking sheet with parchment paper and place the pancakes on the paper. Freeze for 1 to 8 hours or until frozen. Transfer the individually frozen pancakes into a freezer-safe bag and freeze up to 1 month.

6 To reheat, place the individual pancakes in a toaster and heat until crisp and warmed, about 1 to 2 minutes.

PER SERVING: *Calories 305 (From Fat 114); Fat 13g (Saturated 8g); Cholesterol 80mg; Sodium 379mg; Carbohydrate 37g (Dietary Fiber 3g); Protein 13g.*

VARY IT! Try mashed banana or applesauce instead of pumpkin, if you like.

Yogurt Parfaits

PREP TIME: ABOUT 5 MIN	COOK TIME: NONE	YIELD: 8 SERVINGS

INGREDIENTS

One 35.3-ounce container 2% fat plain Greek yogurt

2 tablespoons chia seeds

¼ cup fruit preserves (strawberry, raspberry, apricot, or preferred flavor)

1 cup granola

1 cup blueberries, fresh or frozen

8 teaspoons honey

DIRECTIONS

1 In a medium bowl, stir together the yogurt, chia seeds, and fruit preserves.

2 Divide the mixture between eight 8-ounce Mason jars.

3 Place 2 tablespoons granola into each jar. Top the granola with 2 tablespoons blueberries per jar, and drizzle each with 1 teaspoon honey over the top.

4 Secure the lids, and store in the refrigerator up to 5 days.

PER SERVING: *Calories 229 (From Fat 67); Fat 7g (Saturated 3g); Cholesterol 15mg; Sodium 48mg; Carbohydrate 26g (Dietary Fiber 3g); Protein 16g.*

VARY IT! In fall or winter, opt for apples or pears instead of blueberries. Chop up the apples or pears and stir in lemon juice and honey to help keep the fruit fresh. Dried fruit also works wonderfully — try dates, nectarines, or berries.

Overnight Oats

PREP TIME: ABOUT 5 MIN	COOK TIME: NONE	YIELD: 4 SERVINGS

INGREDIENTS

1½ cups rolled oats

1½ cups whole milk

2 tablespoons chia seeds

¼ cup chopped pitted dates

DIRECTIONS

1 In a medium bowl, stir together all the ingredients.

2 Using four 8-ounce glass Mason jars, divide the mixture between four 8-ounce Mason jars. Secure the lids, and store in the refrigerator up to 5 days.

PER SERVING: *Calories 234 (From Fat 68); Fat 8g (Saturated 3g); Cholesterol 13mg; Sodium 48mg; Carbohydrate 35g (Dietary Fiber 6g); Protein 8g.*

VARY IT! Overnight oats are versatile and fun! Check out the nearby sidebar for some fun twists on this recipe.

VARIATIONS ON A THEME

Try the following variations for a fun twist:

- **European style:** 2 tablespoons chopped dried apple, 1 tablespoon raisins, 1 tablespoon pumpkin seeds, 1 tablespoon honey

- **PB&J:** 1 tablespoon natural peanut butter, 1 tablespoon jam

- **Banana nut:** ¼ medium banana, sliced; 2 tablespoons chopped walnuts; 1 tablespoon honey

- **Carrot cake:** ¼ cup grated carrot, ¼ cup canned crushed pineapple, 1 teaspoon brown sugar, ¼ teaspoon ground cinnamon

- **Coco almond:** 1 tablespoon shredded unsweetened coconut, 2 tablespoons sliced almonds, 1 tablespoon chocolate syrup or chocolate chips

- **Peach pie:** 1 tablespoon peach preserves, ⅛ teaspoon ground ginger or chopped crystallized ginger, ⅛ teaspoon ground cinnamon, ¼ cup chopped canned or fresh peaches

Apple Cinnamon Steel-Cut Oats

PREP TIME: ABOUT 5 MIN	COOK TIME: 20 MIN	YIELD: 8 SERVINGS

INGREDIENTS

1 cup steel-cut oats

3½ cups water

2 large Granny Smith apples, finely chopped

1 teaspoon ground cinnamon

½ teaspoon salt

¼ cup brown sugar

½ cup chopped walnuts

8 tablespoons whole milk, for reheating

DIRECTIONS

1 In a medium saucepan, stir together the oats, water, apples, cinnamon, and salt. Heat over medium-high heat until the mixture begins to bubble; then cover and lower the heat to medium-low and continue to simmer until thickened. Stop cooking after 20 minutes, and remove from the heat.

2 Stir in the brown sugar and chopped walnuts.

3 Let the oatmeal cool; then divide the oatmeal mixture between eight 8-ounce Mason jars. Secure the lids, and store in the refrigerator up to 5 days. Steel-cut oats can be served hot or cold.

4 To reheat, stir in 1 tablespoon milk per jar and microwave (without the lid), for 1 minute or until heated through.

PER SERVING: *Calories 143 (From Fat 55); Fat 6g (Saturated 1g); Cholesterol 2mg; Sodium 154mg; Carbohydrate 21g (Dietary Fiber 3g); Protein 3g.*

VARY IT! Skip the apples and pecans and try adding one of the fun variations in the nearby sidebar instead.

OATMEAL OPTIONS

Try the following variations on steel-cut oatmeal:

- **Tart cherry almond:** 2 tablespoons dried tart cherries, 2 tablespoons almond butter

- **Chocolate peanut butter:** 1 tablespoon natural peanut butter, 1 teaspoon cocoa powder, 1 tablespoon chocolate chips

- **Banana nut:** ¼ medium banana, sliced; 2 tablespoons chopped walnuts

- **Tropical:** ¼ cup chopped macadamia nuts, 2 tablespoons shredded coconut, ¼ cup chopped mango

- **Strawberries and cream:** ¼ cup chopped strawberries (fresh or from frozen), 1 tablespoon cream cheese

Wild Blueberry Smoothie Bowls

PREP TIME: ABOUT 10 MIN	COOK TIME: NONE	YIELD: 8 SERVINGS

INGREDIENTS

2 cups frozen wild blueberries

1 cup apple juice

2 tablespoons chia seeds

2 bananas, divided

¼ cup almond butter

½ cup unsweetened shredded coconut, divided

1 teaspoon lemon juice

¼ cup honey

½ cup sliced almonds

½ cup granola

DIRECTIONS

1 In a blender, place the blueberries, apple juice, chia seeds, 1 of the bananas, almond butter, and ¼ cup of the shredded coconut. Blend until smooth, about 2 minutes.

2 Divide the smoothie between eight 16-ounce Mason jars (wide-mouthed jars, if you have them).

3 Thinly slice the remaining banana into a small bowl and toss with the lemon juice and honey. Divide the mixture between the 8 jars.

4 Top with the remaining coconut, sliced almonds, and granola.

5 Secure the lids, and store in the refrigerator up to 5 days.

PER SERVING: *Calories 277 (From Fat 134); Fat 15g (Saturated 5g); Cholesterol 0mg; Sodium 44mg; Carbohydrate 35g (Dietary Fiber 7g); Protein 5g.*

TIP: If you like, you can freeze the smoothie bowls and defrost overnight in the refrigerator before serving.

TIP: If you prefer your granola to stay crunchy, store on the side instead of mixed into the smoothie bowl.

VARY IT! Add in other fruits (like sliced kiwi, pineapple, or mango), stir in peanut butter, or top with puffed groats (like millet, quinoa, or buckwheat). If you need to get more greens, try blending in spinach or kale with the wild blueberries!

Breakfast Quinoa Porridge

PREP TIME: ABOUT 5 MIN	COOK TIME: 20 MIN	YIELD: 8 SERVINGS

INGREDIENTS

2 cups quinoa

2 cups plus 8 tablespoons whole milk, divided

2 cups water

1 teaspoon cinnamon

¼ teaspoon salt

2 tablespoons brown sugar

½ cup raisins

½ cup chopped pecans

DIRECTIONS

1 Rinse the quinoa under running water for 3 minutes in a sieve before cooking. Shake off excess water.

2 In a medium saucepan, stir together the quinoa, 2 cups of the milk, water, cinnamon, and salt. Heat over medium–high heat until the mixture begins to bubble; then cover, reduce the heat to low, and continue to simmer until thickened. Stop cooking after 20 minutes, and remove from the heat. Stir in the brown sugar.

3 Divide the quinoa mixture between eight 8-ounce Mason jars. Top each with 1 tablespoon raisins and chopped pecans. Secure the lids, and store in the refrigerator up to 5 days. Quinoa can be served hot or cold.

4 To reheat, stir in 1 tablespoon milk per jar and microwave (without the lid), for 1 minute or until heated through.

PER SERVING: *Calories 281 (From Fat 86); Fat 10g (Saturated 2g); Cholesterol 8mg; Sodium 109mg; Carbohydrate 41g (Dietary Fiber 4g); Protein 9g.*

VARY IT! Keep it sweet like oatmeal or make it savory — try stirring in cheddar cheese and green onions, or roasted tomatoes, fresh mozzarella, and balsamic vinegar for a unique twist!

Hearty Berry Muffins

PREP TIME: ABOUT 10 MIN	COOK TIME: 20 MIN	YIELD: 8 SERVINGS

INGREDIENTS

1½ cups whole-wheat pastry flour or all-purpose flour

2 teaspoons baking powder

½ cup granulated sugar

⅓ cup whole milk

⅓ cup melted unsalted butter

1 large egg

½ teaspoon salt

2 cups frozen berries

¼ cup rolled oats

¼ cup brown sugar

DIRECTIONS

1 Preheat the oven to 350 degrees. Place muffin cup liners into 12 muffin cups or use cooking spray.

2 In a medium bowl, stir together the flour, baking powder, and sugar.

3 In another bowl, mix together the milk, butter, egg, and salt.

4 Make a well in the center of the dry ingredients, and pour the wet ingredients into the center. Stir just until combined (lumps should still appear in the batter). Add the frozen berries, and gently combine. Divide the muffin batter between the 12 muffin cups.

5 In a small bowl, mix together the rolled oats and brown sugar. Sprinkle the mixture over the top of the muffins.

6 Bake for 20 to 25 minutes or until set in the center.

7 Cool completely. Store in an airtight container in the refrigerator up to 5 days or in the freezer up to 1 month.

PER SERVING: *Calories 261 (From Fat 81); Fat 9g (Saturated 5g); Cholesterol 48mg; Sodium 284mg; Carbohydrate 42g (Dietary Fiber 2g); Protein 4g.*

NOTE: Whatever berries you have on hand—fresh or frozen—can work!

Greek Yogurt Deviled Eggs

INGREDIENTS

12 large eggs, hard-boiled

¼ cup plain Greek yogurt

2 tablespoons mayonnaise

1 teaspoon mustard

½ teaspoon Worcestershire sauce

1 teaspoon hot sauce

1 green onion, chopped finely

Salt to taste

Freshly ground black pepper to taste

DIRECTIONS

1 Peel the eggs, and slice them down the center. Place the egg yolks in a medium bowl. Add the yogurt, mayonnaise, mustard, Worcestershire sauce, and hot sauce. Using a rubber spatula, stir together all the ingredients until combined, about 2 minutes.

2 Place the egg whites in a storage container. Using a spoon, fill the egg centers with the egg yolk mixture. Top with the onions and season with salt and pepper. Store in the refrigerator up to 3 days.

PER SERVING: *Calories 184 (From Fat 113); Fat 13g (Saturated 4g); Cholesterol 427mg; Sodium 163mg; Carbohydrate 3g (Dietary Fiber 0g); Protein 14g.*

TIP: Serve on toast, as a snack, or on the go with crackers!

TIP: Never made hard-boiled eggs before? In a large saucepan, place the eggs and cover completely with cold water. Over high heat, bring the eggs to a boil; then cover and remove from the heat. Wait 10 minutes; then immediately drain and run the eggs under cold water until cool.

TIP: If hard-boiling your own eggs, be sure to buy your eggs, wait a week, and then make this recipe, instead of using fresh eggs. They'll be easier to peel.

Chapter **7**

Freezer-Friendly Soups

Ready, set, freeze! If time is crunched, the freezer is your friend. Yes, frozen pizzas are great, but when you're ready for some variety, soups are the answer. They're nourishing, hearty, and not just for the cold months. Whether you have a slow cooker or an electric multicooker, like an Instant Pot, you're all set to make and enjoy these soups.

The recipes in this chapter use cooked meats, which keeps food in the safe zone! If you want to save time by using raw meat, be sure to defrost it in the refrigerator overnight before cooking. Also, be sure to write a date on your freezer bags. If you're freezing for a multicooker, be sure to freeze the bag in a bowl that can fit in your pot — an awkward square can't fit into an Instant Pot!

Want to know my secret for keeping soups fun and sassy? Toppings! Yes, the simple addition of fresh, brightly colored toppings are every chef's secret to making their soup *pop!* Add in a squeeze of fresh citrus, chopped fresh herbs, sliced avocados, chopped green onions, or a drizzle of Greek yogurt. Any and all of these additions can elevate the flavor profile and aesthetics of a soup.

Sausage, Spinach, and Lentil Soup

| PREP TIME: ABOUT 10 MIN | COOK TIME: 40 MIN–8 HR | YIELD: 6 SERVINGS |

INGREDIENTS

1 onion, chopped

2 carrots, chopped

2 celery stalks, chopped

1 cup lentils

6 ounces kielbasa, sliced

1 bay leaf

1 teaspoon dried thyme leaves

6 cups chicken or vegetable broth

½ cup water

1 tablespoon red wine vinegar

6 cups fresh baby spinach leaves

Salt to taste

Freshly ground black pepper to taste

½ cup fresh grated Parmesan cheese

DIRECTIONS

1 In a 1-gallon freezer bag, place the onion, carrots, celery, lentils, kielbasa, bay leaf, thyme, and broth. Remove the excess air from the bag. Place the bag in a bowl to freeze. Freeze up to 3 months.

2 To prepare, use either a multi-cooker or a slow cooker.

If using a multicooker, dump the frozen ingredients into the pot, and add the water to the bottom. Secure the lid and select the Pressure Cook for 15 minutes. *Remember:* Frozen ingredients take longer to heat and come to pressure, so give yourself about 40 minutes to cook. After the cooking has completed, you can hold warm until you're ready to serve or do a Quick Release.

If using a slow cooker, dump the frozen ingredients into the pot, and add the water to the bottom. Place the lid on top, select the low heat setting, and cook for 6 to 8 hours.

3 Stir in the vinegar and spinach. Season with salt and pepper. Top with Parmesan, and serve.

PER SERVING: *Calories 291 (From Fat 91); Fat 10g (Saturated 4g); Cholesterol 21mg; Sodium 930mg; Carbohydrate 29g (Dietary Fiber 12g); Protein 21g.*

NOTE: Season bean soups with salt *after* cooking. Broths vary in sodium content — the one you use may be enough seasoning for your taste.

VARY IT! For a vegetarian version, skip the kielbasa and use a vegetarian sausage instead.

TIP: Serve with crusty French bread or grilled-cheese sandwiches to complete the meal.

TIP: Use frozen mirepoix (onion, celery, and carrots) to save time!

Tuscan Kale and Potato Soup

PREP TIME: ABOUT 10 MIN	COOK TIME: 40 MIN–8 HR	YIELD: 8 SERVINGS

INGREDIENTS

1 onion, chopped

8 medium red potatoes, medium diced

4 cloves garlic, chopped

1 bay leaf

2 teaspoons dried oregano

1 pound precooked Italian sausage, sliced

6 cups chicken broth

½ cup water

½ cup heavy cream

8 cups kale, stems removed and thinly sliced

Crushed red pepper to taste

Salt to taste

Freshly ground black pepper to taste

½ cup grated Parmesan cheese

DIRECTIONS

1 In a 1-gallon freezer bag, place the onion, potatoes, garlic, bay leaf, oregano, sausage, and broth. Remove the excess air from the bag. Place the bag in a bowl to freeze. Freeze up to 3 months.

2 To prepare, use either a multicooker or a slow cooker.

If using a multicooker, dump the frozen ingredients into the pot and add the water to the bottom. Secure the lid and select Pressure Cook for 15 minutes. *Remember:* Frozen ingredients take longer to heat and come to pressure, so give yourself about 40 minutes to cook. After the cooking has completed, you can hold warm until you're ready to serve or do a Quick Release.

If using a slow cooker, dump the frozen ingredients into the pot and add the water to the bottom. Place the lid on top, select the low heat setting, and cook for 6 to 8 hours.

3 Stir in the cream and kale. Season with red pepper, salt, and black pepper. Top with Parmesan and serve.

PER SERVING: *Calories 478 (From Fat 212); Fat 24g (Saturated 10g); Cholesterol 58mg; Sodium 1243mg; Carbohydrate 49g (Dietary Fiber 5g); Protein 20g.*

NOTE: Waxy potatoes hold up best in soups. A medium-size potato weighs about 5 ounces.

VARY IT! This recipe can be served vegetarian by using a vegetarian sausage and vegetable broth.

TIP: Serve soup with crusty French bread.

TIP: Use frozen mirepoix (onion, celery, and carrots) to save time!

Hearty Chili with Beans

| PREP TIME: ABOUT 10 MIN | COOK TIME: 40 MIN–8 HR | YIELD: 8 SERVINGS |

INGREDIENTS

1 pound lean ground beef, cooked, drained, and cooled

1 onion, chopped

1 carrot, chopped

1 celery stalk, chopped

One 14.5-ounce can fire-roasted tomatoes

One 15-ounce can kidney beans, drained and rinsed

One 15-ounce can pinto beans, drained and rinsed

1 cup beef or vegetable broth

3 tablespoons chili powder

1 teaspoon cumin powder

1 teaspoon garlic powder

½ cup water

Salt, to taste

½ cup sour cream

½ cup chopped cilantro

DIRECTIONS

1 In a 1-gallon freezer bag, place the ground beef, onion, carrot, celery, tomatoes, kidney beans, pinto beans, broth, chili powder, cumin powder, and garlic powder. Remove the excess air from the bag. Place the bag in a bowl to freeze. Freeze up to 3 months.

2 To prepare, use either a multicooker or a slow cooker.

If using a multicooker, dump the frozen ingredients into the pot and add the water to the bottom. Secure the lid and select Pressure Cook for 15 minutes. *Remember:* Frozen ingredients take longer to heat and come to pressure, so give yourself about 40 minutes to cook. After cooking has completed, you can hold warm until you're ready to serve or do a Quick Release.

If using a slowcooker, dump the frozen ingredients into the pot and add the water to the bottom. Place the lid on top, select the low heat setting, and cook for 6 to 8 hours.

3 Season with salt, as needed. Top with sour cream and cilantro, and serve.

PER SERVING: *Calories 183(From Fat 55); Fat 6g (Saturated 3g); Cholesterol 26mg; Sodium 442mg; Carbohydrate 21g (Dietary Fiber 6g); Protein 12g.*

NOTE: Season bean soups with salt *after* cooking. Broths can vary in sodium content — the one you use may be enough seasoning for your taste.

VARY IT! For a vegetarian version, skip the ground beef and use a vegetarian version instead.

TIP: Serve with chips, cornbread, or grilled-cheese sandwiches to complete the meal.

TIP: Use frozen mirepoix (onion, celery, and carrots) to save time!

Lentil and Chorizo Soup

PREP TIME: ABOUT 10 MIN	COOK TIME: 40 MIN–8 HR	YIELD: 8 SERVINGS

INGREDIENTS

1 onion, chopped

2 carrots, chopped

2 celery stalks, chopped

1 red bell pepper, chopped

1 cup lentils

1 cup diced Spanish chorizo

1 tablespoon tomato paste

1 teaspoon paprika

6 cups chicken or vegetable broth

½ cup water

½ lemon, juiced

½ cup chopped fresh parsley

Salt to taste

Freshly ground black pepper to taste

DIRECTIONS

1 In a 1-gallon freezer bag, place the onion, carrots, celery, bell pepper, lentils, chorizo, tomato paste, paprika, and broth. Remove the excess air from the bag. Place the bag in a bowl to freeze. Freeze up to 3 months.

2 To prepare, use either a multicooker or a slow cooker.

If using a multicooker, dump the frozen ingredients into the pot and add the water to the bottom. Secure the lid and select Pressure Cook for 15 minutes. *Remember:* Frozen ingredients take longer to heat and come to pressure, so give yourself about 40 minutes to cook. After the cooking has completed, you can hold warm until you're ready to serve or do a Quick Release.

If using a slow cooker, dump the frozen ingredients into the pot and add the water to the bottom. Place the lid on top, select the low heat setting, and cook for 6 to 8 hours.

3 Stir in the lemon juice and parsley. Season with salt and pepper. Serve.

PER SERVING: *Calories 203 (From Fat 64); Fat 7g (Saturated 3g); Cholesterol 15mg; Sodium 661mg; Carbohydrate 24g (Dietary Fiber 9g); Protein 11g.*

NOTE: Season bean soups with salt *after* cooking. Broths can vary in sodium content — the one you use may be enough seasoning for your taste.

TIP: Crispy, crunchy crackers and Manchego cheese or garlic bread would make a great side to this soup.

TIP: Use frozen mirepoix (onion, celery, and carrots) to save time! You can also use jarred red bell pepper in place of fresh.

Springtime Pea Soup

PREP TIME: ABOUT 10 MIN | **COOK TIME: 30 MIN–8 HR** | **YIELD: 8 SERVINGS**

INGREDIENTS

One 20-ounce bag frozen baby peas

1 onion, chopped

1 celery stalk, chopped

2 cloves garlic, chopped

1 teaspoon dried thyme leaves

6 cups chicken broth

½ cup water

Salt to taste

Freshly ground black pepper to taste

½ cup sour cream or plain Greek yogurt

½ cup crumbled feta cheese

½ cup chopped fresh parsley

½ lemon, juiced

DIRECTIONS

1 In a 1-gallon freezer bag, place the peas, onion, celery, garlic, thyme, and broth. Remove the excess air from the bag. Place the bag in a bowl to freeze. Freeze up to 3 months.

2 To prepare, use either a multicooker or a slow cooker.

If using a multicooker, dump the frozen ingredients into the pot and add the water to the bottom. Secure the lid and select Pressure Cook for 10 minutes. *Remember:* Frozen ingredients take longer to heat and come to pressure, so give yourself about 30 minutes to cook. After the cooking has completed, hold warm until you're ready to serve or do a Quick Release.

If using a slow cooker, dump the frozen ingredients into the pot and add in 1/2 cup water to the bottom. Place lid on top and select the low heat setting and cook for 6 to 8 hours.

3 Pour the soup into a blender and add the sour cream or yogurt. Place a towel over the blender lid and pulse the soup until the desired consistency is achieved. Season with salt and pepper.

4 In a small bowl, mix together the feta, parsley, and lemon juice.

5 Top the soup with the feta mixture, and serve.

PER SERVING: *Calories 130 (From Fat 46); Fat 5g (Saturated 3g); Cholesterol 16mg; Sodium 615mg; Carbohydrate 16g (Dietary Fiber 4g); Protein 6g.*

NOTE: The citrus and cheese at the end will balance the flavors of the soup.

VARY IT! Try goat cheese or Parmesan cheese in place of the feta.

TIP: Serve with crusty French bread or grilled ham-and-cheese sandwiches to complete the meal.

TIP: If you love ham and pea soup, stir in 2 cups chopped ham after blending and before serving.

Spicy Sweet Potato Soup

| PREP TIME: ABOUT 10 MIN | COOK TIME: 30 MIN–6 HR | YIELD: 8 SERVINGS |

INGREDIENTS

1 onion, chopped

3 medium sweet potatoes, scrubbed and diced with skin on

1 tablespoon tomato paste

½ teaspoon ground ginger

1 teaspoon ground cumin

½ teaspoon turmeric

⅛ teaspoon cayenne pepper

½ teaspoon freshly ground black pepper

¼ cup natural peanut butter

6 cups chicken broth

½ cup water

Salt, to taste

1 lime, juiced

½ cup chopped cilantro

½ cup chopped roasted peanuts

DIRECTIONS

1 In a 1-gallon freezer bag, place the onion, sweet potatoes, tomato paste, ginger, cumin, turmeric, cayenne pepper, black pepper, peanut butter, and chicken brother. Remove the excess air from the bag. Place the bag in a bowl to freeze. Freeze up to 3 months.

2 To prepare, use either a multicooker or a slow cooker.

If using a multicooker, dump the frozen ingredients into the pot and add the water to the bottom. Secure the lid and select Pressure Cook for 10 minutes. *Remember:* Frozen ingredients take longer to heat and come to pressure, so give yourself about 30 minutes to cook. After cooking has completed, hold warm until you're ready to serve or do a Quick Release.

If using a slow cooker, dump the frozen ingredients into the pot and add the water to the bottom. Place the lid on top, select the low heat setting, and cook for 6 hours.

3 Stir in the lime juice and season with salt, as needed. To serve, top with the cilantro and peanuts.

PER SERVING: *Calories 168(From Fat 84); Fat 9g (Saturated 2g); Cholesterol 0mg; Sodium 485mg; Carbohydrate 18g (Dietary Fiber 3g); Protein 5g.*

NOTE: Look for peanut butter without any ingredients other than salt and peanuts.

VARY IT! For a vegetarian version, use vegetable broth instead. For a creamier version, stir in ½ cup to 1 cup canned coconut milk.

Chicken and Roasted Poblano Soup

| PREP TIME: ABOUT 10 MIN | COOK TIME: 20 MIN–4 HR | YIELD: 6 SERVINGS |

INGREDIENTS

1 onion, chopped

2 cloves garlic, chopped

One 12-ounce bag frozen corn

Two 4-ounce cans diced green chilies (mild or spicy)

1 teaspoon cumin

1 bay leaf

4 cups chicken broth

½ cup water

½ cup heavy whipping cream or sour cream

3 cups shredded cooked chicken

Salt to taste

Freshly ground black pepper to taste

½ cup crumbled queso fresco or grated Monterey Jack cheese

DIRECTIONS

1 In a 1-gallon freezer bag, place the onion, garlic, corn, chilies, cumin, bay leaf, and chicken broth. Remove the excess air from the bag. Place the bag in a bowl to freeze. Freeze up to 3 months.

2 To prepare, use either a multicooker or a slow cooker.

If using a multicooker, dump the frozen ingredients into the pot and add in the water to the bottom. Secure the lid and select Pressure Cook for 5 minutes. *Remember:* Frozen ingredients take longer to heat and come to pressure, so give yourself about 20 minutes to cook. After the cooking has completed, hold warm until you're ready to serve or do a Quick Release.

If using a slow cooker, dump the frozen ingredients into the pot and add the water to the bottom. Place the lid on top, select the low heat setting, and cook for 4 hours.

3 Stir in the heavy cream or sour cream. Transfer half of the soup to a blender and pulse for 30 seconds. Return the blended soup to the pot, and stir in the chicken. Place the lid on top and let the soup warm for 5 minutes. Season with salt and pepper, as needed.

4 To serve, top with cheese, and serve.

PER SERVING: *Calories 286 (From Fat 101); Fat 11g (Saturated 6g); Cholesterol 90mg; Sodium 573mg; Carbohydrate 22g (Dietary Fiber 3g); Protein 26g.*

NOTE: This soup is great to keep on hand for when you have a rotisserie chicken or leftover chicken to use up.

TIP: Serve with a quesadilla or cheesy garlic bread.

Southwestern Black Bean Soup

PREP TIME: ABOUT 10 MIN	COOK TIME: 30 MIN–8 HR	YIELD: 8 SERVINGS

INGREDIENTS

1 onion, chopped

2 cloves garlic, chopped

Two 15-ounce cans black beans, drained and rinsed

One 7-ounce can corn

One 14.5-ounce can tomatoes with green chilies

2 teaspoons ground cumin

1 teaspoon coriander

6 cups vegetable or chicken broth

½ cup water

Salt to taste

Freshly ground black pepper to taste

1 lime, zested and juiced

½ cup sour cream or Greek yogurt

1 tablespoon hot sauce

4 cups Fritos corn chips

½ cup chopped cilantro

DIRECTIONS

1 In a 1-gallon freezer bag, place the onion, garlic, black beans, corn, tomatoes with green chilies, cumin, coriander, and broth. Remove the excess air from the bag. Place the bag in a bowl to freeze. Freeze up to 3 months.

2 To prepare, use either a multicooker or a slow cooker.

If using a multicooker, dump the frozen ingredients into the pot and add the water to the bottom. Secure the lid and select Pressure Cook for 5 minutes. *Remember:* Frozen ingredients take longer to heat and come to pressure, so give yourself about 30 minutes to cook. After cooking has completed, hold warm until you're ready to serve or do a Quick Release.

If using a slow cooker, dump the frozen ingredients into the pot and add the water to the bottom. Place the lid on top, select the low heat setting, and cook 6 to 8 hours.

3 Season with salt and pepper.

4 Meanwhile, in a separate bowl, mix together the lime zest, lime juice, sour cream or yogurt, and hot sauce.

5 Place ½ cup corn chips in each bowl, ladle the soup over the chips, and top with the lime-infused sour cream (about 1½ tablespoons per bowl) and cilantro (about 1 tablespoon per bowl).

PER SERVING: *Calories 275 (From Fat 87); Fat 10g (Saturated 3g); Cholesterol 7mg; Sodium 1,203mg; Carbohydrate 41g (Dietary Fiber 8g); Protein 9g.*

NOTE: Season bean soups with salt *after* cooking. Broths vary in sodium content — the one you use may be enough seasoning for your taste.

VARY IT! Need to clean out your fridge? Add in chopped carrots, celery, or bell peppers, too! Add grated cabbage to the soup at the end for a bold addition.

Mediterranean White Bean Soup

PREP TIME: ABOUT 10 MIN | **COOK TIME: 40 MIN–8 HR** | **YIELD: 8 SERVINGS**

INGREDIENTS

1 onion, finely chopped

1 celery stalk, thinly sliced

2 carrots, grated

4 cloves garlic, chopped

1 teaspoon dried oregano

½ teaspoon dried thyme

1 bay leaf

Two 14.5-ounce cans cannellini beans, drained and rinsed

5 cups chicken or vegetable broth

½ cup water

1 lemon, zested and juiced

1 cup chopped fresh parsley

Salt to taste

Freshly ground black pepper to taste

½ cup grated Parmesan

DIRECTIONS

1 In a 1-gallon freezer bag, place the onion, celery, carrots, garlic, oregano, thyme, bay leaf, cannellini beans, and broth. Remove the excess air from the bag. Place the bag in a bowl to freeze. Freeze up to 3 months.

2 To prepare, use either a multicooker or a slow cooker.

If using a multicooker, dump the frozen ingredients into the pot and add the water to the bottom. Secure the lid and select Pressure Cook for 5 minutes. *Remember:* Frozen ingredients take longer to heat and come to pressure, so give yourself about 40 minutes to cook. After cooking has completed, hold warm until you're ready to serve or do a Quick Release.

If using a slow cooker, dump the frozen ingredients into the pot and add the water to the bottom. Place the lid on top, select the low heat setting, and cook for 6 to 8 hours.

3 Stir in the lemon zest, lemon juice, and parsley. Season with salt and pepper.

4 Top with Parmesan, and serve.

PER SERVING: *Calories 143 (From Fat 17); Fat 2g (Saturated 1g); Cholesterol 6mg; Sodium 533mg; Carbohydrate 23g (Dietary Fiber 7g); Protein 9g.*

NOTE: Season bean soups with salt *after* cooking. Broths vary in sodium content — the one you use may be enough seasoning for your taste.

VARY IT! For a meaty version, add shredded chicken or cooked ground sausage.

TIP: Serve with crusty French bread or garlic bread.

TIP: If you prefer a creamier version, blend half the soup. Blended white beans create a velvety texture without adding butter or cream.

Steak and Noodle Soup

PREP TIME: ABOUT 10 MIN | COOK TIME: 40 MIN–8 HR | YIELD: 6 SERVINGS

INGREDIENTS

2 tablespoons extra-virgin olive oil

1½ pounds sirloin steak, cubed

1 teaspoon salt plus more to taste, divided

1 teaspoon freshly ground black pepper plus more to taste, divided

1 onion, sliced

2 carrots, sliced

2 celery stalks, sliced

2 tablespoons tomato paste

1 teaspoon dried rosemary

1 tablespoon Worcestershire sauce

6 cups beef broth

½ cup plus 3 tablespoons cold water, divided

1 tablespoon cornstarch

6 ounces egg noodles

DIRECTIONS

1 In a heavy skillet, heat the olive oil over medium-high heat. Season the cubed steak with 1 teaspoon of the salt and 1 teaspoon of the pepper. Add the seasoned steak to the skillet and stir-fry until fully cooked, about 8 minutes. Remove from the heat and cool completely.

2 In a 1-gallon freezer bag, place the onion, carrots, celery, tomato paste, rosemary, Worcestershire sauce, broth, and cooled steak. Remove the excess air from the bag. Place the bag in a bowl to freeze. Freeze up to 3 months.

3 To prepare, use either a multicooker or a slow cooker.

If using a multicooker, dump the frozen ingredients into the pot and add in 1/2 cup of the water to the bottom. Secure the lid and select Pressure Cook for 5 minutes. *Remember:* Frozen ingredients take longer to heat and come to pressure, so give yourself about 30 minutes to cook. After the cooking has completed, hold warm until you're ready to serve or do a Quick Release.

If using a slow cooker, dump the frozen ingredients into the pot and add in 1/2 cup of the water to the bottom. Place the lid on top, select the low heat setting, and cook for 6 to 8 hours.

4 In a small bowl, stir together the remaining 3 tablespoons of cold water and the cornstarch. Add the cornstarch slurry to the soup, and stir to thicken soup. Add in the egg noodles, and stir. Secure the lid and let the soup sit for 10 minutes. Season with salt and pepper.

PER SERVING: *Calories 356 (From Fat 139); Fat 15g (Saturated 5g); Cholesterol 67mg; Sodium 1,068mg; Carbohydrate 26g (Dietary Fiber 2g); Protein 27g.*

VARY IT! To kick this recipe up a notch, stir in 1 tablespoon horseradish and ½ cup sour cream.

NOTE: Cornstarch, when mixed with cold water, can be added to soups or sauces to thicken.

Thai Coconut Soup with Edamame

PREP TIME: ABOUT 10 MIN | **COOK TIME: 30 MIN–6 HR** | **YIELD: 8 SERVINGS**

INGREDIENTS

1 onion, thinly sliced

1 carrot, thinly sliced

2 cups thinly sliced mushrooms

1 teaspoon ground ginger

1 teaspoon curry powder

2 tablespoons soy sauce

2 cups frozen edamame beans, shelled

5 cups vegetable broth

One 13.5-ounce can coconut milk

½ cup water

1 lime, zested and juiced

½ cup chopped cilantro

Salt to taste

DIRECTIONS

1 In a 1-gallon freezer bag, place the onion, carrot, mushrooms, ginger, curry powder, soy sauce, edamame, broth, and coconut milk. Remove excess air from the bag. Place the bag in a bowl to freeze. Freeze up to 3 months.

2 To prepare, use either a multicooker or a slow cooker.

If using a multicooker, dump the frozen ingredients into the pot and add the water to the bottom. Secure the lid and select Pressure Cook for 5 minutes. *Remember:* Frozen ingredients take longer to heat and come to pressure, so give yourself about 30 minutes to cook. After cooking has completed, you can choose to hold warm until you're ready to serve or do a Quick Release.

If using a slow cooker, dump the frozen ingredients into the pot and add the water to the bottom. Place the lid on top, select the low heat setting, and cook for 4 to 6 hours.

3 Stir in the lime zest, lime juice, and cilantro. Season with salt, and serve.

PER SERVING: *Calories 173 (From Fat 113); Fat 13g (Saturated 9g); Cholesterol 0mg; Sodium 617mg; Carbohydrate 12g (Dietary Fiber 2g); Protein 7g.*

NOTE: Be sure to buy coconut milk in a can, not in a carton. Also, look for varieties that have very few additional ingredients.

VARY IT! Add thinly sliced chicken breast for a meatier version. To spice up the soup, add Sriracha or chili pepper flakes.

Chapter **8**

Salads and Bowls

I f you were to ask me what my go-to meal for busy nights or lunches is, I would quickly reply, "Salads and bowls." Salads and bowls can appeal to all ages. Plus, they give kids the power to choose their own toppings. You can serve them prepared or family-style, allowing everyone to build their own meal. Another advantage of both salads and bowls is the fact that you can use canned goods — including beans, corn, peppers, and tuna — to make them. Stock your pantry well so you can pull together a salad or bowl in a hurry.

In this chapter, I share my family's favorite salads and bowls. The Fiesta Taco Salad is great for a quick dinner, and the Thai Steak Salad makes a simple lunch. Explore different flavors from around the globe, and see how quickly you can pull together fun, ethnic meals. If you have a vegetarian in your family or you're leaning toward a more plant-based menu option, try the Veggie Power Bowls, inspired by a trip I took to Hawaii.

Grab your pack of Mason jars or glass, heat-safe storage containers, and prep in advance. These recipes will be good for up to five days in the fridge.

REMEMBER

Hearty vegetables, like carrots, cabbage, cauliflower, and broccoli, are okay to be prepped in advance with dressing, but vegetables like tomatoes, cucumbers, or lettuce should be kept away from anything liquid until you're ready to eat them.

Fiesta Taco Salad

PREP TIME: ABOUT 10 MIN	COOK TIME: 10 MIN	YIELD: 4 SERVINGS

INGREDIENTS

1 pound ground beef
(93 percent lean)

1 teaspoon cumin powder

1 teaspoon garlic powder

½ teaspoon onion powder

1 tablespoon chili powder

1 teaspoon salt

8 cups chopped or torn
romaine lettuce

2 cups broken tortilla or corn
chips

1 cup shredded red cabbage

1 can black beans, drained and
rinsed

1 Hass avocado, diced

1 cup grape tomatoes, halved

½ red onion, thinly sliced

2 cups shredded cheddar
cheese or Monterey Jack

1 lime, juiced

2 tablespoons extra-virgin
olive oil

½ cup Greek yogurt or sour
cream

1 tablespoon hot sauce

DIRECTIONS

1 In a large skillet, cook the ground beef over medium-high heat for 5 minutes, crumbling the meat as it cooks.

2 Meanwhile, in a small bowl, mix together the cumin powder, garlic powder, onion powder, chili powder, and salt. Then, add the spice mixture to the ground meat and cook for an additional 5 minutes. The meat mixture will be browned and fully cooked.

3 The salad can be served as a layered salad or served at the table family-style, allowing family members to serve themselves and create their own desired version. To serve the salad as a layered salad, place the lettuce at the base of a salad bowl. Top with the tortilla chips, cabbage, black beans, avocado, tomatoes, onion, and shredded cheese. Place the cooked meat on top of the salad.

4 In a small bowl, make the dressing. Whisk together the lime juice, olive oil, Greek yogurt or sour cream, and hot sauce. Drizzle the dressing over the top, or allow people to dress their own salad as desired.

PER SERVING: *Calories 737 (From Fat 394); Fat 44g (Saturated 18g); Cholesterol 132mg; Sodium 1,448mg; Carbohydrate 39g (Dietary Fiber 14g); Protein 49g.*

NOTE: Want to make this salad for lunch? Grab a Mason jar and layer the ingredients — meat, beans, lettuce, cabbage, tomatoes, onions, avocados, dressing, and then cheese!

TIP: Buy preshredded lettuce, cabbage and cheese to save time. To prep in advance, make the spice mix for the meat, make the sauce, and pre-chop vegetables. When you're ready to make it, simply cook the meat and pull the remaining ingredients out for serving. Cut the avocado right before serving to keep it fresh.

Beefy Chop House Salad

PREP TIME: ABOUT 5 MIN | COOK TIME: 10 MIN | YIELD: 4 SERVINGS

INGREDIENTS

1 tablespoon extra-virgin olive oil

1 pound sirloin steaks, thinly sliced

2 teaspoons Worcestershire sauce

½ teaspoon freshly ground black pepper

½ teaspoon salt

8 cups torn butter lettuce

2 carrots, grated

8 baby corn spears, chopped

1 cup grape tomatoes, halved

1 cup diced cucumbers

½ cup canned fried onions

½ cup blue cheese dressing

DIRECTIONS

1 In large skillet, heat the olive oil over medium-high heat. Season the steak with Worcestershire sauce, pepper, and salt, tossing to coat. Add the steak to the skillet, and stir-fry until fully cooked, about 8 minutes. Be sure to continuously stir while cooking. When the steak has browned and fully cooked, remove from the heat.

2 This salad can be served family-style or prepared. To prepare, layer the torn lettuce leaves at the base of a salad bowl. Top with the carrot, corn, tomatoes, and cucumbers. Add the sliced steak over the top and sprinkle the fried onions over the top. Serve the blue cheese dressing on the side or drizzle over the top.

PER SERVING: *Calories 511 (From Fat 314); Fat 35g (Saturated 9g); Cholesterol 105mg; Sodium 789mg; Carbohydrate 15g (Dietary Fiber 3g); Protein 33g.*

NOTE: Want to make this salad for lunch? Grab a Mason jar and layer the ingredients — dressing on the bottom, then steak, carrots, corn, lettuce, beans, lettuce, cucumbers, tomatoes, and onions.

VARY IT! Ranch dressing with cheddar cheese works great for those who don't love blue cheese!

TIP: Save time with preshredded lettuce and carrots.

Thai Steak Salad

PREP TIME: ABOUT 10 MIN | COOK TIME: 8 MIN | YIELD: 4 SERVINGS

INGREDIENTS

¼ cup creamy, natural peanut butter

¼ teaspoon ground ginger powder

1 tablespoon low-sodium soy sauce or Bragg Liquid Aminos

½ lime, zested and juiced

1 tablespoon rice wine vinegar or white wine vinegar

2 to 3 tablespoons water, to thin dressing as needed

1 tablespoon extra-virgin olive oil

1 pound sirloin steaks, thinly sliced

½ teaspoon salt

¼ teaspoon freshly ground black pepper

2 cups shredded red cabbage

4 cups shredded romaine lettuce

1 cup grated carrot

1 cup diced red bell pepper

½ red onion thinly sliced

½ cup chopped cilantro

1 cup chopped peanuts

Sriracha sauce to taste (optional)

DIRECTIONS

1 In a small bowl, whisk together the peanut butter, ground ginger powder, soy sauce or Bragg Liquid Aminos, lime zest, lime juice, and vinegar. Let the dressing sit while preparing the salad. Then thin the dressing, as desired, with water. The dressing should be thinner than a ranch-style dressing.

2 In large skillet, heat the olive oil over medium-high heat. Season the steak with salt and black pepper. Add the steak to the skillet and stir-fry until fully cooked, about 8 minutes. Remove from the heat.

3 The salad can be served family-style or prepared. To prepare, layer the cabbage and shredded lettuce leaves at the base of a salad bowl. Layer the steak on top of the greens. Then top with carrot, bell pepper, onion, cilantro, and peanuts.

4 Drizzle the peanut sauce over the top and Sriracha for added spice, and then serve.

PER SERVING: *Calories 634 (From Fat 392); Fat 44g (Saturated 10g); Cholesterol 96mg; Sodium 708mg; Carbohydrate 20g (Dietary Fiber 8g); Protein 46g.*

NOTE: Want to make this salad for lunch? Grab a Mason jar and layer the ingredients — dressing on the bottom, then steak, carrots, bell pepper, peanuts, cabbage, lettuce, cilantro, and onion.

VARY IT! To make a vegetarian version, replace the sirloin with 2 cups of cooked edamame or fried tofu.

TIP: Save time with preshredded lettuce, cabbage, and carrots. You can also buy peanut dressing at select grocery stores.

Canned Tuna Niçoise Salad

PREP TIME: ABOUT 15 MIN	COOK TIME: 30 MIN	YIELD: 4 SERVINGS

INGREDIENTS

12 small new potatoes, halved

1 tablespoon sea salt, divided

2 cups green beans, trimmed

1 lemon, juiced

3 tablespoons white wine vinegar

1 tablespoon Dijon mustard

½ cup extra-virgin olive oil

¼ teaspoon freshly ground black pepper

4 cups torn romaine lettuce

1 cup grape tomatoes, halved

½ English cucumber, sliced thinly

One 8-ounce jar artichoke hearts, drained and chopped

4 large eggs, hard-boiled and quartered

1 cup mixed, pitted olives

One 16-ounce can or package chunk light tuna, drained

DIRECTIONS

1 In a medium saucepan, place the potato halves and fill with water, just to cover the potatoes. Season the water with 1 teaspoon of the sea salt. Place the pot over high heat and bring to a boil. Then cover the potatoes and reduce the heat to a simmer. Simmer until the potatoes are fork tender, about 15 to 20 minutes. Drain and set aside.

2 In a medium saucepan, bring 4 cups of water with 1 teaspoon of the salt to a boil. Add the green beans, and parboil for 5 minutes. Drain and immediately submerge the green beans in ice water for 1 minute. Drain and set aside.

3 Make the lemon vinaigrette. In a small bowl, whisk together the lemon juice, vinegar, mustard, olive oil, the remaining 1 teaspoon of sea salt, and black pepper.

4 To assemble the salad, place the lettuce on a large serving platter. Top with the potatoes, green beans, tomatoes, cucumbers, artichoke hearts, eggs, olives, and tuna. Drizzle with the lemon vinaigrette and serve immediately.

PER SERVING: *Calories 721 (From Fat 385); Fat 43g (Saturated 7g); Cholesterol 242mg; Sodium 1,407mg; Carbohydrate 48g (Dietary Fiber 7g); Protein 38g.*

NOTE: Want to make this salad for lunch? Grab a Mason jar and layer the ingredients — dressing on the bottom, then tuna, potatoes, green beans, olives, artichoke hearts, eggs, tomatoes, cucumbers, and lettuce on top.

Southwestern Bowls

PREP TIME: ABOUT 5 MIN	COOK TIME: 25 MIN	YIELD: 4 SERVINGS

INGREDIENTS

1¾ cups water

1 lime, zested and juiced

½ teaspoon salt

1 cup basmati or white rice, rinsed

½ cup sour cream

½ teaspoon cumin

2 teaspoons hot sauce (optional)

1 tablespoon extra-virgin olive oil

Salt to taste

4 cups shredded romaine lettuce

One 14.5-ounce can pinto beans, drained and rinsed

2 cups cooked chicken

1 cup pico de gallo (chopped salsa)

1 cup prepared guacamole or 1 avocado, chopped

1 cup shredded Mexican-style cheese

DIRECTIONS

1 In a medium saucepan, add the water, lime zest, and salt. Bring to a boil over high heat. Stir in the rice, cover, and reduce the heat to a simmer until cooked, about 15 to 20 minutes. Remove from the heat.

2 Make the dressing. In a small bowl, mix together the lime juice, sour cream, cumin, hot sauce (if using), and olive oil. Season with salt.

3 To assemble the bowls, either serve family-style or prepared. To prepare, divide the rice, lettuce, beans, chicken, pico de gallo, and guacamole or avocado among 4 bowls. Top each bowl with ¼ cup shredded cheese, and serve with the dressing.

PER SERVING: Calories 649 (From Fat 262); Fat 29g (Saturated 11g); Cholesterol 103mg; Sodium 800mg; Carbohydrate 59g (Dietary Fiber 8g); Protein 38g.

NOTE: Want to make these bowls for lunch? In a glass storage container, mix together the rice, beans, and chicken. In a Mason jar, add the dressing, pico de gallo, cheese, and lettuce. Heat the rice, beans, and chicken in a microwave before serving. Then top with the Mason jar contents to serve. Avocado will not hold well for multiple days — it's best to save the avocado and slice for serving or skip the addition.

TIP: When you've cooked extra chicken or rice, this recipe can come together in a flash! Buy prepared guacamole, pico de gallo, shredded lettuce, and shredded cheese to help pull this meal together in seconds.

TIP: If you have an Instant Pot, cook the rice for 4 minutes (1 cup rice to 1¼ cups water) to save time!

Mediterranean Quinoa Bowls

PREP TIME: ABOUT 5 MIN	COOK TIME: 25 MIN	YIELD: 4 SERVINGS

INGREDIENTS

½ teaspoon salt

2 cups water

1 cup quinoa, rinsed

4 cups arugula, baby spinach, or shredded kale leaves

1 cup diced tomatoes

1 cup chopped cucumbers

½ cup chopped olives

1 cup hummus

1 lemon, juiced

¼ cup extra-virgin olive oil

¼ cup chopped parsley or basil leaves

¼ cup crumbled feta or goat cheese

DIRECTIONS

1 In a medium saucepan, add the salt and water and bring to a boil over high heat. Stir in the quinoa, cover, and reduce to a simmer until cooked, about 20 to 25 minutes. Remove from the heat.

2 To assemble bowls, either serve family-style or prepared. To prepare, divide the quinoa; arugula, spinach, or kale; tomatoes; cucumbers; olives; and hummus among 4 bowls. Squeeze the lemon over each of the bowls and drizzle 1 tablespoon olive oil over each bowl. Top with the chopped parsley or basil and crumbled feta or goat cheese.

PER SERVING: *Calories 446(From Fat 227); Fat 25g (Saturated 5g); Cholesterol 8mg; Sodium 787mg; Carbohydrate 45g (Dietary Fiber 7g); Protein 12g.*

NOTE: Want to make these bowls for lunch? Place the quinoa on the bottom of a Mason jar. Whisk together the lemon juice, olive oil, parsley or basil, and feta or goat cheese. Mix the sauce with the tomatoes and cucumbers and add to the jar. Add in the olives and finish with arugula, spinach, or kale.

TIP: Look for precooked quinoa in the freezer section or instant quinoa in the rice section of your grocery store for a time-saving meal option!

VARY IT! Add roasted red peppers, artichoke hearts, and rotisserie chicken if you like.

Korean Spiced Bowls

PREP TIME: ABOUT 10 MIN | **COOK TIME: 20 MIN** | **YIELD: 4 SERVINGS**

INGREDIENTS

2 cups water

1 cup basmati rice, rinsed

1 pound ground beef, 93 percent lean

1 tablespoon brown sugar

2 tablespoons low-sodium soy sauce

1 teaspoon garlic powder

¼ teaspoon ground ginger

2 tablespoons sesame seeds

2 carrots, julienned or grated

1 English cucumber, thinly sliced

2 green onions, thinly sliced

Sriracha sauce to taste (optional)

DIRECTIONS

1 In a medium saucepan, bring the water to a boil over high heat. Stir in the rice, cover, and reduce the heat to a simmer until cooked, about 15 to 20 minutes.

2 Meanwhile, in a large skillet, add the ground beef, brown sugar, soy sauce, garlic powder, and ginger. Cook over medium heat until browned and completely cooked, about 10 minutes. Stir in the sesame seeds, and remove from the heat.

3 To assemble, divide the rice among 4 bowls. Divide the ground meat and sauce on top of the rice. Top with carrots, cucumbers, and onions. Drizzle Sriracha over the top, if desired.

PER SERVING: *Calories 399(From Fat 75); Fat 8g (Saturated 3g); Cholesterol 70mg; Sodium 371mg; Carbohydrate 50g (Dietary Fiber 3g); Protein 30g.*

NOTE: Want to make these bowls for lunch? Place the cooked rice on the bottom of a glass, heat-safe storage container. Top with ground beef. In another container, mix together the carrots, cucumbers, and green onions. To serve, microwave the rice and meat mixture and top with fresh vegetables.

TIP: Look for precooked rice in the freezer section or bulk cook and freeze your own.

VARY IT! Add a fried egg, *kimchi* (Korean fermented cabbage), or shredded cabbage.

Indian Chicken Bowls

PREP TIME: ABOUT 30 MIN | COOK TIME: 30 MIN | YIELD: 4 SERVINGS

INGREDIENTS

1 cup full-fat plain Greek yogurt

1 tablespoon curry powder

1 teaspoon ground cumin

1 lemon, zested and juiced

1 pound boneless, skinless chicken thighs, thinly sliced

1¾ cups water

½ teaspoon salt

1 cup jasmine or basmati rice, rinsed

¼ cup tahini (ground sesame butter)

1 clove garlic, minced

¼ teaspoon paprika

1 tablespoon honey

¼ cup water (or more as needed to thin dressing)

1 tablespoon vegetable oil

8 cups baby spinach

One 14.5-ounce can garbanzo beans, drained and rinsed

1 cup chopped cashews

DIRECTIONS

1   In a shallow baking dish, mix together the yogurt, curry powder, cumin, and lemon zest. Add the chicken and fully coat with marinade; let the mixture sit at room temperature for 30 minutes.

2   In a medium saucepan, add the water and salt and bring to a boil over high heat. Stir in the rice, cover, and reduce the heat to a simmer until cooked, about 15 to 20 minutes. Remove from the heat.

3   Meanwhile, make the tahini dressing. Whisk together the lemon juice, tahini, garlic, paprika, honey, and water, adding more water as needed to make a thin dressing.

4   Next, in a medium skillet, heat the oil over medium heat. Remove the chicken from the marinade and add to the hot skillet. Cook the chicken until done, stirring frequently, about 8 minutes.

5   Either serve family-style or prepared. To prepare, place the spinach at the base of bowls. Add the rice, chicken, garbanzo beans, and cashews. Drizzle with the dressing, as desired.

PER SERVING: *Calories 768 (From Fat 294); Fat 33g (Saturated 6g); Cholesterol 97mg; Sodium 786mg; Carbohydrate 77g (Dietary Fiber 6g); Protein 45g.*

NOTE: Want to make these bowls for lunch? Place the tahini dressing at the base of a Mason jar. Add the garbanzo beans, cashews, and spinach. In a heat-safe glass storage container, place the chicken and rice. To serve, heat the rice and chicken in a microwave; then toss with the remaining bowl ingredients.

TIP: Look for precooked rice in the freezer section or bulk cook and freeze your own.

VARY IT! Add grated carrots or sliced bell peppers, or replace the spinach with thinly sliced kale.

Chinese Chicken Slaw Bowls

PREP TIME: ABOUT 15 MIN | COOK TIME: NONE | YIELD: 4 SERVINGS

INGREDIENTS

3 tablespoons rice wine vinegar

1 tablespoon sesame oil

1 tablespoon canola oil or vegetable oil

2 tablespoons low-sodium soy sauce

¼ teaspoon ground ginger

½ teaspoon garlic powder

4 cups shredded cabbage

2 cups shredded rotisserie chicken or canned chicken

1 cup grated carrots

4 green onions, finely sliced

½ cup sliced almonds or chopped cashews

1 cup crunchy wontons or fried noodles

8 ounces canned mandarin oranges (in water or juice), drained

DIRECTIONS

1 Make the dressing. In a small bowl, whisk together the vinegar, sesame oil, canola or vegetable oil, soy sauce, ginger, and garlic powder.

2 In a large salad bowl, place the cabbage as the base. Then add the chicken, carrots, onions, almonds or cashews, wontons or fried noodles, and mandarin oranges. Drizzle over the dressing and toss to serve.

PER SERVING: *Calories 390 (From Fat 180); Fat 17g (Saturated 3g); Cholesterol 71mg; Sodium 399mg; Carbohydrate 25g (Dietary Fiber 3g); Protein 28g.*

NOTE: Want to make these bowls for lunch? Place the dressing at the base of a Mason jar. Then add the mandarin oranges, chicken, carrots, onions, almonds or cashews, fried wontons or fried noodles, and cabbage.

TIP: Don't frown at canned chicken. It can help you out when you're in a bind! Costco brand has won taste tests for best canned chicken; one can is 12.5 ounces.

TIP: Bagged shredded cabbage or grated carrots can help pull this recipe together in a pinch.

Lebanese Spiced Veggie Bowls

PREP TIME: ABOUT 25 MIN	COOK TIME: 8 MIN	YIELD: 4 SERVINGS

INGREDIENTS

¼ cup dried bulgur

4 cups chopped fresh parsley

¼ cup chopped fresh mint

1 lemon, juiced

¼ teaspoon ground cloves

2 large tomatoes, chopped

1 English cucumber, chopped

½ red onion, minced

1 teaspoon salt, divided

¼ cup extra-virgin olive oil, divided

1 cup chopped olives

One 14.5-ounce can garbanzo beans, drained and rinsed

¼ cup crumbled feta

Four 8-inch flatbreads

½ teaspoon garlic powder

DIRECTIONS

1 Make the tabbouleh mixture. In a large bowl, mix together the bulgur and ¼ cup boiling water. Let the mixture sit for 5 minutes to soften the bulgur. Next, add the parsley, mint, lemon juice, cloves, tomatoes, cucumbers, onion, ¾ teaspoon of the salt, and 3 tablespoons of the olive oil. Set aside for 15 minutes to reconstitute the bulgur.

2 To assemble the bowls, place tabbouleh mixture on the bottom of 4 bowls. Top with the olives, garbanzo beans, and crumbled feta.

3 Brush the flatbreads with the remaining 1 tablespoon of olive oil. In a heavy skillet, toast the flatbreads over high heat for 1 to 2 minutes on each side. Season the toasted breads with garlic powder and the remaining ¼ teaspoon of salt. Serve with the tabbouleh bowls.

PER SERVING: *Calories 470 (From Fat 223); Fat 25g (Saturated 7g); Cholesterol 20mg; Sodium 1,333mg; Carbohydrate 54g (Dietary Fiber 11g); Protein 13g.*

NOTE: Want to make these bowls for lunch? Place the tabbouleh mixture at the base of a Mason jar. Top with garbanzo beans, olives, and crumbled feta. Heat the flatbreads in a microwave for 5 to 10 seconds to serve warm or use a toaster to heat.

VARY IT! Replace the garbanzo beans with hummus, add in rotisserie chicken, or add in grated carrots.

Veggie Power Bowls

PREP TIME: ABOUT 15 MIN	COOK TIME: 25 MIN	YIELD: 4 SERVINGS

INGREDIENTS

1 pound sweet potatoes, diced into 1-inch cubes

1 tablespoon extra-virgin olive oil

1 teaspoon salt, divided

1 lemon, juiced

¼ cup tahini (ground sesame butter)

1 clove garlic, minced

1 tablespoon honey

2¼ cups water, divided

2 cups Brussels sprouts, shredded, grated, or thinly sliced

1 cup sliced, pickled beets

½ cup sliced almonds

2 green onions, thinly sliced

DIRECTIONS

1 Preheat the oven to 425 degrees. Place the parchment paper on a baking sheet.

2 In a large bowl, toss the sweet potatoes with the olive oil and ½ teaspoon of the salt. Roast for 25 to 30 minutes, stirring every 10 minutes to toast all sides.

3 Make the tahini dressing. In a small bowl, whisk together the lemon juice, tahini, garlic, honey, and ¼ cup of the water, adding more water as needed to make a thin dressing.

4 To assemble the bowls, place the Brussels sprouts at the base of 4 bowls. Top with the sweet potatoes, beets, almonds, and onions. Drizzle with dressing to serve.

PER SERVING: Calories 379 (From Fat 189); Fat 21g (Saturated 3g); Cholesterol 0mg; Sodium 808mg; Carbohydrate 43g (Dietary Fiber 9g); Protein 10g.

NOTE: Want to make these bowls for lunch? Place the dressing at the base of a Mason jar. Next, add the Brussels sprouts, almonds, beets, and sweet potatoes. Top with onions. Don't worry — cold roasted sweet potatoes are still delicious!

TIP: To quicken the meal prep, look for preshredded bags of Brussels sprouts in the bagged lettuce section.

VARY IT! Replace the roasted sweet potatoes with roasted butternut squash, potatoes, or beets. Use shredded cabbage in place of Brussels sprouts. Add in garbanzo or black beans.

On-the-Go Vegetarian Ramen Bowls

PREP TIME: ABOUT 10 MIN	COOK TIME: 5 MIN	YIELD: 4 SERVINGS

INGREDIENTS

4 teaspoons miso

4 teaspoons vegetarian or chicken base paste

4 tablespoons low-sodium soy sauce

4 cups baby spinach

4 large eggs, hard-boiled and halved

4 sheets dried seaweed (like wakame or nori) or ¼ cup crumbled seaweed

2 cups cooked and deshelled edamame

2 packages ramen noodles (discard seasoning package)

4 green onions, thinly sliced

48 ounces boiling water

DIRECTIONS

1 In each of 4 quart-size Mason jars, place 1 teaspoon miso and 1 teaspoon vegetarian or chicken base paste. Add 1 tablespoon soy sauce to each jar. Add 1 cup spinach, 1 egg, 1 crumbled sheet of seaweed or 1 tablespoon crumbled seaweed, and ½ cup cooked edamame (see package for instructions if you buy frozen edamame). Break the ramen noodles in half and place ½ package into each jar. Top with green onions.

2 To serve, pour 12 ounces of boiling water in each jar, secure the lids, and swirl the jars. Gently release the pressure from the lid, and allow the soup to steep for 5 minutes or until reconstituted. Serve immediately.

PER SERVING: *Calories 296 (From Fat 113); Fat 13g (Saturated 4g); Cholesterol 212mg; Sodium 1,326mg; Carbohydrate 25g (Dietary Fiber 5g); Protein 19g.*

NOTE: These bowls are great on cold days. You can also make them ahead of time in a thermos, but the soup will need to be consumed within 3 hours or the noodles will become too soft to enjoy.

VARY IT! Add in frozen peas, green beans, or sliced mushrooms.

4

Time-Saving Meaty Mains

Discover the how to roast a turkey.

Create a fork-tender brisket from the oven.

Revamp your favorite pork roast into zesty new main dishes.

Roast your own rotisserie chicken.

Explore creative ways to serve ham.

Prep ahead and make sheet-pan meals for the week.

Stock your freezer with freezer-friendly main dishes.

Cut back on kitchen time with meals that can be made in less than 20 minutes.

Chapter **9**

Turkey: Today, Tomorrow, and the Next Day

RECIPES IN THIS CHAPTER

* **Oven-Roasted Turkey**

* **Turkey and Vegetable Soup**

* **Turkey and Broccoli Pot Pie**

* **Cream of Turkey with Biscuits**

* **Turkey and Noodles**

Turkey is not just for Thanksgiving! This versatile bird provides ample protein to create delicious leftovers and delectable sandwiches. If you're cooking for just one person, buy a turkey breast and cook that instead of a massive turkey. If you have a larger family, consider purchasing 2 to 2½ pounds per person, so if you have a six-person family, get a 12- to 15-pound bird. This will give you a carcass to make broth, meat for a meal, and enough meat for creative carryovers.

These carryover meals are all family-favorites in our home. Even though the turkey will take some time to cook, the carryover meals are quick and easy to pull together!

Oven-Roasted Turkey

PREP TIME: ABOUT 20 MIN | **COOK TIME: 4 HR** | **YIELD: 12 SERVINGS**

INGREDIENTS

One 15-pound turkey

4 tablespoons chopped fresh rosemary, divided

4 tablespoons chopped fresh thyme, divided

6 cloves garlic, divided

2 lemons, sliced and divided

1 onion, sliced

½ cup unsalted butter

¼ cup white wine or vegetable broth

½ cup extra-virgin olive oil

2 teaspoons salt

2 teaspoons freshly ground black pepper

DIRECTIONS

1 Preheat the oven to 325 degrees. Ready a roasting rack and pan.

2 Remove the giblets from the turkey. Pat the turkey skin dry with paper towels. Place 3 tablespoons of rosemary and 3 tablespoons of thyme inside the cavity of the turkey. Add 3 garlic cloves, 1 of the sliced lemons, and the onion to the cavity.

3 In a small microwave-safe bowl, melt the butter in the microwave for about 1 minute. Whisk together the butter, white wine or broth, the remaining 1 tablespoon of rosemary, the remaining 1 tablespoon of thyme, olive oil, salt, and pepper.

4 Next, chop the remaining 3 garlic cloves. Lift up the skin of the turkey and place the garlic and the remaining lemon slices under the skin. Using a pastry brush, baste the turkey with the sauce. Pour the remaining sauce inside the cavity of the turkey. Place the turkey on the roasting rack, and bake approximately 15 minutes per pound, about 3 hours and 45 minutes. After 3 hours of baking, begin checking the internal temperature; remove when it reaches 165 degrees.

5 Meanwhile, baste the turkey with the pan drippings at least twice while baking.

6 After removing the turkey from the oven, cover immediately with foil and allow to rest for at least 15 minutes prior to carving.

7 Carve the turkey and serve or store for up to 5 days in the refrigerator or up to 1 month in the freezer.

PER SERVING: *Calories 684 (From Fat 309); Fat 34g (Saturated 11g); Cholesterol 391mg; Sodium 593mg; Carbohydrate 0g (Dietary Fiber 0g); Protein 88g.*

NOTE: To cook the carcass, place the turkey bones into an Instant Pot or slow cooker and cover with cold water. Secure the lid and pressure-cook for 1 hour or slow-cook for 8 hours. Strain the broth and refrigerate up to 5 days or freeze up to 6 months.

NOTE: To cook the giblets, place in a medium saucepan and cover with water. Bring to a boil and then reduce to a simmer for 1 hour. The giblet broth can be used for gravy or sauces.

TIP: To cook a turkey breast in a multicooker, place 1 cup chicken stock in the metal pan, place the cooking rack inside, and add a 2- to 3-pound seasoned turkey breast. Pressure-cook on high for 30 minutes with a natural release of pressure; check the internal temperature to ensure the meat is cooked to 165 degrees.

VARY IT! Mix up the fresh herbs with parsley or sage.

TIP

TURKEY TIPS

Here are my top-five tips for cooking a turkey.

- **Buy a better-quality turkey.** Leading brands or butcher-quality turkeys don't need to be brined to give you a tasty, tender piece of meat.

- **Thaw in the refrigerator, estimating one day per 5 pounds.** Yes, it may take up some added fridge space, but it's worth it!

- **Use a thermometer to do temperature checks.** The rule of thumb is cooking about 15 minutes per pound. You want to check the temperature in the meatiest part of the breast, but don't press through to the bone. Insert and look for an internal temperature of 165 degrees; it should hold that temperature for 3 minutes. Then remove the bird, cover with foil, and allow the turkey to rest for 15 minutes before slicing.

- **Only stuff the turkey with vegetables and citrus for flavoring; leave the stuffing on the side for even cooking.** Yes, my grandmother always stuffed her bird, but doing so can really lengthen the cooking time and also risk overcooking the meat in order to fully cook the stuffing. Skip it and keep it on the side.

- **If you don't have a roasting pan, put something under the turkey to create airflow around the bottom of the turkey and to keep it from swimming in the drippings.** Use those drippings to baste your bird twice while cooking!

Turkey and Vegetable Soup

| PREP TIME: ABOUT 10 MIN | COOK TIME: 20 MIN–8 HR | YIELD: 8 SERVINGS |

INGREDIENTS

1 large onion, chopped

2 carrots, diced

2 celery stalks, diced

2 cups frozen green beans

1 cup peas or lima beans

2 russet potatoes, diced

One 10-ounce bag frozen corn

One 29-ounce can chopped tomatoes

3 cups diced, cooked turkey

4 cups turkey or chicken broth

1 bay leaf

2 tablespoons dried parsley or ¼ cup fresh parsley

Salt to taste

Freshly ground black pepper to taste

DIRECTIONS

1 Choose one of the following methods:

In a 6-quart Instant Pot, place all the ingredients in the pot, secure the lid, and select Pressure Cook (High) for 12 minutes. Allow the pot to naturally depressurize for at least 10 minutes before doing a Quick Release.

In a slow cooker, place all the ingredients in the slow cooker, secure the lid, and cook on low for 6 to 8 hours or on high for 4 hours.

On the stovetop, place all the ingredients in a large stock pot and bring to a boil. Lower the heat to a simmer, cover, and allow the soup to simmer for 30 minutes or until the potatoes are fork tender.

2 To serve, season with salt and pepper.

PER SERVING: *Calories 224 (From Fat 20); Fat 2g (Saturated 1g); Cholesterol 51mg; Sodium 525mg; Carbohydrate 31g (Dietary Fiber 6g); Protein 22g.*

NOTE: This recipe is a great way to use the turkey broth prepared from the carcass!

VARY IT! Add in shredded cabbage or diced butternut squash.

TIP: Save time by using frozen vegetables, like a mirepoix mix (onions, celery, and carrots), frozen peas, and frozen green beans.

TIP: This recipe is great for the freezer, too! Place all ingredients in a freezer-safe bag and freeze. To cook, use your preferred cooking method and cook until done.

Turkey and Broccoli Pot Pie

PREP TIME: ABOUT 15 MIN	COOK TIME: 35 MIN	YIELD: 6 SERVINGS

INGREDIENTS

2 russet potatoes, diced

2 teaspoons salt, divided

1 tablespoon extra-virgin olive oil

½ onion, chopped

2 carrots, sliced

2 celery stalks, diced

2 tablespoons unsalted butter

¼ cup all-purpose flour

1 teaspoon dried thyme

½ teaspoon freshly ground black pepper

1¾ cup turkey or chicken broth

¼ cup half-and-half or whole milk

3 cups chopped, cooked turkey

1 cup frozen chopped broccoli

1 prepared single pie crust dough (at room temperature)

DIRECTIONS

1 Preheat the oven to 400 degrees and ready a pie pan or Dutch oven.

2 In a microwave-safe bowl, place the potatoes and 1 teaspoon of the salt, and cover with water. Microwave for 6 minutes.

3 Meanwhile, in a Dutch oven, heat the olive oil over medium-high heat. Sauté the onion, carrots, and celery for 3 minutes. Stir in the butter, flour, thyme, pepper, and the remaining 1 teaspoon of salt. Toast the flour for 3 minutes. Stir in the turkey broth and half-and-half. Turn the heat down to low and let the mixture simmer for 5 minutes, stirring occasionally.

4 Drain the potatoes and add to the pot pie filling. Stir in the turkey and broccoli.

5 Unroll the pie crust. Transfer the filling to a deep-dish pie pan or deep round baking dish. Then place the pie crust over the top. If you're using an oven-safe Dutch oven, simply place the pie dough over the top of the filling. Flute the edges, and cut 3 slits in the top of the pie dough.

6 Bake for 35 minutes or until golden brown and bubbly.

7 Remove from the oven and serve warm.

PER SERVING: *Calories 418 (From Fat 163); Fat 18g (Saturated 7g); Cholesterol 80mg; Sodium 1,108mg; Carbohydrate 38g (Dietary Fiber 4g); Protein 26g.*

NOTE: This recipe freezes beautifully. Cool the filling after cooking. Pour into a freezer-safe pie pan, top with the crust, and freeze. Once frozen, seal with a vacuum sealer or cover with foil completely to protect the crust. Freeze up to 3 months. To bake, defrost overnight and bake for 45 minutes to 1 hour at 350 degrees.

TIP: Save time by using frozen vegetables, like a mirepoix mix (onions, celery, and carrots).

Cream of Turkey with Biscuits

PREP TIME: ABOUT 5 MIN	COOK TIME: 20 MIN	YIELD: 8 SERVINGS

INGREDIENTS

One 16-ounce can biscuits or 8 frozen biscuits

1 tablespoon extra-virgin olive oil

2 tablespoons unsalted butter

½ onion, finely diced

1 celery stalk, finely diced

1 green bell pepper, finely diced

⅓ cup all-purpose flour

1¾ cups turkey broth

½ cup heavy cream or half-and-half

4 cups chopped, cooked turkey

Salt to taste

Freshly ground black pepper to taste

DIRECTIONS

1 Preheat the oven and bake the biscuits according to package directions.

2 In a heavy skillet or Dutch oven, heat the olive oil and butter over medium–high heat. Add the onion, celery, and bell pepper. Cook for 5 minutes, stirring frequently. Add in the flour, stirring to toast or lightly brown the flour for 2 to 3 minutes. Whisk in the broth and cream and reduce the heat to simmer until the sauce thickens, about 8 minutes.

3 If you have a picky eater, consider blending the sauce with a stick blender or in a traditional blender. Otherwise, stir in the chopped turkey and season with salt and black pepper. Cut the biscuits in half to open them; then ladle the cream of turkey over the top to serve.

PER SERVING: *Calories 312 (From Fat 77); Fat 9g (Saturated 3g); Cholesterol 77mg; Sodium 652mg; Carbohydrate 32g (Dietary Fiber 2g); Protein 26g.*

NOTE: As a child, this was my most favorite post-Thanksgiving meal! I craved it more than the Thanksgiving feast. When my nephews were born, they didn't love the peppers, so my mom began blending it for them. This recipe is definitely a favorite for all ages!

TIP: Frozen or canned biscuits have their place! The use of these time-saving ingredients can really keep a busy family sane. If you prefer a homemade biscuit, they can absolutely be used, too!

TIP: To prep in advance, prechop the vegetables, premeasure the flour, and prechop the turkey.

Turkey and Noodles

| PREP TIME: ABOUT 5 MIN | COOK TIME: 13 MIN | YIELD: 6 SERVINGS |

INGREDIENTS

1 tablespoon unsalted butter

½ onion, diced

2 carrots, thinly sliced

2 celery stalks, thinly sliced

6 cups turkey or chicken broth

1 teaspoon dried thyme

1 bay leaf

1 cup frozen peas

3 cups chopped, cooked turkey

One 12- to 16-ounce bag dried egg noodles

Salt to taste

Freshly ground black pepper to taste

DIRECTIONS

In a Dutch oven or large saucepan, heat the butter over medium heat. Add the onion, carrots, and celery, and cook for 5 minutes, stirring occasionally. Add the broth, thyme, bay leaf, peas, and turkey. Increase the heat to high, and bring to a boil. Add the noodles, reduce the heat to medium, and cook until tender, about 8 minutes.

PER SERVING: *Calories 397 (From Fat 61); Fat 7g (Saturated 3g); Cholesterol 122mg; Sodium 519mg; Carbohydrate 50g (Dietary Fiber 5g); Protein 33g.*

NOTE: This is like a thick noodle soup.

VARY IT! Not a pea lover? Replace the peas with 3 cups baby spinach (add it right before serving instead of cooking it down) or stir in 1 cup shredded cabbage. If you want to kick the broth up a notch, swap out 1 cup broth for 1 cup white wine and add cracked red pepper flakes to heat things up!

NOTE: If preparing to store and serve later, slightly undercook the noodles for 6 minutes instead.

TIP: To prep in advance, prechop the vegetables, premeasure the spices, and prechop the turkey.

Chapter **10**

Brisket: Fix It and Revisit It

I love a slow-smoked brisket, but there are many other great ways to prepare and use this inexpensive cut of beef. Preparing a large piece of meat, like brisket, will take a couple hours of cooking time initially, but the rewards are great. Whip up four meals that take less than 20 minutes to pull together or opt for a casserole that you can prep while baking your brisket and then assemble ahead of time and refrigerate later that week.

If time gets away from you, opt for the Street Tacos or French Dip Sandwiches — both take less than ten minutes. If you're looking for a simple side to pair with these dishes, opt for sliced cucumbers, store-bought fruit salad, or a salad kit.

Brisket freezes well. If you prepare too much, wrap it in an airtight freezer bag and freeze up to 3 months.

Roasted Brisket

PREP TIME: 32 MIN	COOK TIME: 3½ HR	YIELD: 12 SERVINGS

INGREDIENTS

2 tablespoons chili powder

1 teaspoon ground cumin

2 teaspoons garlic powder

1 teaspoon onion powder

2 tablespoons brown sugar

¼ cup mustard

1 tablespoon salt

1 tablespoon freshly ground
black pepper

4 pounds beef brisket, trimmed

2 cups beef broth

DIRECTIONS

1 In a small bowl, mix together the chili powder, cumin, garlic powder, onion powder, brown sugar, mustard, salt, and pepper.

2 Place the brisket into a roasting pan. Rub the brisket on all sides with the mustard spice mixture. Let the brisket rest for 30 minutes at room temperature.

3 Meanwhile preheat the oven to 300 degrees.

4 Pour the beef stock into the roasting pan. Cover the pan with foil and bake for 3 hours and 30 minutes. Start checking the meat for doneness around 3 hours; it should be fork tender. Once tender, remove from the oven and allow the meat to rest for 15 minutes. The brisket is fork tender and done when it reaches an internal temperature of 180 degrees.

5 In a slow cooker, cook the meat for 8 to 10 hours on low heat.

PER SERVING: *Calories 201 (From Fat 92); Fat 10g (Saturated 4g); Cholesterol 72mg; Sodium 826mg; Carbohydrate 2g (Dietary Fiber 0g); Protein 24g.*

NOTE: If you want to use an Instant Pot, you'll need to cut the meat down to a 2-pound portion. Reduce the amount of broth to 1½ cups. Place the trivet at the base of the pot, add the liquid, and put the rubbed meat onto the trivet. Secure the lid and set to high pressure for 75 minutes; then do a natural release for at least 15 minutes. (A Quick Release can make the meat more tough.)

TIP: To make a gravy from the pan drippings, pour 2 cups of drippings into a saucepan. Mix together 3 tablespoons cornstarch with 3 tablespoons cold water. Bring the sauce to a simmer and whisk in the cold cornstarch slurry. Season with salt and pepper, as desired.

VARY IT! Mix up the fresh herbs with parsley or sage!

Street Tacos

INGREDIENTS

2 tablespoons extra-virgin olive oil

3 cups beef brisket, chopped

1 teaspoon ground cumin

2 teaspoons chili powder

2 tablespoons water

1 cup chopped cilantro

1 small onion, finely diced

1 jalapeño pepper, finely diced (optional)

2 limes, divided

Twelve 6-inch flour or corn tortillas, heated or warmed

½ cup crumbled cotija cheese or preferred cheese

DIRECTIONS

1 In a heavy-duty or cast-iron skillet, heat the olive oil over high heat. Season the meat with cumin, chili powder, and water. Add the meat to the hot skillet and stir-fry until warmed through and slightly crispy, about 4 to 5 minutes. Remove from the heat.

2 Meanwhile, in a medium bowl, mix together the cilantro, onion, and jalapeño. Squeeze 1 lime over the top. Cut the other lime into 6 wedges to serve with tacos.

3 To assemble the tacos, use about ¼ cup meat per tortilla, top with the cilantro mixture, and crumble cheese over the top. Squeeze the remaining lime over the top.

PER SERVING: *Calories 445 (From Fat 183); Fat 20g (Saturated 7g); Cholesterol 74mg; Sodium 668mg; Carbohydrate 37g (Dietary Fiber 3g); Protein 28g.*

NOTE: Street tacos are fairly simple with onion, cilantro, and jalapeño peppers. Feel free to serve with your favorite toppings or salsa.

VARY IT! Mix up the fresh herbs with parsley or sage.

TIP: To prep in advance, prechop the vegetables.

Enchilada Casserole

PREP TIME: ABOUT 10 MIN	COOK TIME: 35 MIN	YIELD: 8 SERVINGS

INGREDIENTS

One 28-ounce can red enchilada sauce, divided

Twelve 6-inch corn tortillas

3 cups chopped brisket, divided

One 14.5-ounce can pinto beans, drained and rinsed, divided

3 cups shredded Monterey Jack cheese or shredded Mexican cheese, divided

1 Hass avocado, diced

1 lime, juiced

2 medium tomatoes, diced

3 green onions, chopped, or ¼ cup finely diced red onion

4 cups shredded lettuce

DIRECTIONS

1 Preheat the oven to 350 degrees.

2 In a 9-x-13-inch baking dish, pour in one-third of the enchilada sauce. Next, lay a single, overlapping layer of corn tortillas, cutting or tearing the tortillas as needed to cover the bottom. Add 1½ cups of chopped brisket, half of the can of beans, and 1 cup shredded cheese. Pour another one-third of the enchilada sauce over the top of the meaty filling. Add the second layer of tortillas. Add the remaining layer of brisket and beans. Top with 1 cup shredded cheese. Add another layer of tortillas and the remaining enchilada sauce, spreading the sauce with the back of a spoon over the tortilla shells; then add the remaining 1 cup of shredded cheese. Cover the casserole with foil. Bake for 20 minutes. Then remove the foil and bake until bubbly and the cheese has completely melted, about 10 to 15 minutes. Allow the casserole to rest for 10 minutes before cutting and serving.

3 Meanwhile, mix together the avocado, lime, tomatoes, and onions. To serve, cut the casserole into squares and top with shredded lettuce and the avocado and tomato mixture.

PER SERVING: *Calories 549 (From Fat 314); Fat 35g (Saturated 17g); Cholesterol 120mg; Sodium 402mg; Carbohydrate 30g (Dietary Fiber 7g); Protein 31g.*

NOTE: The casserole can be made into personal-size baking dishes and frozen for up to 1 month. To cook, simply defrost overnight in the refrigerator and bake as noted in the recipe. The cooked casserole is good up to 4 days in the refrigerator.

TIP: Spray the foil with cooking spray to prevent the cheese from sticking to the foil while baking.

VARY IT! Add corn to the casserole, swap out pinto beans for black beans, or add in canned jalapeños. For the topping, add sour cream and black olives.

TIP: To prep in advance, prechop the vegetables (except the avocado) and prechop the meat. The uncooked casserole can be made 3 days in advance.

Sweet Potato and Brisket Hash

INGREDIENTS

2 tablespoons extra-virgin olive oil

2 medium sweet potatoes, scrubbed clean and diced (with skin on)

1 red, yellow, or orange bell pepper, finely chopped

½ medium onion, finely chopped

½ teaspoon salt

½ teaspoon freshly ground black pepper

2 cups chopped brisket

DIRECTIONS

In a heavy skillet, heat the oil over medium–high heat. Add the sweet potatoes and cook for 4 minutes, stirring frequently to evenly brown on all sides. Add the bell pepper and onion, and continue to cook for 8 minutes. Season with salt and black pepper, and stir in the brisket. Reduce the heat to medium–low and cover the pan with a lid. Cook covered for 4 to 6 minutes or until the brisket is heated and the sweet potatoes are fork tender, stirring occasionally.

PER SERVING: Calories 299 (From Fat 145); Fat 16g (Saturated 4g); Cholesterol 62mg; Sodium 481mg; Carbohydrate 17g (Dietary Fiber 3g); Protein 21g.

TIP: Frozen sweet potatoes or prechopped sweet potatoes can work in this dish and help cut back on prep and cook times.

VARY IT! Replace the sweet potatoes with butternut squash or russet potatoes. Make a nest and add in eggs for a hearty breakfast or breakfast-for-dinner option. With eggs, cover the pan with a lid to cook the eggs or place in a 400-degree oven for 10 minutes or until the eggs are fully cooked.

TIP: To prep in advance, prechop the vegetables (store sweet potatoes in water) and prechop the meat.

Black Bean and Brisket Tostadas

PREP TIME: ABOUT 10 MIN	COOK TIME: 16 MIN	YIELD: 4 SERVINGS

INGREDIENTS

2 tablespoons extra-virgin olive oil

Eight 6-inch corn tortillas

One 14.5-ounce can black beans, drained and rinsed

2 cups chopped brisket

1 cup shredded Mexican cheese or Monterey Jack

2 cups shredded lettuce or cabbage

½ cup salsa

1 Hass avocado, diced

¼ cup sour cream or Greek yogurt

½ lime, juiced

1 tablespoon hot sauce

DIRECTIONS

1 Preheat the oven to 400 degrees. Place foil onto 2 baking sheets.

2 In a heavy skillet, heat the olive oil over medium–high heat. Heat the corn tortillas 30 seconds on each side. Spread out the heated tortillas onto the baking sheets.

3 To assemble for baking, evenly top the tortillas with black beans. Divide the brisket over the top of the beans. Finally, add the cheese. Bake for 8 to 10 minutes or until the cheese has melted.

4 To serve, top the tostadas with shredded lettuce, salsa, and avocado. Next, in a small bowl make the Mexican crema by mixing the sour cream, lime juice, and hot sauce. Drizzle the sauce over the top and serve.

PER SERVING: *Calories 609 (From Fat 314); Fat 35g (Saturated 12g); Cholesterol 95mg; Sodium 598mg; Carbohydrate 41g (Dietary Fiber 12g); Protein 36g.*

NOTE: Buy premade tostada shells for a faster meal prep.

VARY IT! Swap out black beans with refried beans. Add in sliced olives or canned corn.

TIP: To prep in advance, prechop the vegetables (except avocado), pre-rinse the beans, make the sauce up to 3 days in advance, and prechop the meat.

French Dip Sandwiches

PREP TIME: ABOUT 5 MIN	COOK TIME: 8 MIN	YIELD: 6 SERVINGS

INGREDIENTS

6 French rolls, split

12 teaspoons plus 1 tablespoon unsalted butter

3 cups thinly shredded brisket

1 teaspoon Worcestershire sauce

2 cups beef broth, divided

1 teaspoon cornstarch

Salt to taste

Freshly ground black pepper to taste

DIRECTIONS

1 Preheat the oven to 450 degrees.

2 Place the French rolls onto a foil-lined baking sheet. Butter each side of the rolls with 1 teaspoon butter.

3 Meanwhile, in a saucepan heat the Worcestershire sauce and 1½ cups beef broth over medium heat until it begins to simmer. In a small bowl, whisk together the remaining ½ cup of beef broth with the cornstarch. Add the cornstarch mixture to the beef broth and whisk in the remaining 1 tablespoon of butter, and turn to a low heat. This will give the sauce a shine. Season with salt and pepper.

4 In a medium bowl, place ¼ cup of the broth mixture with the shredded brisket. Top each French roll with ½ cup sliced brisket. Place the rolls into the oven and reduce the heat to 400 degrees. Bake until the bread is toasted and the meat is warmed, about 5 to 8 minutes.

5 Serve the heated sandwiches with the remaining broth to dip into or drizzle over the top and serve.

PER SERVING: *Calories 349 (From Fat 172); Fat 19g (Saturated 9g); Cholesterol 88mg; Sodium 649mg; Carbohydrate 19g (Dietary Fiber 1g); Protein 24g.*

NOTE: Serve with a side salad. Buy a quick salad kit to pull this meal together in minutes!

VARY IT! Add in fresh thyme or rosemary to season the broth. Brush the bread with garlic butter for a savory addition.

TIP: To prep in advance, shred the meat and premeasure the cornstarch and keep in a covered bowl.

Chapter **11**

Pork Dishes to Please Everyone

Discover the versatility of pork! In this chapter, you jump into pork by braising a butt or shoulder roast. These cuts are meaty, flavorful, and absolutely delicious. There are many simple ways to braise a pork roast, from simple salt and pepper to barbecue sauce. My most favorite way is with citrus. The oranges give the pork subtle sweet and tangy notes, but don't alter it so much that it can't be made into a variety of cultural dishes, from Barbecue Pork Pizza to Shredded Pork Rice Paper Rolls.

In this chapter, I share some of my treasured recipes, many of which were inspired by fun restaurant dining experiences. I've simplified the recipes to help create a faster carryover meal, but feel free to deck these out if you have more time!

Rest assured, you'll have a greater appreciation of pork after trying out these recipes.

Braised Pork Butt

PREP TIME: 30 MIN	COOK TIME: 1 HR 20 MIN TO 8 HR	YIELD: 8 SERVINGS

INGREDIENTS

3 pounds pork butt or shoulder (boneless)

2 teaspoons salt

2 teaspoons freshly ground black pepper

2 teaspoons ground cumin

2 oranges, cut into wedges

One 12-ounce lager beer or chicken broth

DIRECTIONS

1 Preheat the oven to 400 degrees. Bring the pork to room temperature for at least 30 minutes prior to cooking. Rub the pork with salt, pepper, and cumin.

2 To cook, choose one of the following methods:

Heavy-duty Dutch oven or deep cast-iron skillet: Heat a heavy-duty Dutch oven or deep cast-iron skillet over high heat. Add the pork and sear on all sides, about 3 minutes total. Add in the oranges and beer and cover with a lid or foil. Transfer the Dutch oven to the oven, reduce the heat to 325 degrees, and roast until you're able to shred the meat, about 3 hours.

Instant Pot: Cut the meat into 3-inch pieces. Add the meat to the Instant Pot and brown using the Sauté function. Then add the beer and oranges over the top of the meat. Secure the lid and select Pressure Cook (High) for 1 hour and 20 minutes. Then naturally release the pressure for about 20 minutes.

Slow cooker: In a skillet, sear the meat; then transfer to a slow cooker. Pour the beer over the top and add the oranges. Place the lid on top and cook on low until the meat can be shredded with a fork, about 8 to 10 hours.

PER SERVING: *Calories 293 (From Fat 140); Fat 16g (Saturated 6g); Cholesterol 125mg; Sodium 845mg; Carbohydrate 0g (Dietary Fiber 0g); Protein 36g.*

NOTE: Overly flavorful beers will impact the flavor, which is why I recommend a lager.

TIP: If you want to use a larger piece of meat (up to 5 pounds), cut meat into 3-inch pieces and cook in a slow cooker for 10 to 14 hours or in the oven up to 5 hours. Most multicookers can't hold meat much larger than 2 to 3 pounds.

VARY IT! Don't have citrus on hand? Add in ½ cup apple cider vinegar instead.

Carnitas

INGREDIENTS

3 tablespoons extra-virgin olive oil

1 teaspoon garlic powder

1 teaspoon onion powder

½ teaspoon ground cumin

3 cups cooked and shredded pork butt or shoulder

Salt to taste

Twelve 6-inch corn tortillas

½ cup chopped cilantro

½ medium red onion, chopped

1 lime, juiced

DIRECTIONS

1 In heavy skillet, heat the olive oil over medium-high heat.

2 In a medium bowl, mix together the garlic powder, onion powder, and cumin. Add the pork and toss to flavor the meat. Add the meat to the hot skillet and brown the meat, stirring frequently for 4 minutes, or place under a broiler for 4 to 5 minutes. The browning will give the meat a slightly crispy texture. Season with salt if needed.

3 Meanwhile, coat a medium skillet with cooking spray, and heat the tortillas one at a time until warm and pliable, about 30 seconds to 1 minute. Transfer to a towel and wrap the heated tortillas while heating the remaining ones.

4 In a small bowl, mix together the cilantro, onion, and lime juice.

5 To serve, place ¼ cup pork into each tortilla and top with the cilantro and onion mixture.

PER SERVING: *Calories 320 (From Fat 146); Fat 16g (Saturated 4g); Cholesterol 66mg; Sodium 126mg; Carbohydrate 22g (Dietary Fiber 3g); Protein 21g.*

TIP: To prep in advance, prechop the cilantro, onion, and meat.

TIP: If you prefer a faster method, dampen a tea towel with water, wrap up the tortillas in the dampened towel, and microwave for 30 seconds. Check the heat of the tortillas. If hot, pull them out. If not, rewrap in the towel and continue microwaving in 30-second intervals until warm.

Pulled Pork Sandwiches

PREP TIME: ABOUT 5 MIN | COOK TIME: 5 MIN | YIELD: 6 SERVINGS

INGREDIENTS

3 cups cooked and shredded pork butt or shoulder

1 cup barbecue sauce

2 tablespoons apple cider vinegar

3 cups shredded purple cabbage

¼ cup chopped cilantro

1 lime, juiced

2 tablespoons extra-virgin olive oil

½ cup Greek yogurt or sour cream

1 teaspoon salt

¼ teaspoon cumin powder

6 brioche hamburger buns

DIRECTIONS

1 In medium saucepan, heat the meat with the barbecue sauce and vinegar over medium-low heat, about 5 minutes, stirring frequently to avoid burning. If you prefer a saucier meat, add more barbecue sauce.

2 In a medium bowl, mix together the cabbage, cilantro, lime juice, olive oil, Greek yogurt, salt, and cumin.

3 To assemble, serve ½ cup meat and ½ cup cabbage slaw on buns.

PER SERVING: *Calories 456 (From Fat 180); Fat 20g (Saturated 5g); Cholesterol 115mg; Sodium 767mg; Carbohydrate 42g (Dietary Fiber 2g); Protein 26g.*

TIP: To prepare in advance, prechop the meat and make the coleslaw (up to 4 days in advance).

VARY IT! Try a variety of barbecue sauces to change up the flavor profile.

Shredded Pork Rice Paper Summer Rolls

PREP TIME: 30 MIN	COOK TIME: NONE	YIELD: 6 SERVINGS

INGREDIENTS

Twelve 8-inch rice paper wrappers

1 cup shredded pork

8 ounces dried thin rice noodles, reconstituted according to package directions

12 small butter lettuce leaves

1 small cucumber, thinly sliced lengthwise

12 basil leaves

24 mint leaves

½ cup natural peanut butter

1 tablespoon low-sodium soy sauce

1 lime, juiced

⅛ teaspoon ground ginger or 1 teaspoon grated fresh ginger

¼ teaspoon garlic powder or 1 clove garlic, minced

DIRECTIONS

1 Prepare and have the ingredients ready to go — this step is critical.

2 Add warm water to a large bowl. Working one at a time, place a rice paper wrapper into the bowl for 5 seconds. They'll still be slightly stiff — you don't want them to get mushy.

3 Remove the rice paper wrapper and lay it onto a cutting board. Add 1 tablespoon shredded pork on top of the circle. Next add 2 tablespoons rice noodles. Then, next to the noodles lay the lettuce leaf. Top with the thin cucumber slices, 1 basil leaf, and 2 mint leaves. Leave room around the edges to tuck as you roll. To roll, start at the meat edge and roll down, tucking the sides as you go. Place the wrapped spring roll to the side and cover with a slightly damp towel. Repeat with the remaining rolls.

4 After all the rolls are done, make the sauce. In a small bowl, whisk together the peanut butter, soy sauce, lime juice, ginger, garlic powder, and 5 tablespoons of warm water. Add more water if you prefer a thinner sauce.

5 Serve the rolls with the peanut butter dip and enjoy!

PER SERVING: *Calories 422 (From Fat 128); Fat 14g (Saturated 3g); Cholesterol 22mg; Sodium 287mg; Carbohydrate 60g (Dietary Fiber 3g); Protein 15g.*

TIP: To prepare in advance, prechop the meat and vegetables and pre-make the dipping sauce. Store the vegetables in small, separate containers to keep them fresh.

TIP: To store leftover spring rolls, place parchment paper underneath and on top of them; then dampen a paper towel and lay it across the top of the parchment paper to keep the moisture in the storage container. Store in the refrigerator up to 2 days.

Pork and Beans Empanadas

PREP TIME: ABOUT 15 MIN | **COOK TIME: 25 MIN** | **YIELD: 10 SERVINGS**

INGREDIENTS

1 Hass avocado, peeled and pitted

½ cup Greek yogurt or sour cream

2 teaspoons hot sauce

½ lime, juiced

½ cup chopped cilantro, divided

2½ cups cooked, shredded pork butt or shoulder

½ teaspoon ground cumin

½ teaspoon garlic powder

1 teaspoon chili powder

1 can black beans, drained and rinsed

10 frozen empanada wrappers, defrosted overnight in the refrigerator

DIRECTIONS

1 Preheat the oven to 400 degrees.

2 In a food processor or blender, blend together the avocado, Greek yogurt or sour cream, hot sauce, lime juice, and ¼ cup of the chopped cilantro until creamy, about 1 minute. Set aside or refrigerate until serving.

3 In a medium bowl, mix together the remaining ¼ cup of cilantro, shredded pork, cumin, garlic powder, chili powder, and black beans.

4 Working one at a time, place a heaping spoonful of mixture into the center of an empanada dough disc. Wet the edges of the dough lightly with water. Fold the dough in half, creating a half-moon shape. Use a fork to crimp the edges. Place onto a baking sheet lined with parchment paper. Repeat with the remaining empanadas.

5 Spray the empanadas with cooking spray and bake until gold brown, about 20 to 25 minutes.

6 Serve the empanadas with the avocado crema drizzled on top or as a dip.

PER SERVING: *Calories 229 (From Fat 108); Fat 12g (Saturated 4g); Cholesterol 34mg; Sodium 237mg; Carbohydrate 17g (Dietary Fiber 3g); Protein 13g.*

TIP: To prepare in advance, make the avocado sauce up to 3 days ahead. Place a piece of plastic wrap or parchment paper across the surface for storing in the refrigerator. Prechop the meat and premeasure spices for quick preparation. Empanadas can be made in advance and frozen raw. Defrost overnight or bake for 40 minutes from frozen.

TIP: If empanada wrappers are hard to find in your area, you can use pie crust dough instead.

VARY IT! Try a variety of different additions, like cooked, chopped sweet potatoes or potatoes, olives, boiled eggs, and chopped bell peppers.

Barbecue Pork Pizza

PREP TIME: ABOUT 10 MIN	COOK TIME: 10 MIN	YIELD: 4 SERVINGS

INGREDIENTS

¾ cup barbecue sauce, divided

One 16-ounce ready-to-prepare pizza dough

1 cup cooked, shredded pork butt or shoulder

¼ cup thinly sliced red onion

2 cups shredded mozzarella cheese

DIRECTIONS

1 Preheat the oven to 500 degrees. Place a heavy-duty baking sheet or pizza stone into the oven while it heats.

2 In a small bowl, mix together ¼ cup of the barbecue sauce with the meat, tossing to coat.

3 On a lightly floured surface, roll out the pizza dough to the size of your baking sheet or stone.

4 Carefully remove the baking sheet or stone from the hot oven. Place the rolled dough onto the hot pan. Spread the remaining ½ cup of barbecue sauce over the surface of the dough, all the way to the edges. Top with barbecue meat, then shredded onions, and then shredded mozzarella cheese. Work fast, because the hot pan can begin to cook the dough, creating a misshaped pizza.

5 Place the pizza in the oven and bake until the cheese has slightly browned and the pizza dough is cooked, about 8 to 10 minutes.

PER SERVING: *Calories 596 (From Fat 171); Fat 19g (Saturated 9g); Cholesterol 63 mg; Sodium 1,537mg; Carbohydrate 73g (Dietary Fiber 2g); Protein 33g.*

TIP: To prepare in advance, prechop the meat.

VARY IT! Add in other veggies, like chopped broccoli, spiralized zucchini, or thinly sliced boiled potatoes. Barbecue chicken pizzas are great, too!

Chapter 12

Chicken Dishes to Chow Down On

Leftover or store-bought rotisserie chicken is your best ally to creating fast, nutritious, and delicious meals on a dime! Many large-chained grocery stores sell rotisserie chickens for less than it can cost to buy and roast your own. If that's easiest for you, stick to something simple to jump-start these recipes. If you prefer to roast your own, I have you covered with three different methods of making a tender and juicy rotisserie-style chicken!

In this chapter I share my favorite tortilla soup, a simple sheet-pan quesadilla, the classic chicken and dumplings, and delicious buffalo chicken wraps that are perfect for lunch or dinner!

TIP

To prep in advance, take time to prechop vegetables on one day and keep them in your refrigerator so they're ready to go whenever you need them! Crêpes can be store-bought or made in advance. Cool and place them in between sheets of parchment paper for quick assembly. Freeze any leftovers, and go sweet or savory later!

Rotisserie-Style Chicken

PREP TIME: ABOUT 5 MIN	COOK TIME: 35 MIN–6 HR	YIELD: 6 SERVINGS

INGREDIENTS

4 pounds chicken, giblets removed

1 teaspoon sea salt

1 teaspoon paprika

1 teaspoon freshly ground black pepper

1 teaspoon garlic powder

½ teaspoon onion powder

1 teaspoon dried thyme

1 tablespoon dried parsley, crushed

2 tablespoons unsalted butter

¼ cup white wine (if using an Instant Pot or slow cooker)

DIRECTIONS

1 Preheat the oven to 275 degrees (if cooking in an oven).

2 Place the chicken in a roasting pan (if cooking in an oven).

3 In a small bowl, mix together the salt, paprika, pepper, garlic powder, onion powder, thyme, and parsley. Rub all over the chicken skin and inside the chicken cavity.

4 Place the butter inside the chicken cavity.

5 To cook, choose one of the following methods:

Oven: Place the roasting pan in the oven and roast the chicken until the internal temperature reads 165 degrees, about 3 to 3½ hours. (If using a convection oven, begin checking around 2½ hours.)

Instant Pot: Place the trivet inside the metal bowl. Pour the white wine and 1 cup water into the bowl. Place the chicken inverted, with the cavity hole facing upward, to keep the butter from falling out. Secure the lid and select Pressure Cook (High) for 35 minutes with a natural release of pressure.

Slow cooker: Place the white wine and ½ cup water in the bottom of the dish and place the chicken inside. Secure the lid and slow-cook for 4 to 6 hours.

PER SERVING: *Calories 378 (From Fat 219); Fat 24g (Saturated 8g); Cholesterol 157mg; Sodium 499mg; Carbohydrate 0g (Dietary Fiber 0g); Protein 38g.*

NOTE: This recipe is the perfect one to double or triple if you're cooking in an oven. If you're cooking for more than 6 people, I suggest cooking 2 or 3 small whole chickens to ensure you have ample leftovers for the carryover meals. You can't cook multiple chickens in a multicooker at one time; in most slow cookers, you can cook up to 2.

Tortilla Soup

PREP TIME: ABOUT 10 MIN | COOK TIME: 18 MIN | YIELD: 6 SERVINGS

INGREDIENTS

1 tablespoon extra-virgin olive oil

1 medium red bell pepper, finely diced

One 14.5-ounce can fire-roasted tomatoes or diced tomatoes

4 cups chicken broth

1 teaspoon ground cumin

½ teaspoon garlic powder

½ teaspoon onion powder

1 teaspoon chili powder

3 cups shredded, cooked chicken

3 cups broken or slightly crushed tortilla or corn chips

1 cup chopped cilantro

½ cup crumbled cotija cheese or shredded Mexican cheese

2 Hass avocados, diced

1 teaspoon salt

1 lime, juiced

DIRECTIONS

1 In a large saucepan, heat the olive oil over medium–high heat and add the bell peppers; sauté to soften, about 5 minutes. Add the tomatoes, chicken broth, cumin, garlic powder, onion powder, chili powder, and chicken. Bring the mixture to a low boil; then lower the temperature to medium–low and simmer for 15 minutes.

2 Meanwhile, divide the broken chips evenly among 6 bowls. Top with the cilantro, cheese, and avocado.

3 Season the soup with the salt and stir in the lime juice. Adjust the seasonings, as desired. Ladle the soup into bowls and serve.

PER SERVING: *Calories 382 (From Fat 187); Fat 21g (Saturated 5g); Cholesterol 64mg; Sodium 1,045mg; Carbohydrate 23g (Dietary Fiber 6g); Protein 26g.*

TIP: To prepare in advance, measure out the seasonings and prepare all toppings except the avocado due to browning,

VARY IT! Stir in the sour cream for a creamy addition. If avocados aren't in season, you can use prepared guacamole as a topping. For added spice, top or stir in chopped jalapeño peppers.

Sheet-Pan Quesadillas

PREP TIME: ABOUT 10 MIN	COOK TIME: 22 MIN	YIELD: 8 SERVINGS

INGREDIENTS

Eight 10-inch flour tortillas

One 14.5-ounce can refried beans

1 teaspoon chili powder

1 teaspoon ground cumin

1 teaspoon salt

2 cups salsa, divided

3 cups shredded, cooked chicken

3 cups shredded Mexican or Monterey Jack cheese

½ chopped cilantro

½ cup sour cream

DIRECTIONS

1 Preheat the oven to 425 degrees. Spray a 13-x-18-inch baking sheet (also called a half sheet pan) with cooking spray. Cover the bottom with 5 to 6 tortillas, overlapping the tortillas and hanging half over the edge to fold over the filling later. Save 2 tortillas to overlap on the top later.

2 Spread the refried beans over the bottom layer of tortillas.

3 In a medium bowl, mix together the chili powder, cumin, salt, and 1 cup of the salsa. Next, mix in the chicken. Spread this mixture over the refried beans. Top with the cheese.

4 Fold over edges of the tortillas, and top with the 2 remaining tortillas to cover any gaps. Spray the top with cooking spray. Cover with parchment paper or foil and add another sheet pan or heavy, oven-safe pan to the top. (This will help press the quesadilla, rendering a crispy edge.)

5 Place the baking sheet in the oven and bake for 18 minutes. Remove the top pan and parchment paper or foil and continue baking until golden brown, about 5 to 8 minutes.

6 To serve, invert onto a cutting board and rest for 5 minutes. Using scissors or a pizza cutter, cut 8 servings. Top each quesadilla with 1 tablespoon of cilantro, 1 tablespoon of sour cream, and 2 tablespoons salsa, or serve the toppings on the table.

PER SERVING: *Calories 543 (From Fat 214); Fat 24g (Saturated 12g); Cholesterol 85mg; Sodium 1,604mg; Carbohydrate 47g (Dietary Fiber 6g); Protein 34g.*

TIP: To prepare in advance, make the quesadillas as directed and refrigerate for up to 3 days before reheating in the oven at 350 degrees for 15 minutes.

VARY IT! Add a dollop of guacamole, avocado slices, or hot sauce.

Shredded Buffalo-Style Chicken Wraps

PREP TIME: ABOUT 5 MIN	COOK TIME: 5 MIN	YIELD: 6 SERVINGS

INGREDIENTS

1 tablespoon unsalted butter

1 tablespoon extra-virgin olive oil

½ cup hot sauce

3 cups shredded, cooked chicken

Six 10-inch flour tortillas

6 cups shredded romaine or iceberg lettuce

3 celery stalks, thinly sliced lengthwise

¾ cup crumbled blue cheese or preferred cheese

DIRECTIONS

1 In a small saucepan, heat the butter and olive oil over medium heat until butter has melted. Add the hot sauce and chicken and toss to coat. Remove from the heat and let cool for 5 minutes.

2 Meanwhile, lay out the tortillas. Top with shredded lettuce down the center. Cut the celery stalks to fit, and place them on top of the lettuce. Top with ½ cup of the chicken mixture per wrap. Crumble 2 tablespoons cheese over the top of each wrap.

3 Fold up like a burrito. Beginning on the sides, fold them in. Then lift up the bottom edge and roll it over to the top creating a wrap. Chill or serve immediately.

PER SERVING: *Calories 438 (From Fat 158); Fat 18g (Saturated 7g); Cholesterol 70mg; Sodium 1,254mg; Carbohydrate 39g (Dietary Fiber 3g); Protein 29g.*

TIP: To prepare in advance, toss the meat in hot sauce and store in the refrigerator. Chop and store vegetables and cheese separately.

TIP: To store prepared wraps, lay flat in a storage container in a single layer, top with paper towel, and add another layer of wraps. They can be made up to 2 days in advance.

VARY IT! Add in other great vegetables, like shredded carrots, cabbage, or spiralized zucchini or cucumbers. If you can't find blue cheese, use 1 tablespoon prepared blue cheese dressing instead.

Savory Chicken and Mushroom Crêpes

PREP TIME: ABOUT 10 MIN	COOK TIME: 30 MIN	YIELD: 6 SERVINGS

INGREDIENTS

6 large eggs

2¼ cups whole milk (plus 1 to 2 tablespoons more if needed to thin sauce), divided

1 cup all-purpose flour

¾ cup whole-wheat flour

½ teaspoon salt

5 tablespoons unsalted butter, melted

1 tablespoon extra-virgin olive oil

2 cup sliced mushrooms

4 cups chopped baby spinach

2 cups shredded chicken

½ cup cream cheese with chives and onions

DIRECTIONS

1 In a medium bowl, whisk together the eggs, 2 cups of the milk, all-purpose flour, whole-wheat flour, salt, and butter. Set aside to rest.

2 In a heavy skillet, heat the olive oil over medium heat. Add the mushrooms, and sauté for 4 minutes, stirring frequently. Add the spinach and stir to wilt, about 2 minutes. Add the chicken and toss to warm, about 2 minutes. Stir in the cream cheese and the remaining ¼ cup of milk, stirring to melt the cream cheese and create a thick saucy filling. Add more milk, if needed to thin the sauce. Keep warm over low heat, stirring occasionally.

3 Spray a 10-inch skillet with cooking spray and heat over medium-high heat. Add ¼ cup of the crêpe mixture, lift up the pan, and tilt to swirl in the skillet to create a flat pancake. Return to the heat, and when the edges begin to crisp and pull from the pan, flip the crêpe. Continue cooking for 30 seconds. Place the crêpe on a plate and cover with a towel to keep it warm. Continue with the remaining batter, to make about 24 crêpes.

4 To serve, place ⅓ cup of the filling on ½ a crêpe, fold the crêpe in half, and then fold in quarters. Another way to serve crêpes is to place the filling down the center and roll up like a taquito.

PER SERVING: *Calories 505 (From Fat 260); Fat 29g (Saturated 14g); Cholesterol 302mg; Sodium 407mg; Carbohydrate 34g (Dietary Fiber 3g); Protein 29g.*

TIP: Premade crêpes can be found in many grocery stores or specialty markets.

VARY IT! Replace the mushrooms and spinach with shredded kale, roasted butternut squash, or spiralized zucchini.

Old-Fashioned Chicken and Dumplings

PREP TIME: ABOUT 10 MIN	COOK TIME: 25 MIN	YIELD: 6 SERVINGS

INGREDIENTS

2 cups plus 3 tablespoons all-purpose flour, divided

1 tablespoon baking powder

1 teaspoon dried thyme or dried rosemary

¼ cup room-temperature salted butter, cubed

¾ cup whole milk

2 tablespoons unsalted butter

1 tablespoon extra-virgin olive oil

1 small onion, finely diced

1 carrot, finely diced

1 celery stalk, finely diced

4 cups chicken broth

½ cup whipping cream

3 cups chopped, cooked chicken

1 cup frozen peas or green beans

Salt to taste

Freshly ground black pepper to taste

DIRECTIONS

1 In a medium bowl, mix together 2 cups of the flour, baking powder, and thyme or rosemary. Cut in the salted butter until pea-size crumbs are formed. Stir in the milk to form a wet dough. Set aside.

2 In a Dutch oven, heat the unsalted butter and olive oil over medium-high heat until melted, about 1 minute. Add the onion, carrots, and celery, and sauté for 2 minutes. Whisk in the remaining 3 tablespoons of flour until lightly golden brown, about 2 minutes. Add the broth, and stir for 3 minutes. Add the whipping cream, chicken, and peas. Stir and reduce the heat to medium. Add a heaping tablespoon of the wet dough onto the surface, ladling the soup over the dumplings. Lower the temperature to a low simmer, cover, and cook until the dumplings are cooked through, about 12 to 15 minutes. The smaller the dumplings, the quicker they'll cook.

3 Season with salt and pepper, and serve warm.

PER SERVING: *Calories 518 (From Fat 231); Fat 26g (Saturated 14g); Cholesterol 113mg; Sodium 414mg; Carbohydrate 43g (Dietary Fiber 4g); Protein 28g.*

TIP: You can make the biscuit dough 2 days in advance. You can also chop the vegetables and chicken in advance.

TIP: Use premade biscuits, cut into quarters for a fast fix! Also, swap out fresh chopped onions, carrots, and celery with a frozen mix.

VARY IT! Swap out frozen peas or green beans with frozen spinach or chopped broccoli.

Chicken Salad Croissant Sandwiches

PREP TIME: ABOUT 10 MIN	COOK TIME: NONE	YIELD: 4 SERVINGS

INGREDIENTS

¼ cup mayonnaise

¼ cup sour cream or Greek yogurt

2½ cups chopped, cooked chicken

½ cup chopped celery

¼ cup chopped red onion

¼ cup chopped pecans

½ cup quartered red grapes

½ teaspoon salt

½ teaspoon freshly ground black pepper

4 croissants, split open for sandwiches

4 leaves butter lettuce

DIRECTIONS

1 In a medium bowl, mix the mayonnaise and sour cream or yogurt. Next, stir in the chicken, celery, onion, pecans, grapes, salt, and pepper.

2 Divide the filling among the four croissants, top with a leaf of lettuce, and serve.

PER SERVING: *Calories 445 (From Fat 226); Fat 25g (Saturated 9g); Cholesterol 106mg; Sodium 774mg; Carbohydrate 26g (Dietary Fiber 2g); Protein 29g.*

TIP: Serve with your favorite kettle chips and fresh fruit to complete the meal.

VARY IT! Love curry? Add ½ teaspoon curry powder and ¼ teaspoon cumin to the chicken salad for a curried twist and replace the pecans with cashews! If you can't get grapes, try diced apple instead.

Chapter 13

Making the Most out of a Ham Bone

RECIPES IN THIS CHAPTER

* **Roasted Ham Bone**
* **Ham and Potato Soup**
* **Cobb Salad**
* **Baked Ham Sammies**
* **Ham and Broccoli Quiche**
* **Ham Pancit**

Much like turkey, ham seems to get made on holidays and ignored the rest of the year. This bulk meat is a gem in the prep world! With each salty, savory bite, ham delivers big flavor in each bite. For the amount of meat you can get with each 10-pound ham, it's a budget-friendly protein food.

In this chapter, I share how to ditch the sauce pack and make your own delicious roasted ham. Plus, I included a warm Ham and Potato Soup, fresh and popular Cobb Salad, and a picnic favorite, Baked Ham Sammies.

Next time you're at the market, grab a precooked ham and give these recipes a whirl.

TIP Ham freezes beautifully! Freeze the sliced meat in an airtight container or plastic wrap for up to 3 months, and don't toss the bone — the ham bone is a perfect addition to any pea or potato soup.

Roasted Ham Bone

PREP TIME: ABOUT 5 MIN	COOK TIME: 3 HR 15 MIN	YIELD: 20 SERVINGS

INGREDIENTS

One 10-pound presliced ham with bone in

½ cup Dijon mustard

¼ cup brown sugar

DIRECTIONS

1 Preheat the oven to 325 degrees.

2 Place the ham on a roasting rack. Rub the ham with mustard and sprinkle with brown sugar.

3 Pour 1 cup of water into the base of the roasting pan and wrap with foil. Bake the ham for 20 minutes per pound, about 3 hours and 15 minutes for a 10-pound ham. (If you bake a smaller ham, decrease the baking time.)

4 Let the ham rest for 20 minutes before removing the foil and serving.

PER SERVING: *Calories 397 (From Fat 158); Fat 18g (Saturated 6g); Cholesterol 173mg; Sodium 487mg; Carbohydrate 2g (Dietary Fiber 0g); Protein 54g.*

NOTE: If you enjoy the sauce packet that comes with many store-bought hams, feel free to use that in place of the mustard and brown sugar mix.

Ham and Potato Soup

INGREDIENTS

2 cups diced peeled potatoes

1 teaspoon salt

1 tablespoon extra-virgin olive oil

½ small onion, chopped

2 tablespoons all-purpose flour

3 cups chicken broth

1 cup whole milk

1 cup cubed ham

1 cup frozen peas

½ teaspoon dried thyme

Salt to taste

Freshly ground black pepper to taste

DIRECTIONS

1 In a microwave-safe bowl, place the potatoes, 2 cups water, and 1 teaspoon salt. Microwave for 5 minutes or until tender. Drain and set aside.

2 Meanwhile, in a large saucepan, heat the olive oil and onion over medium-high heat for 2 minutes. Add the flour, and stir for 1 minute. Whisk in the chicken broth and milk. Add the ham, peas, and drained potatoes. Season with thyme, and simmer for 10 minutes.

3 Season with salt and pepper before serving.

PER SERVING: *Calories 226 (From Fat 60); Fat 7g (Saturated 2g); Cholesterol 38mg; Sodium 1,026mg; Carbohydrate 25g (Dietary Fiber 4g); Protein 17g.*

NOTE: This soup is for 2-cup servings, meant for a larger meal. You can also serve it as a smaller lunch with a salad or grilled-cheese sandwich.

TIP: To speed up the cooking time use frozen, cubed potatoes.

VARY IT! For a broccoli and cheddar version, add 2 cups shredded cheddar and frozen broccoli instead of peas.

Cobb Salad

PREP TIME: ABOUT 15 MIN	COOK TIME: NONE	YIELD: 6 SERVINGS

INGREDIENTS

3 tablespoons red wine vinegar

3 tablespoons extra-virgin olive oil

2 teaspoons prepared mustard

1 teaspoon honey

¼ teaspoon garlic powder

½ teaspoon salt

½ teaspoon freshly ground black pepper

2 tablespoons chopped fresh parsley

8 cups torn butter lettuce

4 large eggs, hard-boiled and chopped

1 cup cubed cooked ham

½ red onion, thinly sliced

1 cup chopped tomatoes

1 Hass avocado, diced

½ cup crumbled blue cheese

DIRECTIONS

1 In a small bowl or Mason jar, mix the red wine vinegar, olive oil, mustard, honey, garlic powder, salt, pepper, and parsley. Set aside.

2 On a serving platter, layer the lettuce, eggs, ham, onion, tomatoes, avocado, and blue cheese.

3 Serve with dressing over the top or toss before serving. Serve immediately.

PER SERVING: *Calories 259 (From Fat 173); Fat 19g (Saturated 5g); Cholesterol 171mg; Sodium 469mg; Carbohydrate 7g (Dietary Fiber 3g); Protein 15g.*

NOTE: To prep in advance for a lunch, make the dressing and divide into 6 quart-size jars. Next, add in the chopped ham. Use cherry tomatoes instead, and add those. Then add the onion, lettuce, and blue cheese. Cut the avocado immediately before serving to avoid unwanted browning.

TIP: Buy red wine vinaigrette instead of making your own for a time-saving swap. You can also buy hard-boiled eggs in most grocery stores.

VARY IT! Add bacon, chopped broccoli, grated carrots, or diced celery for added vegetables. If blue cheese isn't your favorite, use shredded cheddar instead!

Baked Ham Sammies

PREP TIME: ABOUT 10 MIN	COOK TIME: 25 MIN	YIELD: 6 SERVINGS

INGREDIENTS

12 Hawaiian rolls

½ cup mayonnaise

1 tablespoon Dijon mustard

1 tablespoon dried oregano

1 teaspoon garlic powder

2 teaspoons Worcestershire sauce

½ pound sliced ham

½ pound sliced Swiss cheese

DIRECTIONS

1 Preheat the oven to 350 degrees.

2 Slice the rolls in half to make sandwiches. Place the bottoms of the rolls into a 9-x-9-inch baking dish.

3 In a bowl, stir together the mayonnaise, mustard, oregano, garlic powder, and Worcestershire sauce.

4 Brush the bottoms of the rolls with the mayonnaise mixture. Next, layer ½ of the ham on the rolls. Top with Swiss cheese slices. Top with the remaining ham, and then add the roll tops. Brush the tops of the rolls with the remaining mayonnaise mixture.

5 Cover with foil and bake for 20 minutes. Uncover and bake for 5 minutes to crisp the tops of the rolls.

PER SERVING: *Calories 499 (From Fat 270); Fat 30g (Saturated 11g); Cholesterol 114mg; Sodium 554mg; Carbohydrate 33g (Dietary Fiber 1g); Protein 25g.*

NOTE: These are perfect for breakfast, lunch, or dinner! After storing in the refrigerator, serve cold or wrap in a paper towel and microwave for 30 seconds to 1 minute before serving.

NOTE: After baking, these sweet little sandwiches can be frozen for later. Wrap them individually or in pairs and freeze up to 1 month. Reheat in the oven at 350 degrees until heated through, about 10 minutes (or microwave in a paper towel for 45 seconds to 1 minute).

TIP: You can make these up to 3 days in advance and keep them in the refrigerator before baking.

TIP: Serve these with a tossed salad or tomato soup to complete the meal.

VARY IT! Use shredded cheese instead of slices and use your favorite variety of cheese.

Ham and Broccoli Quiche

PREP TIME: ABOUT 5 MIN | COOK TIME: 35 MIN | YIELD: 6 SERVINGS

INGREDIENTS

1 premade pie crust dough

5 large eggs

½ cup whole milk

1 cup cubed ham

1 cup chopped broccoli

½ teaspoon onion powder

¼ cup chopped parsley

1 cup shredded cheddar cheese

¼ cup grated Parmesan cheese

DIRECTIONS

1 Preheat the oven to 400 degrees. Place a baking sheet in the oven while the oven heats.

2 Place the pie crust into a pie pan.

3 In a medium bowl, whisk the eggs. Stir in the remaining ingredients. Pour the egg mixture into the pie crust.

4 Place the pie pan directly onto a hot baking sheet and bake for 35 minutes or until fully cooked (with an internal temperature of 160 degrees). Let the quiche rest for 10 minutes before slicing and serving.

PER SERVING: *Calories 350 (From Fat 197); Fat 22g (Saturated 9g); Cholesterol 223mg; Sodium 421mg; Carbohydrate 17g (Dietary Fiber 1g); Protein 21g.*

NOTE: Double this recipe and bake 2. Freeze for up to 3 months. To reheat a frozen quiche, bake at 350 degrees for 15 to 20 minutes or until fully heated on the inside.

TIP: Quiche can be served any time of the day! Complete the meal with a side salad or soup.

VARY IT! Use a variety of shredded cheeses instead of cheddar. Swap out broccoli with frozen spinach or peas.

Ham Pancit

PREP TIME: ABOUT 10 MIN | **COOK TIME: 15 MIN** | **YIELD: 6 SERVINGS**

INGREDIENTS

One 12-ounce package thin rice noodles

1 tablespoon vegetable oil

2 carrots, sliced

2 celery stalks sliced

One 6-ounce package mushrooms, quartered

½ teaspoon garlic powder

2 cups shredded green cabbage

1 cup diced ham

3 tablespoons low-sodium soy sauce

½ cup chicken broth

1 lemon, juiced

6 green onions, thinly sliced

DIRECTIONS

1 In a large bowl, soak the noodles in warm water for about 10 minutes or until pliable. Drain and set aside.

2 Meanwhile, in a large skillet or wok, heat the vegetable oil over medium–high heat. Add the carrots, celery, and mushrooms, and sauté for 5 minutes, stirring frequently. Sprinkle with garlic powder. Add the cabbage and ham, and sauté for 3 minutes. Add the soy sauce, broth, fresh lemon juice, and noodles; toss and heat thoroughly, about 3 minutes. Top with onions and serve.

PER SERVING: *Calories 310 (From Fat 44); Fat 5g (Saturated 1g); Cholesterol 21mg; Sodium 495mg; Carbohydrate 55g (Dietary Fiber 3g); Protein 11g.*

NOTE: Pancit is a traditional Filipino dish and can be made with a variety of protein foods, such as chicken, shrimp, tofu, or beef. Ham is saltier, so less is needed to go a long way for flavor. This dish is perfect for potlucks or for lunches. It reheats well and can last in the refrigerator up to 5 days.

TIP: Place leftover pancit in wide-mouthed pint jars for easy storage and grab-and-go lunches!

TIP: Grab a bag of pre-shredded coleslaw mix to use in this recipe to save on chopping time.

VARY IT! Add pan-fried tofu, edamame, shitake mushrooms, onion, peas, snow peas, or bean sprouts for added veggie options. If you want more vegetables, add them in. The sky's the limit on the creativity of this dish.

Chapter 14

All-in-One Sheet-Pan Meals

Sheet-pan meals are all-in-one-pan, baked meals. Typically, it's best to use a heavy-duty, 18-x-26-inch sheet pan, but if you're cooking for one, you can use a smaller size. From a meal-prep standpoint, sheet-pan meals are the perfect match for prepping ahead and getting a meal on the table faster. The fastest meals are seafood based (think thin fish fillets and shrimp). Seafood needs to be used within 48 hours of prep time. I recommend storing seafood containers in ice to keep them very cold and fresh. If you're using frozen shrimp, keep it in the freezer until you're ready to cook. When adding in a starch, like potatoes, you'll want to preboil your potatoes (or microwave them) to cut the cooking time. To prep ahead, cut up vegetables and portion and season proteins. Store in an airtight container and keep the meals together and labeled, so you can find them with ease.

In this chapter, I offer a variety of options, from vegetarian dishes like the Sheet-Pan Tofu Buddha Bowls and the Indian Spiced Cauliflower and Garbanzo Beans to quick meals like the Spiced Pecan Shrimp and Sugar Snap Peas and the Baked Salmon with Capers and Zucchini. My family voted the Moroccan Mini Meatloaves with Cauliflower their favorite, and my personal favorite is the Cherry Balsamic Pork Tenderloin with Brussels Sprouts.

If you want to make your own meal kits, where you prep ahead for the week, this chapter is a great place to start! Prep each component in individual containers, season, and spread onto a baking sheet to cook!

Lemony Salmon and Asparagus

PREP TIME: ABOUT 5 MIN	COOK TIME: 15 MIN	YIELD: 4 SERVINGS

INGREDIENTS

2 tablespoons chopped fresh dill or 2 teaspoons dried dill

3 tablespoons extra-virgin olive oil, divided

1 tablespoon unsalted butter, melted

½ teaspoon garlic powder

1¼ teaspoons sea salt, divided

1 pound asparagus, ends trimmed

4 salmon fillets, totaling about 1¼ to 1½ pounds

½ pound French baguette (about 8 to 12 inches in length)

1 Roma tomato

1 lemon

DIRECTIONS

1 Preheat the oven to 400 degrees.

2 Place a piece of parchment paper on a baking sheet.

3 In a small bowl, mix together the dill, 2 tablespoons of the olive oil, butter, garlic powder, and 1 teaspoon of the sea salt.

4 Place the asparagus on one side of the sheet pan. Place the salmon on the other side of sheet pan. Drizzle the sauce over both the asparagus and the salmon, using your hands to coat the asparagus and salmon fillets.

5 Bake for 15 minutes. The salmon should flake easily when it's done cooking.

6 Meanwhile, slice the French baguette in half lengthwise. Place the baguette in the oven directly on the oven rack. Bake for 10 minutes.

7 Remove both the sheet pan and the baguette from the oven. Cut the Roma tomato in half and rub the cut half directly onto the baguette. Sprinkle with the remaining ¼ teaspoon of sea salt and drizzle with the remaining 1 tablespoon of olive oil. Slice the lemon in half and squeeze over the fish and asparagus. Serve immediately.

PER SERVING: Calories 470 (From Fat 243); Fat 27g (Saturated 6g); Cholesterol 75mg; Sodium 461mg; Carbohydrate 26g (Dietary Fiber 3g); Protein 31g.

NOTE: Look for salmon fillets that are all about the same thickness to ensure even cooking times for all the fillets.

TIP: Really rub the toasted bread with the tomato, leaving just the tomato skin behind. This technique is popular in Spain.

VARY IT! You can use halibut, trout, or tuna instead of salmon if you prefer.

Sausage and Bell Peppers

INGREDIENTS

1 pound small new potatoes, halved

One 1-pound kielbasa (pork, beef, or turkey)

2 red, orange, yellow, or green bell peppers

½ sweet onion

1 tablespoon extra-virgin olive oil

½ teaspoon paprika

½ teaspoon garlic powder

1 teaspoon sea salt

1 teaspoon freshly ground black pepper

DIRECTIONS

1 Preheat the oven to 400 degrees.

2 Place the halved potatoes in a heat-safe bowl, cover with water, and microwave on high for 3 minutes.

3 Meanwhile, slice the kielbasa, bell peppers, and sweet onion into bite-size pieces.

4 Place a piece of parchment paper on a baking sheet. Place the potatoes, peppers, onions, and kielbasa onto the baking sheet. Drizzle with olive oil and sprinkle with paprika, garlic powder, sea salt, and black pepper. Toss to coat.

5 Bake for 15 minutes or until the potatoes are tender. Serve immediately.

PER SERVING: *Calories 512 (From Fat 312); Fat 35g (Saturated 11g); Cholesterol 75mg; Sodium 1,620mg; Carbohydrate 33g (Dietary Fiber 4g); Protein 17g.*

NOTE: Smoked sausages are precooked, so they can last longer in the fridge and reduce food waste.

TIP: Prechopped bell peppers or baby peppers make for quick meal prep!

VARY IT! Grab spiralized sweet potatoes or cubed butternut squash to replace the potatoes if you want.

Spiced Pecan Shrimp and Sugar Snap Peas

| PREP TIME: ABOUT 10 MIN | COOK TIME: 10 MIN | YIELD: 4 SERVINGS |

INGREDIENTS

1 pound jumbo shrimp, deveined

2 tablespoons low-sodium soy sauce, divided

¼ cup cornstarch

2 large egg whites

1 cup finely chopped pecans

2 tablespoons honey

1 pound sugar snap peas

1 lime, zested and juiced

1 teaspoon sesame oil

3 green onions, finely chopped

DIRECTIONS

1 Preheat the oven to 425 degrees. Line a baking sheet with parchment paper.

2 In a large bowl, place the shrimp. Toss the shrimp with 1 tablespoon of the soy sauce.

3 In a second bowl, place the cornstarch.

4 In a third bowl, whisk the egg whites until they're frothy.

5 In a fourth bowl, place the chopped pecans.

6 Working with 1 shrimp at a time, dip the shrimp into the cornstarch and thoroughly shake off the excess. Next, dip it into the frothy egg whites. Finally, dip it into the finely chopped pecans. Place the shrimp onto the baking sheet. Repeat with the remaining shrimp.

7 Drizzle the honey over all the shrimp. Place the sugar snap peas to the side of the shrimp. Place the pan in the oven and bake until the shrimp are pink and fully cooked, but still tender, about 10 minutes.

8 While the shrimp is baking, whisk together the remaining 1 tablespoon of soy sauce, the lime zest, the lime juice, and the sesame oil.

9 When the sheet pan is out of the oven, toss the sugar snap peas with the soy sauce mixture. Sprinkle the green onions over the top of the sheet pan and serve immediately.

PER SERVING: *Calories 391 (From Fat 182); Fat 20g (Saturated 2g); Cholesterol 166mg; Sodium 753mg; Carbohydrate 29g (Dietary Fiber 6g); Protein 26g.*

NOTE: This recipe is a spin-off of the popular honey walnut shrimp dish found in Chinese restaurants. Pecans hold up better for higher-temperature baking than walnuts do, and they impart a great, complementary flavor to the shrimp and sugar snap peas.

TIP: If you're using frozen, raw shrimp, defrost it under cold running water right before using.

VARY IT! You can use spiralized zucchini or green beans instead of sugar snap peas if you prefer. If you have a nut allergy, skip the pecans, egg whites, and cornstarch, and instead dip the shrimp in soy sauce and then in semolina flour — this technique will give the shrimp a great texture.

Sheet-Pan Tofu Buddha Bowls

PREP TIME: ABOUT 15 MIN	COOK TIME: 30 MIN	YIELD: 4 SERVINGS

INGREDIENTS

One 14-ounce package extra-firm tofu, drained

2 teaspoons ground cumin

1½ teaspoons garlic powder

1 teaspoon paprika

1 teaspoon turmeric

¼ cup red wine vinegar

½ cup extra-virgin olive oil, divided

2 cups chopped cauliflower

One 14.5-ounce can garbanzo beans, drained and rinsed

2 cups peeled and cubed butternut squash

1 tablespoon tahini sauce (sesame seed paste)

1 lemon, juiced

4 cups thinly shredded kale leaves

4 teaspoons sesame seeds

DIRECTIONS

1 Preheat the oven to 400 degrees. Line a baking sheet with parchment paper.

2 Thinly slice the tofu cube in half so you have 2 steaks. Place the tofu steaks on a tea towel, fold half the tea towel over the top, and place a sheet pan on top of the tea towel with something heavy (like a book) placed on the sheet pan. Press the moisture out of the tofu for 10 minutes.

3 While the tofu is being pressed, in a small bowl mix together the cumin, garlic powder, paprika, turmeric, red wine vinegar, and ¼ cup of the olive oil. Divide the spice mixture in half; place half of the mixture in a large bowl and add the cauliflower, garbanzo beans, and butternut squash. Stir to coat the vegetables and beans. Pour this mixture onto the sheet pan.

4 Brush the remaining spice mixture onto the tofu steaks on both sides. Cut the tofu into cubes. Place the cubes onto the baking sheet with the vegetables. Roast for 25 to 30 minutes or until the vegetables are tender and the tofu is golden.

5 While the tofu is baking, in a small bowl, whisk together the tahini sauce, the remaining ¼ cup of olive oil, and the lemon juice. Toss the kale leaves with the sauce.

6 To serve, place the greens on the bottom of 4 bowls. Add the roasted vegetables and tofu, top with 1 teaspoon sesame seeds per bowl, and serve immediately.

PER SERVING: Calories 495 (From Fat 299); Fat 33g (Saturated 5g); Cholesterol 0mg; Sodium 321mg; Carbohydrate 38g (Dietary Fiber 8g); Protein 15g.

NOTE: Roasted vegetables can keep in the refrigerator up to 5 days. Tofu can be pressed and marinated 3 days prior to baking.

Indian Spiced Cauliflower and Garbanzo Beans

PREP TIME: ABOUT 10 MIN	COOK TIME: 30 MIN	YIELD: 4 SERVINGS

INGREDIENTS

1 cup whole-fat plain yogurt (4 percent to 5 percent fat)

1 tablespoon curry powder

1½ teaspoons sea salt

1 teaspoon paprika

1 tablespoon tomato paste

¼ cup extra-virgin olive oil, divided

One 14.5-ounce can garbanzo beans, drained and rinsed

1 head cauliflower, cut into bite-size pieces

1 lemon, juiced

4 flatbreads or pita

¼ cup chopped parsley or cilantro

DIRECTIONS

1 Preheat the oven to 400 degrees. Line a baking sheet with parchment paper.

2 In a small bowl, mix together the yogurt, curry powder, salt, paprika, tomato paste, and 3 tablespoons of the olive oil.

3 In a large bowl, place the garbanzo beans and cauliflower.

4 Pour 1 cup of the yogurt mixture over the cauliflower mixture, reserving the remaining sauce in the refrigerator. Toss the beans and cauliflower to coat with the sauce.

5 Pour onto the prepared baking sheet and roast for 30 minutes.

6 Meanwhile, with the remaining sauce, whisk in the remaining 1 tablespoon of olive oil and the lemon juice.

7 Place the flatbread or pita in the oven the final 3 minutes of baking to heat through.

8 Drizzle the sauce over the roasted vegetables and top with chopped parsley or cilantro. Serve with the toasted flatbread or pita bread.

PER SERVING: *Calories 342 (From Fat 149); Fat 17g (Saturated 3g); Cholesterol 7mg; Sodium 1,145mg; Carbohydrate 40g (Dietary Fiber 7g); Protein 11g.*

NOTE: This is a great plant-forward dish full of flavor and nourishing spices. If you're looking for a meatless Monday dish, start here! If you feel like you need a bit more, serve the vegetables over a bed of baby spinach or shredded kale leaves.

TIP: To prepare this dish in advance, make the sauce and prechop the cauliflower (or buy prechopped cauliflower). Don't toss the vegetables and beans with the sauce until it's time to bake, though.

VARY IT! You can use broccoli or sweet potatoes instead of cauliflower if you prefer.

Peachy Pork Tenderloin with Green Beans and Carrots

PREP TIME: ABOUT 10 MIN | **COOK TIME: 25 MIN** | **YIELD: 6 SERVINGS**

INGREDIENTS

1½ pounds pork tenderloins

1 teaspoon sea salt, divided

1 teaspoon garlic powder, divided

1 pound green beans

3 carrots, cut in half lengthwise

½ cup peach preserves

2 tablespoons balsamic vinegar

DIRECTIONS

1 Preheat the oven to 450 degrees. Line a baking sheet with parchment paper.

2 Pat pork tenderloins with a paper towel. Season the pork tenderloins with ½ teaspoon of the sea salt and ½ teaspoon of the garlic powder.

3 Place the green beans and carrots onto the baking sheet, and sprinkle with the remaining ½ teaspoon of sea salt and the remaining ½ teaspoon of garlic powder.

4 Place the pork tenderloins over the vegetables, spaced apart.

5 In a small bowl, whisk together the peach preserves and balsamic vinegar. Spoon over the pork tenderloins.

6 Bake until an internal temperature of 145 degrees is reached, about 20 to 25 minutes. If the vegetables begin to brown, reduce the temperature to 425 degrees or pull the cooked vegetables off and place in a serving bowl, holding warm with a plate over the top. Let the pork rest for 5 minutes before thinly slicing. Pour the pan drippings over the top and serve.

PER SERVING: Calories 263 (From Fat 51); Fat 6g (Saturated 2g); Cholesterol 80mg; Sodium 480mg; Carbohydrate 26g (Dietary Fiber 3g); Protein 28g.

NOTE: To make a richer sauce to serve over the top, place the pan drippings into a small skillet with 2 tablespoons of butter and heat over medium heat until bubbly. Drizzle over the pork and vegetables.

NOTE: If your vegetables are getting too brown while baking, reduce the temperature to 425 degrees.

TIP: You can purchase prewashed and cleaned green beans for an easy dinner fix.

VARY IT! Parboiled new potatoes and broccoli are great vegetables to use for a change. You can also try cherry preserves instead of peach preserves.

Sage–Spiced Chicken and Butternut Squash

PREP TIME: ABOUT 5 MIN	COOK TIME: 20 MIN	YIELD: 4 SERVINGS

INGREDIENTS

4 boneless chicken thighs (skin on)

1½ teaspoons sea salt

½ teaspoon freshly ground black pepper

¼ teaspoon paprika

1 tablespoon minced fresh sage or 1 teaspoon dried sage

4 cups peeled and cubed butternut squash

3 tablespoons extra-virgin olive oil

DIRECTIONS

1 Preheat the oven to 450 degrees. Line a baking sheet with parchment paper. Pat the chicken dry.

2 In a small bowl, mix together the salt, pepper, paprika, and sage. Sprinkle 1 tablespoon of the mixture over the chicken and rub it all over.

3 Place the butternut squash on the baking sheet and sprinkle the rest of the spice mixture over the butternut squash; toss to coat. Place the chicken on the baking sheet. Drizzle the pan with olive oil.

4 Bake for 20 minutes. The internal temperature of the chicken should be 165 degrees and it should have a crisped skin; the butternut squash should be slightly browned, but not burned. Serve immediately.

PER SERVING: *Calories 306 (From Fat 179); Fat 20g (Saturated 4g); Cholesterol 58mg; Sodium 930mg; Carbohydrate 16g (Dietary Fiber 3g); Protein 17g.*

NOTE: Make sure the butternut squash is even in size and no larger than 1-inch cubes to cook within 20 minutes.

TIP: To speed up the cook time, use prechopped butternut squash, and measure out spices in advance.

VARY IT! You can use sweet potatoes, pumpkins, kabocha squash, or delicata squash instead of butternut squash if you like.

Poblano Chicken and Zucchini

PREP TIME: ABOUT 15 MIN	COOK TIME: 20 MIN	YIELD: 4 SERVINGS

INGREDIENTS

2 medium sweet potatoes

4 boneless, skinless chicken breasts, cubed

2 poblano peppers

4 cloves garlic

3 medium zucchini

½ teaspoon paprika

1 teaspoon cumin powder

1½ teaspoons sea salt, divided

½ teaspoon freshly ground black pepper

2 tablespoons extra-virgin olive oil

2 tablespoons unsalted butter

2 tablespoons all-purpose flour

1 cup whole milk

¼ cup cilantro

1 lime, juiced

DIRECTIONS

1 Preheat the oven to 450 degrees. Line a baking sheet with parchment paper.

2 Cut the sweet potatoes in 1-inch pieces. Place in a microwave-safe bowl and cover with water. Microwave on high for 5 minutes. Drain the sweet potatoes with a strainer and set aside.

3 Meanwhile, place the cubed chicken breasts on half of the parchment paper. In the center, place the peppers (whole) and the garlic.

4 Slice the zucchinis in half lengthwise, and then cut into 2-inch pieces. Place the zucchini on the other side of the parchment paper. Work the sweet potatoes into the sheet pan around the chicken.

5 In a small bowl, mix together the paprika, cumin powder, 1 teaspoon of the salt, and black pepper. Sprinkle the food with the spice mixture, and drizzle with the olive oil. Give the food a little stir to fully coat with oil and spices. Bake for 20 minutes.

6 Meanwhile, in a small saucepan or skillet, heat the butter and flour over medium heat until lightly golden, about 3 minutes, stirring occasionally. While stirring, add the milk and allow the mixture to bubble for 1 minute. Then remove from the heat.

7 Remove the pan from the oven. Place the chicken, sweet potatoes, and zucchini on a serving platter.

8 Remove the stems from the poblano peppers. Place the peppers, garlic, the remaining ½ teaspoon of salt, the pan drippings from the sheet pan (chicken broth juices), and the thickened milk in a blender; pulse until smooth. Add the cilantro and lime juice, and blend for 20 seconds. Serve the sauce over the chicken and zucchini.

PER SERVING: *Calories 502 (From Fat 184); Fat 20g (Saturated 7g); Cholesterol 147mg; Sodium 1,543mg; Carbohydrate 27g (Dietary Fiber 4g); Protein 52g.*

NOTE: Poblanos are not spicy hot like jalapeños; instead, they have a smoky flavor. If you prefer less spice, remove the seeds from the pepper before blending.

TIP: To prep ahead, precut the chicken and store in a container. Prechop the sweet potatoes and store in water in the refrigerator. Prechop the zucchini and store in a separate container in the refrigerator. Premix the seasonings.

VARY IT! If you like it spicier, add in a jalapeño pepper while roasting and in the sauce. Top with crumbled cotija or goat cheese.

Meatballs and Caramelized Onion Green Beans

PREP TIME: ABOUT 10 MIN	COOK TIME: 22 MIN	YIELD: 4 SERVINGS

INGREDIENTS

2 tablespoons whole milk

½ cup whole-wheat breadcrumbs

1 large egg

1 pound ground beef (93 percent lean)

1 cup canned kidney beans, drained and rinsed

1 teaspoon garlic powder

½ teaspoon onion powder

1 teaspoon dried oregano

1½ teaspoons sea salt, divided

¼ cup grated Parmesan cheese

1 sweet onion, thickly sliced

2 teaspoons granulated sugar

2 tablespoons extra-virgin olive oil

1 pound green beans

DIRECTIONS

1 Preheat the oven to 425 degrees. Line a baking sheet with parchment paper.

2 In a large bowl, mix together the milk, breadcrumbs, and egg. Add the kidney beans and mash with a fork or potato masher. Add the ground beef, garlic powder, onion powder, oregano, 1 teaspoon of the sea salt, and the Parmesan cheese.

3 In a medium bowl, toss together the onions, sugar and olive oil. Place the thin onion slices on one side of the sheet pan. Place the green beans on the other side of the sheet pan and top with the remaining ½ teaspoon of sea salt. Roll out 16 1½–inch meatballs, and place the meatballs on top of the green beans.

4 Bake for 10 minutes, stir the onions and turn over the meatballs, and cook another 10 minutes. Check to make sure that the insides of the meatballs are completely cooked.

5 To serve, plate the green beans with the onions on top and the meatballs on the side.

PER SERVING: *Calories 435 (From Fat 154); Fat 17g (Saturated 5g); Cholesterol 128mg; Sodium 1,231mg; Carbohydrate 37g (Dietary Fiber 8g); Protein 35g.*

NOTE: Meatballs are often served with pasta, but this dish is hearty enough without it. The beans add the starch and fiber.

TIP: Make meatballs in advance and freeze uncooked meatballs. Then just defrost overnight in the refrigerator before baking. Onions can be presliced and stored in water in the refrigerator.

VARY IT! Kidney beans are great in Italian-style dishes, but lentils, garbanzo beans, and cannellini beans work great as well.

Hearty Berry Muffins (Chapter 6)

Tar 18)

Sausage, Spinach, and Lentil Soup (Chapter 7)

Street Tacos (Chapter 10) and Roasted Brisket (Chapter 10)

Shredded Pork Rice Paper Summer Rolls (Chapter 11)

Shredded Buffalo-Style Chicken Wraps (Chapter 12)

Tortilla Soup (Chapter 12)

Ham and Broccoli Quiche (Chapter 13)

Moroccan Mini Meatloaves with Cauliflower (Chapter 14)

Cilantro Shrimp with Spicy Guacamole (Chapter 16)

Loaded Baked Potatoes (Chapter 16)

Dinner Charcuterie Board (Chapter 16)

Chocolate Avocado Mousse (Chapter 19) and No-Bake Lemon and

Moroccan Mini Meatloaves with Cauliflower

PREP TIME: ABOUT 10 MIN	COOK TIME: 35 MIN	YIELD: 4 SERVINGS

INGREDIENTS

1½ pounds lean ground beef (93 percent lean)

2 large eggs

½ cup whole-wheat panko breadcrumbs

3 teaspoons curry powder, divided

1½ teaspoons sea salt, divided

1 cup tomato chutney or tomato jam

½ head cauliflower, cut into bite-size pieces

¼ cup red wine vinegar

1 teaspoon freshly ground black pepper

½ teaspoon turmeric

1 tablespoon extra-virgin olive oil

DIRECTIONS

1 Preheat the oven to 400 degrees. Line a baking sheet with parchment paper.

2 In a large bowl, mix together the ground beef, eggs, breadcrumbs, 2 teaspoons of the curry powder, and 1 teaspoon of the salt. Form into 4 mini loaves and place onto the parchment paper. Top each loaf with ¼ cup chutney or jam.

3 In another bowl, mix together the cauliflower, the remaining 1 teaspoon of curry powder, red wine vinegar, pepper, turmeric, and olive oil. Place the cauliflower on the sheet pan around the meatloaves.

4 Bake until the meat reaches an internal temperature of 160 degrees, about 30 to 35 minutes. The cauliflower should be golden and toasted, but not blackened in color. If the cauliflower cooks too fast, remove from the pan and hold warm until the meat is finished cooking.

PER SERVING: *Calories 544 (From Fat 140); Fat 16g (Saturated 5g); Cholesterol 209mg; Sodium 1,157mg; Carbohydrate 62g (Dietary Fiber 3g); Protein 41g.*

NOTE: Can't find tomato chutney or tomato jam? No problem! Make a curry ketchup instead: Mix together 1 cup ketchup, 1 teaspoon curry powder, and ½ teaspoon black pepper. Spread on top of the meatloaves equally prior to baking.

TIP: These meatloaves are perfect for the freezer — you can bake and freeze or freeze unbaked. If heating a frozen, unbaked meatloaf, cook for at least 1 hour (check to make sure an internal temperature of 160 degrees is reached). If reheating a frozen and baked meatloaf, bake for at least 40 minutes, or defrost baked meatloaves in the refrigerator overnight and reheat for 25 minutes or until heated through.

VARY IT! Add chopped mushrooms or cooked lentils for a boost of nutrition. Go Greek and add chopped olives and mozzarella cheese, top with Roma tomato slices, and bake.

Baked Salmon with Capers and Zucchini

PREP TIME: ABOUT 10 MIN	COOK TIME: 18 MIN	YIELD: 4 SERVINGS

INGREDIENTS

Four 6-ounce salmon fillets

1 tablespoon capers, chopped

2 cloves garlic, chopped

¼ cup extra-virgin olive oil

1 teaspoon sea salt

¼ cup chopped flat-leaf parsley

1 lemon, zested and sliced thin

4 small zucchinis

1 cup cherry tomatoes

4 tablespoons grated Parmesan cheese

DIRECTIONS

1 Preheat the oven to 425 degrees. Line a baking sheet with parchment paper.

2 Place the salmon fillets on the baking sheet.

3 In a small bowl, mix together the capers, garlic, olive oil, sea salt, parsley, and lemon zest. Take half of this mixture and divide among the salmon fillets, spreading it across the top. Next, place the lemon slices evenly over the salmon fillets.

4 Slice the zucchinis lengthwise. Cut the cherry tomatoes in half, lengthwise. Toss the vegetables with the remaining caper mixture. Place the vegetables around the salmon on the baking sheet.

5 Bake until the fish flakes easily, about 15 to 22 minutes. Top the vegetables with grated Parmesan cheese, and serve immediately.

PER SERVING: *Calories 437 (From Fat 281); Fat 31g (Saturated 6g); Cholesterol 85mg; Sodium 811mg; Carbohydrate 7g (Dietary Fiber 2g); Protein 32g.*

NOTE: If your fillets have skin on them, place them skin side down on the baking sheet.

TIP: Look for presliced zucchini to speed up the slicing time.

VARY IT! You can use any firm fish in place of the salmon. Try yellow-crookneck squash or pattypan squash in place of the zucchini.

Skewer-Free Chicken Kabobs

PREP TIME: 8 HR	COOK TIME: 20 MIN	YIELD: 4 SERVINGS

INGREDIENTS

1 pound new potatoes

1½ pounds chicken breasts, cubed

One 15-ounce bottle Italian dressing, divided

2 red, yellow, or orange bell peppers, cut into bite-size pieces

One 6-ounce package cremini (baby bella) or button mushrooms, cleaned

1 sweet onion, cut into bite-size pieces

DIRECTIONS

1 Poke the potatoes with a fork and microwave on high for 3 minutes, which slightly starts the cooking process for the potatoes. (The potatoes will not be soft at this point —they'll fully cook later.)

2 Place the chicken in an airtight container or bag and pour in half the bottle of Italian dressing.

3 Place the bell peppers, mushrooms, onions, and potatoes in another container or bag and pour the remaining Italian dressing over the top. Shake to fully coat. Refrigerate for at least 8 hours or up to 48 hours in advance of cooking.

4 Preheat the oven to 425 degrees. Line two baking sheets with parchment paper.

5 Drain the marinade and discard. Place half the veggie mix onto one baking sheet and the other half of the veggie mix on the other baking sheet. Divide the chicken between the two sheets.

6 Bake for 20 minutes, stirring halfway through the baking time. Serve immediately.

PER SERVING: *Calories 444 (From Fat 135); Fat 15g (Saturated 3g); Cholesterol 107mg; Sodium 1,107mg; Carbohydrate 33g (Dietary Fiber 5g); Protein 44g.*

NOTE: Italian dressing makes for a great shortcut marinade! Use it on pork, beef, or tofu.

TIP: Serve kabobs with crusty French bread or flatbread and steamed rice.

TIP: To prep in advance, prechop all vegetables and store in a container until ready to marinate. Vegetables and chicken can be marinated up to 2 days before cooking time.

VARY IT! Add grape tomatoes, pineapple chunks, or parboiled sweet potatoes for more colors and flavors.

Spicy Meatballs with Roasted Potatoes and Bell Peppers

PREP TIME: ABOUT 10 MIN	COOK TIME: 24 MIN	YIELD: 6 SERVINGS

INGREDIENTS

½ cup rolled oats

3 tablespoons whole milk

1 pound ground beef (93 percent lean)

½ pound ground pork or sausage

¼ teaspoon crushed red pepper flakes

1 teaspoon garlic powder

2 large eggs

1 teaspoon onion powder

¼ cup chopped fresh parsley

1 teaspoon Worcestershire sauce

1½ teaspoons sea salt, divided

1½ teaspoons freshly ground black pepper, divided

1 pound new potatoes

2 large green, red, yellow, or orange bell peppers

¼ cup extra-virgin olive oil

DIRECTIONS

1 Preheat the oven to 400 degrees. Line 2 baking sheets with parchment paper.

2 In a large bowl, mix together the oats and milk. Let this mixture sit for 5 minutes.

3 To the bowl with the oats, add the beef, pork or sausage, red pepper flakes, garlic powder, eggs, onion powder, parsley, Worcestershire sauce, ½ teaspoon of the salt, and ½ teaspoon of the black pepper. Using your hands, work the ingredients into the meat and fully combine, about 2 minutes. Roll the meat into 24 meatballs and place 12 meatballs on each baking sheet.

4 Quarter the new potatoes and cut the bell peppers into 1-inch bite-sized pieces. Toss the vegetables with the remaining 1 teaspoon of salt, the remaining 1 teaspoon of black pepper, and the olive oil.

5 Place half the vegetable mixture on each baking sheet.

6 Bake until the meat reaches an internal temperature of 160 degrees and the potatoes are golden, about 20 to 24 minutes. Serve immediately.

PER SERVING: *Calories 395 (From Fat 162); Fat 18g (Saturated 4g); Cholesterol 139mg; Sodium 696mg; Carbohydrate 27g (Dietary Fiber 4g); Protein 30g.*

NOTE: If you don't have two baking sheets, use a baking sheet and Dutch oven to accommodate the quantity. You don't want to crowd the meat and potatoes in one pan, or they may turn out more steamed than roasted.

TIP: Use frozen meatballs for a simple meal swap! To prep in advance, chop the potatoes and store in water in a container in the refrigerator. Chop the bell peppers and store in a container in the refrigerator.

VARY IT! Use cauliflower, kohlrabi, or carrots instead of potatoes if you want more-fibrous options.

Cherry Balsamic Pork Tenderloin with Brussels Sprouts

PREP TIME: ABOUT 8 MIN	COOK TIME: 20 MIN	YIELD: 6 SERVINGS

INGREDIENTS

2 pork tenderloins, totaling around 2 pounds

1 teaspoon sea salt, divided

1 teaspoon freshly ground black pepper, divided

2 tablespoons extra-virgin olive oil, divided

1 pound Brussels sprouts

1 cup cherry preserves

1 tablespoon balsamic vinegar

1 tablespoon Dijon mustard

1 tablespoon fresh thyme leaves

1 tablespoon cornstarch

3 tablespoons cold water

DIRECTIONS

1 Preheat the oven to 500 degrees. Line a baking sheet with parchment paper.

2 Season the pork tenderloins with ½ teaspoon of the salt and ½ teaspoon of the pepper. Place the pork tenderloins onto the baking sheet. Brush the top of the tenderloins with 1 tablespoon of the olive oil.

3 Cut the Brussels sprouts into thin slices, discarding the tough base. Toss the Brussels sprouts with the remaining ½ teaspoon of salt, the remaining ½ teaspoon of the pepper, and the remaining 1 tablespoon of olive oil. Spread the shredded Brussels sprouts onto the baking sheet around the pork tenderloins.

4 Place into the oven and immediately lower the oven temperature to 425 degrees. Bake until the pork reaches an internal temperature of 145 degrees, about 20 to 25 minutes. Tent the meat with foil and let it rest for 5 minutes before slicing.

5 Meanwhile, in a small saucepan, place the cherry preserves, balsamic vinegar, Dijon mustard, and thyme. Heat and stir the mixture over medium heat for 3 minutes.

6 While the mixture is cooking, in a small bowl whisk together the cornstarch and cold water. After 3 minutes of cooking the sauce, add the cornstarch mixture to the cherry mixture and stir to slightly thicken the sauce, stirring constantly. Serve the sauce over the pork and Brussels sprouts. Serve immediately.

PER SERVING: *Calories 388 (From Fat 79); Fat 9g (Saturated 2g); Cholesterol 81mg; Sodium 516mg; Carbohydrate 45g (Dietary Fiber 4g); Protein 32g.*

NOTE: The very high heat will sear the edges of the pork tenderloin when you place it in the oven. If you prefer not to cook at such a high heat, sear the meat in a skillet prior to baking.

TIP: Use preshredded Brussels sprouts, often found in the salad section of the grocery store, for a quick fix.

Sheet-Pan Mediterranean Pasta

PREP TIME: ABOUT 5 MIN	COOK TIME: 30 MIN	YIELD: 6 SERVINGS

INGREDIENTS

1 pint cherry tomatoes

½ cup halved olives (black or green)

½ cup chopped fresh parsley

2 tablespoons capers

1 tablespoon fresh thyme leaves or 1 teaspoon dried thyme leaves

4 cloves garlic, chopped

¼ cup extra-virgin olive oil

3 teaspoons sea salt, divided

1 teaspoon freshly ground black pepper

One 8-ounce block feta (sheep or cow milk)

8 ounces penne pasta (or cavatappi or preferred shape)

DIRECTIONS

1 Preheat the oven to 425 degrees.

2 In a 9-x-13-inch baking dish, place the cherry tomatoes. Top with the olives, parsley, capers, thyme, garlic, olive oil, 1 teaspoon of the salt, and the pepper; toss to mix. Nest the block of feta into the center of the tomato mixture. Bake until the feta is slightly golden and soft, about 25 to 30 minutes. The tomatoes should have slightly browned and be very soft.

3 Meanwhile, while the sauce is cooking, add 4 quarts of water to a large stock pot and bring to a rolling boil. Add the remaining 2 teaspoons of salt and the pasta. Cook according to package instructions, about 9 to 11 minutes. Drain in a colander and set aside until the sauce is done cooking.

4 Remove the baking dish from the oven and use tongs to mix up the sauce and cheese. Add the cooked pasta, toss, and serve immediately.

PER SERVING: Calories 345 (From Fat 170); Fat 19g (Saturated 7g); Cholesterol 34mg; Sodium 1,007mg; Carbohydrate 33g (Dietary Fiber 2g); Protein 11g.

NOTE: This is one of my most frequently made pasta dishes. I prep it on Sunday and bake it by Wednesday for a quick weeknight meal!

TIP: Place all the ingredients (except the pasta and the salt for the pasta water) in a baking dish, cover with plastic wrap, and refrigerate until you're ready to make the dish. You can make it 3 days in advance. Buying fresh pasta can cut the boil time down to 3 minutes.

VARY IT! Add chopped spinach, kale, or Swiss chard leaves for more greens. Mix up the sauce by using goat cheese or cream cheese instead of feta. If you love sardines, toss some in for extra protein and essential fatty acids.

Chapter **15**

Freezer-Friendly Mains

When it comes to meal prep, your freezer is your friend! Whether it's frozen entrees, frozen veggies, or your favorite ice cream, the freezer helps maintain meal-prep sanity. Weeknights have you feeling rushed? Needing an easy weekend meal? You've found the right chapter. Freezer-friendly main dishes are baked straight from the freezer. These are great recipes to make as double dishes — one you enjoy the day you make it, and the other goes straight into the freezer. Or, here's another option: Spend one day prepping all these meals, and your freezer will be fit for the next month! It's a win-win for the nights you find yourself in a bind and needing an easy meal option.

These recipes include meals you can prep and store in the freezer for up to three months prior to cooking. I dish out two ways of preparing them, both in a multicooker (like an Instant Pot) or in a slow cooker.

REMEMBER

If you use a slow cooker, you'll need to defrost overnight and cook all day. Why? Because putting frozen, raw meat into a slow cooker isn't safe or recommended. It hangs out at an unsafe temp for too long, creating a possible risk of foodborne illness. When using a multicooker, you don't need to defrost overnight, but you do need to allow for extra cooking time, because frozen foods take longer to reach pressure.

This chapter has something for everyone, from Indian dishes, like Butter Chicken and Chicken Korma, to Mediterranean meals, like Chicken Cacciatore and Greek Meatballs in Tomato Sauce. Check out the tips at the ends of the recipes for suggestions on what to serve with these meaty mains if you need inspiration!

Butter Chicken

| PREP TIME: ABOUT 10 MIN | COOK TIME: 25 MIN–6 HR | YIELD: 6 SERVINGS |

INGREDIENTS

6 boneless, skinless chicken thighs, cut into bite-size pieces, totaling about 1½ pounds

1 cup tomato sauce

3 cloves garlic, chopped

1 teaspoon ground ginger

1 teaspoon ground turmeric

1 teaspoon ground cumin

1 teaspoon paprika

1 teaspoon garam masala

1 teaspoon sea salt

½ teaspoon freshly ground black pepper

1 cup chicken broth

1 cup full-fat plain yogurt (4 percent to 5 percent fat)

¼ cup cubed unsalted butter

½ cup chopped cilantro or parsley (optional)

DIRECTIONS

1 In a gallon-size freezer bag, place the chicken, tomato sauce, garlic, ginger, turmeric, cumin, paprika, garam masala, salt, and pepper. If you'll be using a multicooker, place the bag in a bowl that will fit in your multicooker, and then place the bowl in the freezer. If you'll be using a slow cooker, you can freeze the bag flat. Freeze up to 3 months.

2 To cook, choose one of the following methods:

Multicooker: Place the frozen contents in the multicooker, and add the chicken broth. Secure the lid. Pressure-cook on high for 15 minutes. Naturally release the pressure for 10 minutes before doing a Quick Release. To serve, remove 1 cup of liquid from the sauce and discard. Stir in the yogurt and butter. Top with cilantro or parsley before serving.

Slow cooker: Defrost the frozen contents in the refrigerator overnight. Place the contents in the slow cooker, and add the chicken broth. Secure the lid. Slow-cook for 6 to 8 hours on low. To serve, remove 1 cup of liquid from the sauce and discard. Stir in the yogurt and butter. Top with cilantro or parsley before serving.

PER SERVING: *Calories 284 (From Fat 165); Fat 18g (Saturated 8g); Cholesterol 106mg; Sodium 762mg; Carbohydrate 5g (Dietary Fiber 1g); Protein 25g.*

TIP: If your chicken thighs are previously frozen, keep them frozen and add them to the bag as whole chicken thighs. The meat will be tender when cooked and easy to shred.

NOTE: If you prefer a soupy sauce, don't discard the liquid before adding the yogurt and butter. If you prefer a thicker sauce, discard more of the liquid before adding the yogurt and butter.

TIP: Serve with steamed rice, sautéed spinach, and flatbread. Or keep it simple by serving with rice and a salad.

Chicken Korma

PREP TIME: ABOUT 15 MIN	COOK TIME: 25 MIN–6 HR	YIELD: 6 SERVINGS

INGREDIENTS

4 boneless, skinless chicken breasts, cut into bite-size pieces, totaling about 2 pounds

¼ cup whole-fat yogurt (4 percent to 5 percent fat)

2 teaspoons paprika

1 teaspoon chili powder

1 teaspoon sea salt

½ teaspoon garlic powder

1 teaspoon ground ginger

1 teaspoon ground cinnamon

1 teaspoon ground cumin

1 teaspoon ground coriander

½ teaspoon ground cardamom

1 cup cashews

2 cups chopped onions

2 bay leaves

1 cup chicken broth

DIRECTIONS

1 In a gallon-size freezer bag, place the chicken, yogurt, paprika, chili powder, and salt.

2 In a blender or food processor, place the garlic powder, ginger, cinnamon, cumin, coriander, cardamom, cashews, and onions, and pulse until smooth, about 1 minute. Pour the contents into a second freezer bag. Add the bay leaves. If you'll be using a multicooker, place the bag in a bowl that will fit in your multicooker, and then place the bowl in the freezer. If you'll be using a slow cooker, you can freeze the bags flat. Freeze up to 3 months.

3 To cook, choose one of the following methods:

Multicooker: Place the frozen contents in the multicooker, and add the chicken broth. Secure the lid. Pressure-cook on high for 15 minutes. Naturally release the pressure for 10 minutes before doing a Quick Release. Top with cilantro or parsley before serving.

Slow cooker: Defrost the frozen contents in the refrigerator overnight. Place the contents in the slow cooker, and add the chicken broth. Secure the lid. Slow-cook for 6 to 8 hours on low. Top with cilantro or parsley before serving.

PER SERVING: *Calories 357 (From Fat 134); Fat 15g (Saturated 3g); Cholesterol 98mg; Sodium 618mg; Carbohydrate 16g (Dietary Fiber 2g); Protein 40g.*

VARY IT! You can use chicken thighs instead of chicken breasts if you prefer. If you can't find cashews, you can use almonds instead.

TIP: Serve with steamed rice and steamed broccoli. Or keep it simple by serving with rice and a salad.

Chipotle Braised Beef Short Ribs

PREP TIME: ABOUT 5 MIN	COOK TIME: 1–8 HR	YIELD: 6 SERVINGS

INGREDIENTS

3 pounds beef short ribs, bone in

1 teaspoon sea salt

1 teaspoon freshly ground black pepper

1 cup chopped tomatoes (canned or fresh)

2 green bell peppers, chopped

1 cup chopped onions

2 teaspoons chipotle powder or 2 canned chipotle peppers, chopped

1 cup beef broth

3 tablespoons cornstarch

¼ cup cold water

1 cup chopped cilantro

½ lime, juiced

DIRECTIONS

1 In a gallon-size freezer bag, place the short ribs, salt, black pepper, tomatoes, bell peppers, onions, and chipotle. If you'll be using a multicooker, place the bag in a bowl that will fit in your multicooker, and then place the bowl in the freezer. If you'll be using a slow cooker, you can freeze the bag flat. Freeze up to 3 months.

2 To cook, choose one of the following methods:

Multicooker: Place the frozen contents in the multicooker, and add the beef broth. Secure the lid. Pressure-cook high for 45 minutes. Naturally release the pressure for 10 minutes before doing a Quick Release. Remove the meat and place on a serving dish. Using an immersion blender or a blender, puree the sauce until smooth. In a small bowl, whisk together the cornstarch and water; add to the sauce and blend. Stir in the cilantro and lime juice. Pour the sauce over the meat and serve immediately.

Slow cooker: Defrost the frozen contents in the refrigerator overnight. Place the contents in the slow cooker, and add the beef broth. Secure the lid. Slow-cook for 8 to 10 hours on low. Remove the meat and place on a serving dish. Using an immersion blender or a blender, puree the sauce until smooth. In a small bowl, whisk together the cornstarch and water; add to the sauce and blend. Stir in the cilantro and lime juice. Pour the sauce over the meat and serve immediately.

PER SERVING: *Calories 260 (From Fat 119); Fat 13g (Saturated 6g); Cholesterol 66mg; Sodium 736mg; Carbohydrate 11g (Dietary Fiber 2g); Protein 23g.*

NOTE: Look for small cans of chipotle peppers in adobo sauce. Leftover chipotle can be frozen for another meal.

TIP: If you prefer a less spicy sauce, reduce or skip the chipotle pepper seasoning and use 1 tablespoon chili powder instead. You can top the meat with sour cream or yogurt to cut the spice, too.

TIP: Serve this dish with mashed potatoes and salad or coleslaw and potato salad.

Beef Paprikash

PREP TIME: ABOUT 10 MIN	COOK TIME: 45 MIN–6 HR	YIELD: 8 SERVINGS

INGREDIENTS

2 pounds cubed beef stew meat

1 onion, diced

1 red bell pepper, diced

1 green bell pepper diced

1 cup diced tomatoes (canned or fresh)

1 tablespoon paprika

1 teaspoon garlic powder

1 teaspoon salt

1 teaspoon freshly ground black pepper

1½ cups beef broth

3 tablespoons cornstarch

3 tablespoons cold water

½ cup sour cream or Greek yogurt

¼ cup chopped parsley

DIRECTIONS

1 In a gallon-size freezer bag, place the meat, onions, bell peppers, tomatoes, paprika, garlic powder, salt, and black pepper. If you'll be using a multicooker, place the bag in a bowl that will fit in your multicooker, and then place the bowl in the freezer. If you'll be using a slow cooker, you can freeze the bag flat. Freeze up to 3 months.

2 To cook, choose one of the following methods:

Multicooker: Place the frozen contents in the multicooker, and add the beef broth. Secure the lid. Pressure-cook on high for 30 minutes. Naturally release the pressure for 10 minutes before doing a Quick Release. In a small bowl, whisk together the cornstarch and water; add to the paprikash and stir well. Stir in the sour cream and parsley to serve.

Slow cooker: Defrost the frozen contents in the refrigerator overnight. Place the contents in the slow cooker, and add the beef broth. Secure the lid. Slow-cook for 6 to 8 hours on low. Before serving, in a small bowl, whisk together the cornstarch and water; add to the paprikash and stir well. Stir in the sour cream and parsley to serve.

PER SERVING: Calories 267 (From Fat 112); Fat 12g (Saturated 5g); Cholesterol 90mg; Sodium 784mg; Carbohydrate 9g (Dietary Fiber 1g); Protein 29g.

NOTE: Any color bell peppers can work in this dish.

TIP: Serve with egg noodles and steamed broccoli or mashed potatoes and a salad.

Sloppy Joes

PREP TIME: ABOUT 5 MIN | COOK TIME: 20 MIN–6 HR | YIELD: 8 SERVINGS

INGREDIENTS

2 pounds lean ground beef

1 onion, finely chopped

1 green, yellow, or red bell pepper, finely chopped

1 carrot, finely chopped

1 cup tomato sauce

2 tablespoons Worcestershire sauce

1 tablespoon prepared mustard

¼ cup ketchup

1 tablespoon granulated sugar

½ teaspoon garlic powder

½ teaspoon paprika

1 teaspoon salt

½ teaspoon freshly ground black pepper

½ cup water or beef broth

8 toasted hamburger buns

DIRECTIONS

1 In a gallon-size freezer bag, place the ground beef, onion, bell pepper, carrot, tomato sauce, Worcestershire sauce, mustard, ketchup, sugar, garlic powder, paprika, salt, and black pepper. If you'll be using a multicooker, place the bag in a bowl that will fit in your multicooker, and then place the bowl in the freezer. If you'll be using a slow cooker, you can freeze the bag flat. Freeze up to 3 months.

2 To cook, choose one of the following methods:

Multicooker: Place the frozen contents in the multicooker, and add the water or broth. Secure the lid. Pressure-cook on high for 10 minutes. Naturally release the pressure for 10 minutes before doing a Quick Release. Serve on the toasted buns.

Slow cooker: Defrost the frozen contents in the refrigerator overnight. Place the contents in the slow cooker and add in the water or broth. Secure the lid. Slow-cook for 6 hours on low. Serve on the toasted buns.

PER SERVING: *Calories 229 (From Fat 45); Fat 5g (Saturated 2g); Cholesterol 38mg; Sodium 816mg; Carbohydrate 29g (Dietary Fiber 2g); Protein 17g.*

TIP: To toast the hamburger buns, place the opened buns on a baking sheet. Place under a broiler, cut side up, about 5 inches from broiler, for 3 to 5 minutes. Be sure to watch the buns closely so they don't burn. You can also pan-toast them in butter over a medium-high heat in a heavy pan.

VARY IT! Sloppy Joes are a great way to add more vegetables into the whole family's meal. Chop up and add in 8 ounces mushrooms, too!

TIP: Serve these sandwiches with steamed veggies or coleslaw.

Pineapple Chicken

PREP TIME: ABOUT 5 MIN	COOK TIME: 20 MIN–6 HR	YIELD: 6 SERVINGS

INGREDIENTS

8 chicken thighs or breasts, cubed, totaling about 2 pounds

1 cup pineapple juice

1 cup cubed pineapple

¼ cup low-sodium soy sauce

3 cloves garlic, chopped

1 teaspoon ground ginger

½ cup ketchup

¼ cup brown sugar

½ cup water

3 tablespoons cornstarch

3 tablespoons cold water

½ lime, juiced, or 1 tablespoon rice wine vinegar

Red pepper flakes, to taste (optional)

DIRECTIONS

1 In a gallon-size freezer bag, place the chicken, pineapple juice, cubed pineapple, soy sauce, garlic, ginger, ketchup, and brown sugar. If you'll be using a multicooker, place the bag in a bowl that will fit in your multicooker, and then place the bowl in the freezer. If you'll be using a slow cooker, you can freeze the bag flat. Freeze up to 3 months.

2 To cook, choose one of the following methods:

Multicooker: Place the frozen contents in the multicooker, and add the ½ cup water. Secure the lid. Pressure-cook on high for 10 minutes. Naturally release the pressure for 10 minutes before doing a Quick Release. In a small bowl, stir together the cornstarch and cold water; stir into the sauce, along with the lime juice and red pepper flakes. Serve immediately or hold warm until ready to serve.

Slow cooker: Defrost the frozen contents in the refrigerator overnight. Place the contents in the slow cooker and add the ½ cup water. Secure the lid. Slow-cook for 6 hours on low. In a small bowl, stir together the cornstarch and cold water; stir into the sauce, along with the lime juice and red pepper flakes. Serve immediately or hold warm until ready to serve.

PER SERVING: *Calories 289 (From Fat 38); Fat 4g (Saturated 1g); Cholesterol 96mg; Sodium 664mg; Carbohydrate 25g (Dietary Fiber 1g); Protein 37g.*

NOTE: I used canned pineapple in this recipe.

NOTE: This dish is popular in Hawaii, often served in pineapple boats.

TIP: Serve with steamed rice and grilled bell peppers or sautéed carrots.

Creamy Peanut Chicken

PREP TIME: ABOUT 5 MIN | COOK TIME: 20 MIN–6 HR | YIELD: 6 SERVINGS

INGREDIENTS

1 cup chopped peanuts

4 chicken breasts

1 cup coconut milk

½ cup creamy peanut butter

1 teaspoon garlic powder

1 tablespoon soy sauce

1 teaspoon ground ginger

1 cup chicken broth

3 tablespoons cornstarch

3 tablespoons cold water

½ lime, juiced, or 1 tablespoon rice wine vinegar

DIRECTIONS

1 In a small resealable bag, place the peanuts. Set aside until ready to cook. (This step ensures you have peanuts when cooking this meal and they don't get used in another recipe!)

2 In a gallon-size freezer bag, place the chicken, coconut milk, peanut butter, garlic powder, soy sauce, and ginger; massage to mix the ingredients together, working to break up the peanut butter. If you'll be using a multicooker, place the bag in a bowl that will fit in your multicooker, and then place the bowl in the freezer. If you'll be using a slow cooker, you can freeze the bag flat. Freeze up to 3 months.

3 To cook, choose one of the following methods:

Multicooker: Place the frozen contents in the multicooker, and add the broth. Secure the lid. Pressure-cook on high for 10 minutes. Naturally release the pressure for 10 minutes before doing a Quick Release. In a small bowl, stir together the cornstarch and water; stir into the sauce, along with the lime juice or vinegar. Top with the chopped peanuts. Serve immediately or hold warm until ready to serve.

Slow cooker: Defrost the frozen contents in the refrigerator overnight. Place the contents into the slow cooker, and add the broth. Secure lid. Slow-cook for 6 hours on low. In a small bowl, stir together the cornstarch and water; stir into the sauce, along with the lime juice or vinegar. Top with the chopped peanuts. Serve immediately or hold warm until ready to serve.

PER SERVING: *Calories 547 (From Fat 314); Fat 35g (Saturated 12g); Cholesterol 97mg; Sodium 330mg; Carbohydrate 13g (Dietary Fiber 4g); Protein 49g.*

NOTE: Be sure to use full-fat coconut milk from a can, not from a refrigerated carton. These two products are very different.

NOTE: You can use chicken thighs in this dish instead of chicken breasts.

TIP: Serve with steamed rice and a green salad or steamed vegetables.

Creamy Pork and Mushrooms

PREP TIME: ABOUT 5 MIN	COOK TIME: 20 MIN–6 HR	YIELD: 6 SERVINGS

INGREDIENTS

6 boneless pork chops, about 1-inch thick

2 cups thinly sliced mushrooms

1 cup chopped onion

2 tablespoons Worcestershire sauce

1 teaspoon freshly ground black pepper

1 teaspoon dried oregano, rosemary, or thyme

1 cup chicken broth

3 tablespoons cornstarch

3 tablespoons cold water

½ cup heavy whipping cream

¼ cup chopped parsley (optional)

DIRECTIONS

1 In a gallon-size freezer bag, place the pork chops, mushrooms, onion, Worcestershire sauce, pepper, and oregano, rosemary, or thyme. If you'll be using a multicooker, place the bag in a bowl that will fit in your multicooker, and then place the bowl in the freezer. If you'll be using a slow cooker, you can freeze the bag flat. Freeze up to 3 months.

2 To cook, choose one of the following methods:

Multicooker: Place the frozen contents in the multicooker, and add the chicken broth. Secure the lid. Pressure-cook on high for 10 minutes. Naturally release the pressure for 10 minutes before doing a Quick Release. In a small bowl, stir together the cornstarch and water; stir into the sauce, along with the heavy cream. Top with the parsley. Serve immediately or hold warm until ready to serve.

Slow cooker: Defrost the frozen contents in the refrigerator overnight. Place the contents in the slow cooker and add the broth. Secure the lid. Slow-cook for 6 hours on low. In a small bowl, stir together the cornstarch and water; stir into the sauce, along with the heavy cream. Top with the chopped parsley. Serve immediately or hold warm until ready to serve.

PER SERVING: *Calories 288 (From Fat 142); Fat 16g (Saturated 8g); Cholesterol 94mg; Sodium 183mg; Carbohydrate 10g (Dietary Fiber 1g); Protein 25g.*

NOTE: Heavy whipping cream is very thick and can withstand higher heats; however, cream under pressure doesn't work well. Be sure to keep cream on hand in the refrigerator for this dish!

NOTE: If you can only find bone-in pork chops, increase the time to 15 minutes if using a multicooker.

TIP: Serve with egg noodles or mashed potatoes and a salad.

Chicken Cacciatore

INGREDIENTS

6 chicken breasts, cubed, totaling about 3 pounds

½ teaspoon salt

½ teaspoon freshly ground black pepper

1 tablespoon dried oregano

2 tablespoons extra-virgin olive oil

2 large green, yellow, or red bell peppers, chopped

1 onion, chopped

6 cloves garlic, chopped

¼ cup capers, drained and rinsed

½ cup white wine

One 28-ounce can diced tomatoes

1 cup chicken broth

½ cup chopped fresh parsley or basil

½ cup grated Parmesan cheese

DIRECTIONS

1 In a gallon-size freezer bag, place the chicken, salt, black pepper, oregano, olive oil, bell peppers, onion, garlic, capers, white wine, and tomatoes. If you'll be using a multicooker, place the bag in a bowl that will fit in your multicooker, and then place the bowl in the freezer. If you'll be using a slow cooker, you can freeze the bag flat. Freeze up to 3 months.

2 To cook, choose one of the following methods:

Multicooker: Place frozen contents in the multicooker, and add the chicken broth. Secure the lid. Pressure-cook on high for 12 minutes. Naturally release the pressure for 10 minutes before doing a Quick Release. Top with the chopped parsley or basil. Serve immediately with the grated Parmesan.

Slow cooker: Defrost the frozen contents in the refrigerator overnight. Place the contents in the slow cooker and add the broth. Secure the lid. Slow-cook for 6 hours on low. Top with the chopped parsley or basil. Serve immediately with the grated Parmesan.

PER SERVING: *Calories 329 (From Fat 91); Fat 10g (Saturated 3g); Cholesterol 114mg; Sodium 661mg; Carbohydrate 11g (Dietary Fiber 3g); Protein 44g.*

VARY IT! If you want this dish to have an added kick in spice, add crushed red peppers.

TIP: Serve with pasta or mashed potatoes and a salad.

Greek Meatballs in Tomato Sauce

PREP TIME: ABOUT 15 MIN	COOK TIME: 25 MIN–6 HR	YIELD: 4 SERVINGS

INGREDIENTS

1 pound lean ground beef

1 cup cooked rice

1 teaspoon cumin

1 teaspoon coriander

1 teaspoon dried oregano

1 cup mushrooms, sliced

1 onion, chopped

2 red bell peppers, chopped

3 cloves garlic, chopped

One 14.5-ounce can chopped tomatoes

2 cups beef stock

DIRECTIONS

1 In a large bowl, mix together the ground beef, rice, cumin, coriander, and oregano. Form 16 meatballs, about the size of golf balls. Place the meatballs on a cookie sheet or plate lined with parchment paper, and freeze for 30 minutes. Then transfer to a gallon-size freezer bag. Add the mushrooms, onion, bell peppers, garlic, and tomatoes to the bag. If you'll be using a multicooker, place the bag in a bowl that will fit into your multicooker, and then place the bowl in the freezer. If you'll be using a slow cooker, you can freeze the bag flat. Freeze up to 3 months.

2 To cook, choose one of the following methods:

Multicooker: Place the trivet inside the bowl of the multicooker. Place the frozen contents in the bowl, and add the beef stock. Secure the lid. Pressure-cook on high for 15 minutes. Naturally release the pressure for 15 minutes before doing a Quick Release. Remove the meatballs to a serving platter. Using an immersion blender or a blender, puree the sauce until smooth. Serve the sauce over the meatballs.

Slow cooker: Defrost the frozen contents in the refrigerator overnight. Place the contents in the slow cooker and add the beef stock. Secure the lid. Slow-cook for 6 hours on low. Remove the meatballs to a serving platter. Using an immersion blender or a blender, puree the sauce until smooth. Serve the sauce over the meatballs.

PER SERVING: *Calories 293 (From Fat 58); Fat 6g (Saturated 3g); Cholesterol 69mg; Sodium 455mg; Carbohydrate 30g (Dietary Fiber 3g); Protein 29g.*

NOTE: This recipe is great doubled and cooked in a slow cooker. If you're trying to double the recipe in a multicooker, you'll need at least an 8-quart multicooker.

TIP: Serve with a side salad and a crusty baguette.

Chapter **16**

Twenty-Minute Main Meals

This chapter is all about meal hacks that cut lengthy cook times in half. These recipes are less about prepping ahead than other chapters, but they still require some prep. Shopping smart and having a well-stocked kitchen will mean these meals can be on your menu rotation any time.

In this chapter, I break down my top eight meals to make when it's crunch time. Before the family hits "hangry," break out eggs, frozen shrimp, or smoked salmon for a quick protein-packed dinner. If you're looking for more plant-forward quick-fixes, consider Zesty Bean and Cheese Tostadas or Loaded Baked Potatoes. If you're a pasta-loving crew, definitely try the Smoked Salmon Pasta with Greens or Caprese Pasta.

Move over cheese and crackers — now there's something better: charcuterie boards! This is my family's go-to on nights when I don't want to cook. I hope this chapter helps you on those crazy nights when you're needing easy dinner options, too!

Ham and Cheese Omelet with Avocado Toast

PREP TIME: ABOUT 5 MIN | **COOK TIME: 10 MIN** | **YIELD: 4 SERVINGS**

INGREDIENTS

8 large eggs, whisked, divided

¾ cup shredded cheddar cheese, divided

¾ cup chopped ham, divided

¾ teaspoon sea salt, divided

¼ teaspoon freshly ground black pepper

4 slices whole-grain sourdough or crusty French-style bread

1 Hass avocado

1 tablespoon lemon juice

DIRECTIONS

1 Heat a 6- to 8-inch skillet over medium heat. Spray with cooking spray.

2 Working in batches, pour ½ cup of the whisked eggs into the heated skillet and swirl the pan. Stir the eggs until you notice them beginning to set, about 20 seconds. Stop stirring and place 3 tablespoons of the cheese and 3 tablespoons of the ham down the center of the omelet. Turn off the heat. Fold one side toward the middle and the opposite side toward the middle, creating a tri-fold omelet. Let the omelet sit for 1 minute; then transfer to a plate. Repeat 3 more times, yielding 4 omelets.

3 Put each omelet onto a plate and sprinkle them with ½ teaspoon of the salt and the pepper.

4 Toast the bread in a toaster or in the oven under a broiler.

5 While the bread is toasting, in a small bowl, mash the avocado using a fork. Add in the lemon juice, and season with the remaining ¼ teaspoon salt.

6 Divide the mashed avocado among the 4 pieces of toast, and immediately serve with the omelets.

PER SERVING: *Calories 411 (From Fat 214); Fat 24g (Saturated 9g); Cholesterol 459mg; Sodium 1,242mg; Carbohydrate 22g (Dietary Fiber 3g); Protein 28g.*

NOTE: Breakfast for dinner? Yes, please! Omelets are such an easy and satisfying meal. If they seem too complex, turn it into an open-faced sandwich instead, with bread, avocado, cheese, ham, and egg on top!

VARY IT! If you're looking for more vegetables, add baby spinach leaves with the eggs or add chopped broccoli! Replace the cheddar with your favorite cheese, or skip the cheese altogether.

Zesty Bean and Cheese Tostadas

PREP TIME: ABOUT 5 MIN	COOK TIME: 8 MIN	YIELD: 4 SERVINGS

INGREDIENTS

One 14.5-ounce can black beans, drained and rinsed

8 tostada shells (flat, fried corn tortillas)

2 cups shredded Mexican cheese or Monterey Jack

One 8-ounce bag shredded lettuce

1 cup salsa

DIRECTIONS

1 Preheat the oven to 350 degrees. Ready a baking sheet with parchment paper. If you can only fit 6 tostada shells on 1 sheet, ready 2 baking sheets.

2 In a small bowl, place the black beans and mash with a fork. Spread the mashed beans onto the tostada shells. Top each tostada shell with ¼ cup shredded cheese. Bake for 8 minutes.

3 To serve, top with the shredded lettuce and salsa.

PER SERVING: *Calories 407 (From Fat 209); Fat 23g (Saturated 13g); Cholesterol 50mg; Sodium 1,021mg; Carbohydrate 32g (Dietary Fiber 7g); Protein 20g.*

NOTE: If you can't find precooked tostada shells, you can fry corn tortillas at 375 degrees in corn or avocado oil for 1 to 2 minutes, or bake at 400 degrees sprayed with cooking spray.

TIP: You can use canned refried beans in place of the mashed black beans if you like.

VARY IT! Have fun with these tostadas! They're quick and satisfying and really quite versatile. Here are some toppings you can add to this recipe: chopped olives, chopped tomatoes, jalapeño slices, chopped tomatoes, sliced avocado or guacamole, canned corn, shredded cabbage, crumbled cotija cheese, shredded chicken or ground beef, or sour cream or plain yogurt.

Loaded Baked Potatoes

PREP TIME: ABOUT 5 MIN	COOK TIME: 10 MIN	YIELD: 4 SERVINGS

INGREDIENTS

4 large russet potatoes

6 slices raw bacon

½ cup raw broccoli, finely chopped

1 cup sour cream or plain Greek yogurt

1 cup shredded cheddar cheese

2 green onions, chopped

DIRECTIONS

1 Wash the potato skins well. Using a fork, poke holes on all sides of the potatoes, including the ends. Place the potatoes in the microwave and microwave on high for 4 minutes; turn the potatoes and continue cooking for about 2 to 4 minutes, checking every minute for doneness. Check the firmness; the potatoes should give with gentle squeezing. If necessary, microwave longer (time may vary based on your microwave and the size of the potatoes).

2 Place 2 pieces of paper towel on a heat-safe plate. Place the bacon slices on 1 piece of paper towel and cover with the other piece of paper towel. Microwave the bacon for 3 minutes and check for doneness; continue baking, to desired doneness, about 2 minutes. (Times vary based on microwaves.) Chop the cooked bacon for crumbling into the potatoes.

3 Cut the baked potatoes open lengthwise. Squeeze the potatoes to break up the inside. Add 2 tablespoons raw broccoli and ¼ cup sour cream and cheese to each potato, and stir to mix with the potato. Top with onions, and serve immediately.

PER SERVING: Calories 585 (From Fat 238); Fat 26g (Saturated 14g); Cholesterol 73mg; Sodium 533mg; Carbohydrate 67g (Dietary Fiber 7g); Protein 21g.

NOTE: Cook the bacon in large batches and store in the refrigerator for up to 5 days or freezer for up to 1 month.

TIP: Baked potatoes are family pleasers! Serve them family-style with a variety of toppings. Here are some toppings you can add to this recipe: chopped olives; chopped tomatoes; salsa; sliced avocado or guacamole; crumbled, cooked sausage; chopped chives; sour cream or plain yogurt; broccoli and cheese soup; chili; or creamed spinach or spinach and artichoke dip.

Cilantro Shrimp with Spicy Guacamole

PREP TIME: ABOUT 8 MIN	COOK TIME: 10 MIN	YIELD: 4 SERVINGS

INGREDIENTS

1 pound frozen, deveined, and deshelled jumbo shrimp

¼ cup unsalted butter

¼ cup extra-virgin olive oil

4 cloves garlic chopped

½ teaspoon cumin

1 teaspoon sea salt

¼ cup chopped cilantro

2 avocados, pitted and peeled

1 tablespoon hot sauce

¼ cup Greek yogurt or sour cream

1 lime, juiced and divided

½ bag (about 6 ounces) corn tortilla chips

DIRECTIONS

1 Preheat the oven to 375 degrees. Line a baking sheet with parchment paper.

2 In a colander, place the shrimp and run them under cold water, just to separate the shrimp. Pat dry, and place the shrimp in a single layer on the parchment paper.

3 In a microwave-safe bowl, melt the butter in the microwave for about 1 minute. Stir in the olive oil, garlic, cumin, sea salt, and cilantro. Pour this mixture over the top of the shrimp, and bake until the shrimp are opaque and pink, about 6 to 8 minutes.

4 Meanwhile, in a bowl, place the avocados, hot sauce, yogurt or sour cream, and ½ of the lime juice. Using a fork, mash together.

5 Squeeze the remaining lime juice over the shrimp and toss. On the serving platter, plate the guacamole, place the shrimp around the sides of the guacamole, and serve with the chips.

PER SERVING: *Calories 683 (From Fat 479); Fat 53g (Saturated 14g); Cholesterol 155mg; Sodium 615mg; Carbohydrate 35g (Dietary Fiber 7g); Protein 20g.*

NOTE: This dish is inspired by many trips down to Baja California and savoring the seafood!

TIP: You can serve this like nachos with tortilla chips as the base, shrimp (with sauce) on top, and dolloped with guacamole. Or skip the tortilla chips and serve these like tacos in soft flour tortillas. Either way, you'll be making this shrimp dish a lot!

VARY IT! Create a more Mediterranean inspired shrimp dish with capers, olives, parsley, and lemon instead. Kick up the heat with crushed red pepper flakes instead of hot sauce, and serve with crusty bread.

Pan-Fried Burgers with Creamy Feta Green Salad

PREP TIME: ABOUT 10 MIN	COOK TIME: 8 MIN	YIELD: 4 SERVINGS

INGREDIENTS

1 pound lean ground beef

½ teaspoon sea salt

½ teaspoon freshly ground black pepper

4 ounces feta

¼ cup plain yogurt

⅓ cup mayonnaise

2 teaspoons dried dill

1 clove garlic, chopped

1 pound bagged salad

½ cup chopped tomatoes

½ cup chopped olives

DIRECTIONS

1 Season the meat with salt and pepper. Make 4 patties with the ground meat. Make a hole in the center of each patty, creating more of a doughnut shape (this helps the burger cook evenly).

2 Heat a heavy skillet over medium-high heat. Add the patties to the skillet, and cook until seared and cooked to an internal temperature of 160 degrees, about 3 to 4 minutes on each side.

3 Meanwhile, in a food processor, blend together the feta, yogurt, mayonnaise, dill, and garlic.

4 Plate this family-style or on individual plates. Place the lettuce on a plate, top with the cooked burger, top with the dressing, and finish with the chopped tomatoes and olives. Serve immediately.

PER SERVING: *Calories 400 (From Fat 257); Fat 29g (Saturated 9g); Cholesterol 106mg; Sodium 944mg; Carbohydrate 8g (Dietary Fiber 2g); Protein 29g.*

VARY It! You can use ground beef, turkey, or lamb in this dish.

TIP: Keep bagged salads on hand for those meals you need to pull together quick, like this one!

VARY IT! Open up the pantry and add ingredients to the salad! Try adding canned roasted red bell peppers, artichoke hearts, baby corn, or croutons.

Smoked Salmon Pasta with Greens

PREP TIME: ABOUT 5 MIN	COOK TIME: 10 MIN	YIELD: 4 SERVINGS

INGREDIENTS

1 pound dried angel hair pasta

1 tablespoon salt (for boiling pasta)

3 tablespoons extra-virgin olive oil

2 tablespoons unsalted butter

½ cup chopped onion

4 cups thinly sliced kale, Swiss chard, or spinach leaves

¼ cup heavy whipping cream

2 tablespoons capers

4 ounces smoked salmon, flaked

½ lemon, juiced

Salt to taste

Freshly ground black pepper to taste

DIRECTIONS

1 Bring a large stock pot full of water to a boil. Add the salt and pasta. Cook according to the package directions, about 3 to 5 minutes. Drain the pasta in a colander; set aside.

2 Meanwhile, in a heavy skillet, heat the olive oil and butter over medium heat. Add the onions and sauté for 3 minutes. Add the kale, Swiss chard, or spinach leaves, and toss. Cover with the lid for 2 minutes. Stir in the heavy cream, capers, and salmon.

3 Place the pasta in a serving bowl, and top with the smoked salmon sauce. Squeeze fresh lemon over the top. Season with salt and pepper. Serve immediately.

PER SERVING: Calories 694 (From Fat 224); Fat 25g (Saturated 9g); Cholesterol 42mg; Sodium 395mg; Carbohydrate 96g (Dietary Fiber 6g); Protein 23g.

NOTE: Grab a bag of prechopped kale or baby spinach to make this dish even faster!

TIP: Angel hair pasta cooks the quickest of all the pastas. If you prefer a thicker pasta, use fresh linguini or spaghetti instead. Fresh pastas often cook in less than 3 minutes.

Caprese Pasta

PREP TIME: ABOUT 5 MIN | **COOK TIME: 5 MIN** | **YIELD: 4 SERVINGS**

INGREDIENTS

1 pound dried angel hair pasta

1 tablespoon salt (for boiling pasta)

2 tablespoons balsamic vinegar

1 teaspoon granulated sugar

¼ cup extra-virgin olive oil

2 cups cherry tomatoes, halved

8 ounces fresh mozzarella (stored in water, drained), cut into cubes

¼ cup thinly sliced basil leaves

Salt to taste

Freshly ground black pepper to taste

DIRECTIONS

1 Bring a large stock pot full of water to a boil. Add the salt and pasta. Cook according to package directions, about 3 to 5 minutes. Drain in a colander; set aside.

2 Meanwhile, in a small saucepan, heat the vinegar, sugar, and olive oil over medium heat, about 3 to 5 minutes.

3 Place the pasta in a serving bowl, and toss with the olive oil mixture. Add the tomatoes, mozzarella, and basil and toss. Season with salt and pepper. Serve immediately.

PER SERVING: *Calories 735 (From Fat 252); Fat 28g (Saturated 10g); Cholesterol 45mg; Sodium 368mg; Carbohydrate 91g (Dietary Fiber 5g); Protein 28g.*

NOTE: Angel hair pasta cooks in 3 to 4 minutes and fresh pasta can often be cooked in less than 3 minutes. Check packages and keep quick-cooking pasta on hand!

TIP: If you need a meaty addition, thinly slice salami or ham to mix in.

Dinnertime Charcuterie Board

| PREP TIME: ABOUT 15 MIN | COOK TIME: NONE | YIELD: 8 SERVINGS |

INGREDIENTS

2 cups broccoli flowers, cut into bite-size pieces

1 cucumber, thinly sliced

2 carrots, halved and sliced lengthwise into 2-inch pieces

1 apple, sliced

1 bunch grapes, washed

1 cup walnuts

1 cup almonds

1 cup hummus

8 ounces sliced cheese (cheddar, mozzarella, Monterey Jack, or provolone)

1 pound various lunch meats (ham, salami, or prosciutto)

1 pound crackers

8 olives

8 gherkin pickles

DIRECTIONS

1 On a large serving platter, place each item grouped together. Serve family–style and enjoy!

PER SERVING: *Calories 722 (From Fat 338); Fat 37g (Saturated 9g); Cholesterol 55mg; Sodium 1,632mg; Carbohydrate 68g (Dietary Fiber 8g); Protein 32g.*

NOTE: My dad always enjoyed cheese and crackers for dinner, but in this century, cheese and crackers have gotten a face-lift! It's more like a meze platter of fun fridge and pantry items. For this, I stuck with heartier fruits and vegetables (ones that can be in the refrigerator longer). Keep nuts, crackers, olives, and pickles on hand just for these types of nights!

TIP: Let your imagination take you away when creating charcuterie boards. Here are some fun additions to consider: Brie, berries, candied nuts, dried fruits (apricots, raisins, cranberries, cherries), more vegetables (cherry tomatoes, celery, cauliflower, snap peas, canned baby corn), dips (artichoke dip, mustards, guacamole, bean dips, jams, honey), nuts (pistachios, hazelnuts, pine nuts, peanuts, cashews), and sliced bread or a variety of crackers.

5

Creating Simple Sides and Sweets

Discover side dishes that take less than ten minutes to pull together.

Redesign your snack drawer with good-for-you snacks made from scratch.

Explore easy and elegant desserts for everyday enjoyment.

Chapter **17**

Sides in Ten Minutes or Less

Make half your plate greens! Fruits and vegetables should be stars on the plate, because of their added nutritional value from vitamins, minerals, and fiber. However, a rainbow of fruits and vegetables is out there, so go bold and explore the full color spectrum of these delicious additions.

From a meal-prep perspective, if you have a protein, a starch, and this chapter, you're set with a complete meal. Whether you make a rotisserie-style chicken or buy one at the store, pair it with Zesty Cabbage Slaw and a microwave baked potato for a quick meal fix. Consider pairing a steak with Nutty Herbed Couscous and Lemony Broccoli. And next time you make rice, make a big batch and freeze it — frozen rice can turn into a quick Cilantro Lime Rice.

Our family favorites are the cruciferous variety. Why? Cabbage and broccoli can hang out in the refrigerator a while and still be great side dishes! Whenever I make Miso and Lemon Kale Salad, everyone asks me for the recipe — I hope you give it a try!

TIP

If you love to grill vegetables, grill them dry (without oil). Then, as soon as you pull them from the grill, give them a quick toss in your favorite vinaigrette. Vegetables like zucchini, eggplant, and sweet potatoes will retain their texture and fast become a star-studded-side!

Lemony Broccoli

PREP TIME: ABOUT 5 MIN | **COOK TIME: 5 MIN** | **YIELD: 6 SERVINGS**

INGREDIENTS

4 cups broccoli florets

1½ cups water

1 teaspoon salt

3 tablespoons unsalted butter

1 lemon, zested and juiced

DIRECTIONS

1 In a Dutch oven or large skillet with lid, place the broccoli florets, water, and salt. Turn the heat to medium-high and secure the lid. When the water begins to steam, cook the broccoli for 3 to 5 minutes; if you prefer softer broccoli, cook it up to 7 minutes.

2 Meanwhile, in a small skillet or saucepan, melt the butter over medium-low heat; then add the lemon zest and lemon juice, stir, and remove from the heat.

3 Strain the broccoli and transfer to a serving dish. Pour the lemony butter sauce over the top and toss the broccoli. Serve immediately.

PER SERVING: *Calories 73 (From Fat 54); Fat 6g (Saturated 4g); Cholesterol 15mg; Sodium 408mg; Carbohydrate 5g (Dietary Fiber 2g); Protein 2g.*

NOTE: Frozen broccoli can work in this recipe, too! Frozen broccoli is pre-cooked, so the cooking time will be shorter.

TIP: To prepare in advance, prechop the broccoli and store in a resealable bag or airtight container in the refrigerator.

VARY IT! Grab a bag of prechopped broccoli and cauliflower instead of just broccoli.

Grilled Balsamic Asparagus

PREP TIME: ABOUT 6 MIN	COOK TIME: 3 MIN	YIELD: 4 SERVINGS

INGREDIENTS

1 pound asparagus

½ cup balsamic vinaigrette or dressing

¼ cup grated Parmesan cheese

DIRECTIONS

1 Take a vegetable peeler to the ends of the asparagus or snap off the tough ends, leaving a lengthy stalk.

2 To cook, choose one of the following methods:

Grill: Heat a gas grill to high. Place the asparagus on the grill across the grates so they don't fall through. Grill for 3 minutes, rotating after 2 minutes on one side.

Broiler: Heat the broiler to high. Place the asparagus on a baking sheet and place in the oven 3 to 5 inches from the heat element. Broil for 3 to 5 minutes.

3 Place the vinaigrette in a serving dish. Place the hot asparagus into the dressing and toss. Top with grated Parmesan cheese, and serve immediately or at room temperature.

PER SERVING: *Calories 129 (From Fat 95); Fat 11g (Saturated 2g); Cholesterol 6mg; Sodium 584mg; Carbohydrate 5g (Dietary Fiber 1g); Protein 5g.*

TIP: To prepare in advance, trim the ends from the asparagus, wrap in a lightly dampened paper towel, and place in a resealable bag in the refrigerator.

VARY IT! Cooked broccoli, cauliflower, green beans, or carrots all work with this dressing.

Zesty Cabbage Slaw

PREP TIME: ABOUT 5 MIN	COOK TIME: NONE	YIELD: 8 SERVINGS

INGREDIENTS

½ medium head red cabbage

½ cup Greek yogurt or sour cream

2 tablespoons mayonnaise

1 lime, juiced

½ teaspoon salt

¼ teaspoon ground cumin

1 to 2 teaspoons hot sauce or Sriracha (optional)

¼ cup chopped cilantro or parsley

DIRECTIONS

1 Using a mandoline or chef's knife, thinly slice the cabbage to shred.

2 In a large bowl, whisk together the yogurt or sour cream, mayonnaise, lime juice, salt, cumin, and hot sauce. Add the cabbage and toss.

3 Place the cabbage in a serving dish, top with chopped cilantro or parsley, and serve.

PER SERVING: *Calories 60 (From Fat 37); Fat 4g (Saturated 2g); Cholesterol 8mg; Sodium 197mg; Carbohydrate 6g (Dietary Fiber 1g); Protein 1g.*

NOTE: This is a perfect side dish at picnics or barbecues.

TIP: To prepare in advance, shred the cabbage and place in a resealable bag in the refrigerator up to 4 days in advance.

VARY IT! You can use shredded white cabbage, shredded broccoli, or shredded Brussels sprouts in place of red cabbage for a fun twist.

Braised Cabbage

PREP TIME: ABOUT 1 MIN | COOK TIME: 9 MIN | YIELD: 6 SERVINGS

INGREDIENTS

½ medium head red or white cabbage

1½ cups vegetable or chicken broth

2 tablespoons salted butter

1 tablespoon red wine vinegar or apple cider vinegar

Salt to taste

Freshly ground black pepper to taste

DIRECTIONS

1 Cut the cabbage into 6 wedges.

2 Place the cabbage and broth into a Dutch oven, secure the lid, and heat over medium-high heat for 6 to 8 minutes. Add the butter and vinegar. Stir the cabbage and return the lid for 1 minute.

3 Season with salt and pepper, and serve.

PER SERVING: *Calories 61 (From Fat 36); Fat 4g (Saturated 2g); Cholesterol 10mg; Sodium 146mg; Carbohydrate 5g (Dietary Fiber 2g); Protein 2g.*

NOTE: Braised cabbage pairs well with fish, pork, or roasted meats.

VARY IT! Having a glass of white wine? Add ½ cup Chardonnay or Sauvignon Blanc in place of the broth for a subtle change in flavor.

Cilantro Lime Rice

PREP TIME: ABOUT 5 MIN	COOK TIME: 5 MIN	YIELD: 6 SERVINGS

INGREDIENTS

1 tablespoon extra-virgin olive oil

¼ teaspoon ground cumin

2 cups leftover cooked white or brown rice

½ lime, zested and juiced

¼ cup chopped cilantro or parsley

2 green onions, chopped

DIRECTIONS

1 In a large skillet, heat the olive oil over medium heat. Add the cumin and stir to toast and release the flavors. Add the cold rice and stir–fry until heated through, about 3 to 5 minutes. Add in a splash of water if the rice begins to stick.

2 Place the rice in a serving dish and add the lime zest, lime juice, cilantro or parsley, and onions. Toss and serve.

PER SERVING: *Calories 94 (From Fat 26); Fat 3g (Saturated 0g); Cholesterol 0mg; Sodium 4mg; Carbohydrate 16g (Dietary Fiber 1g); Protein 2g.*

NOTE: Leftover rice is a must for stir-fried rice. Freshly cooked rice will get soggy and clump when stir-fried.

TIP: To freeze rice, place cooled rice onto a baking sheet, freeze for 30 minutes, and then break into clumps and transfer to a freezer bag. Use within 6 months of freezing. Many large grocery outlets carry frozen rice.

VARY IT! Add toasted, flaked coconut for coconut lime rice. Use sesame oil and add 1 scrambled egg, ½ cup of peas, and 1 tablespoon of soy sauce for a quick Asian-inspired rice.

Nutty Herbed Couscous

PREP TIME: ABOUT 2 MIN	COOK TIME: 8 MIN	YIELD: 6 SERVINGS

INGREDIENTS

1¾ cups vegetable or chicken broth

1 cup dried couscous

2 teaspoons extra-virgin olive oil

2 tablespoons chopped almonds, walnuts, or pine nuts

Salt to taste

1 teaspoon chopped fresh thyme or rosemary or ½ teaspoon chopped dried thyme or rosemary

2 tablespoons chopped fresh parsley

DIRECTIONS

1 In a medium saucepan, bring the broth to a boil. Add the couscous, stir, cover with a lid, and remove from the heat. Let the couscous rest for 5 minutes. Then fluff with a fork.

2 Meanwhile, in a small skillet, heat the olive oil over medium heat and add the chopped nuts, stirring constantly. As soon as you can smell the nuts, remove from the heat and add the salt, thyme or rosemary, and parsley.

3 Pour the nutty herbed mixture over the couscous, toss, and serve.

PER SERVING: *Calories 148 (From Fat 32); Fat 4g (Saturated 0g); Cholesterol 0mg; Sodium 120mg; Carbohydrate 23g (Dietary Fiber 2g); Protein 5 g.*

NOTE: Couscous is technically pasta, made from semolina or durum wheat. Quinoa may be a healthier alternative, but couscous takes the cake for time!

TIP: Fresh herbs go a long way toward adding aroma and flavor to a dish. Keep fresh herbs in the refrigerator by placing the stems in a water glass and covering the glass with a plastic resealable bag. The herbs can stay fresh this way for up to 2 weeks.

VARY IT! Most any fresh herb and nut combination can work in this recipe. My favorites are pine nuts with thyme, slivered almonds with rosemary, chopped walnuts with sage, and cashews with curry powder and parsley. Add sautéed garlic, green peas, sautéed mushrooms, or grated carrot for fun additions.

Asian Pickled Cucumbers

PREP TIME: ABOUT 5 MIN	COOK TIME: NONE	YIELD: 4 SERVINGS

INGREDIENTS

1 English cucumber, thinly sliced

½ small red onion, thinly sliced

1 teaspoon toasted sesame oil or canola oil

1 tablespoon rice wine vinegar or white wine vinegar

1 tablespoon black sesame seeds or toasted white sesame seeds

Salt to taste

DIRECTIONS

In a serving bowl, place the cucumbers and onions. Toss with oil and vinegar, and stir. Top with sesame seeds, season with salt, and serve immediately or within 8 hours.

PER SERVING: *Calories 48 (From Fat 22); Fat 2g (Saturated 0g); Cholesterol 0mg; Sodium 6mg; Carbohydrate 6g (Dietary Fiber 1g); Protein 1g.*

NOTE: Black sesame seeds are bold in color and nuttier in flavor. If you can find them, use them — Their color really makes a dish pop! If you can't, don't dismay, white sesames are still fun and have a great flavor. Check the Asian section of most markets for sesame seeds or the spice aisle.

TIP: You can use any cucumbers, but English cucumbers have fewer seeds. If you're using a standard cucumber, consider peeling the cucumber and removing the seeds before slicing.

VARY IT! For a Southern favorite, use apple cider vinegar and a sweet onion and skip the sesame seeds.

Carrot and Cilantro Salad

PREP TIME: ABOUT 5 MIN	COOK TIME: NONE	YIELD: 4 SERVINGS

INGREDIENTS

4 carrots, grated

½ cup chopped cilantro

¼ teaspoon ground cumin

½ teaspoon sea salt

1 lime, juiced

2 tablespoons extra-virgin olive oil

DIRECTIONS

In a serving bowl, mix together the carrot, cilantro, cumin, sea salt, lime juice, and olive oil. Toss and serve.

PER SERVING: *Calories 92 (From Fat 62); Fat 7g (Saturated 1g); Cholesterol 0mg; Sodium 342mg; Carbohydrate 8g (Dietary Fiber 2g); Protein 1g.*

NOTE: When shopping for carrots, look for ones with the green tops still on for the freshest flavors.

TIP: Grab a bag of preshredded carrots at the market to make this side dish in 2 minutes!

VARY IT! If you don't care for cilantro, try fresh parsley instead. The color really makes this side dish pop!

VARY IT! This cilantro dressing works great on roasted sweet potatoes or butternut squash as well.

Garlicky Greens

PREP TIME: ABOUT 5 MIN	COOK TIME: 2 MIN	YIELD: 8 SERVINGS

INGREDIENTS

1 tablespoon extra-virgin olive oil

2 cloves garlic, chopped

½ lemon, juiced

8 cups thinly sliced kale

¼ cup grated Parmesan cheese

DIRECTIONS

1 In a small skillet, heat the olive oil over medium heat. Add the garlic and sauté just until fragrant, about 1 to 2 minutes. Immediately remove from the heat to avoid burning the garlic.

2 Meanwhile, in a serving bowl, place the lemon juice and sliced kale. Massage the kale with your hands to coat with lemon juice (this helps tenderize this tougher green). Next, pour the garlic oil over the top of the greens and toss well.

3 Top the greens with grated Parmesan, and serve.

PER SERVING: *Calories 64 (From Fat 28); Fat 3g (Saturated 1g); Cholesterol 3mg; Sodium 77mg; Carbohydrate 8g (Dietary Fiber 1g); Protein 4g.*

NOTE: If your garlic becomes brown, dump it and start over. Burnt garlic has a very bitter flavor.

TIP: Look for lacinato or Tuscan kale at the market. It's a flatter leaf and more tender in texture. Remove the tough stems from the kale. Next, lay the kale leaves on top of each other and roll up like a cigar. Then thinly slice or chiffonade the kale to get strands of greens.

VARY IT! Spinach, beet greens, Swiss chard greens, and collard greens can all be used in this recipe instead of kale. Use whatever you prefer and can get at a local market.

Parmesan Spiralized Zucchini Noodles

PREP TIME: ABOUT 10 MIN	COOK TIME: NONE	YIELD: 4 SERVINGS

INGREDIENTS

2 medium zucchini, stems and ends removed

1 cup cherry tomatoes, halved

½ cup cubed, fresh mozzarella

3 tablespoons prepared pesto

DIRECTIONS

1 Using a spiralizer or box grater, make long noodle strands with the zucchini. Place the zucchini in a serving bowl.

2 Add the tomatoes and mozzarella, and toss with the pesto. Serve at room temperature or refrigerated. This dish will keep for 2 days in the refrigerator.

PER SERVING: *Calories 128 (From Fat 88); Fat 10g (Saturated 3g); Cholesterol 15mg; Sodium 215mg; Carbohydrate 5g (Dietary Fiber 2g); Protein 6g.*

NOTE: You don't need to cook zucchini noodles! The acid in the pesto and tomatoes will soften the zucchini slightly.

NOTE: Fresh mozzarella is a soft cheese often found stored in water. Drain off the water and dice or slice to use.

TIP: You can buy pre-spiralized zucchini at most grocery stores. This recipe will come together in 3 minutes if you go that route.

VARY IT! No pesto on hand? No problem! Whisk together 1 tablespoon red wine vinegar, 1 teaspoon mustard, ½ teaspoon garlic powder, ¼ teaspoon onion powder, 1 teaspoon honey, and 2 tablespoons extra-virgin olive oil. Season with salt and pepper to serve. A simple red wine vinaigrette goes a long way on zucchini!

Tropical Fruit Salad

PREP TIME: ABOUT 5 MIN	COOK TIME: 1 MIN	YIELD: 4 SERVINGS

INGREDIENTS

1 fresh or canned mango, diced

2 cups canned or fresh pineapple, diced

1 banana, thinly sliced

¼ cup shredded, unsweetened coconut

¼ cup chopped macadamia nuts

2 tablespoons honey

½ lime, juiced

DIRECTIONS

1 In a large serving bowl, mix together the mango, pineapple, banana, coconut, and macadamia nuts.

2 In a microwaveable bowl, microwave the honey for 10 seconds. Stir in the lime juice. Pour this mixture over the fruit salad and serve, or store in the refrigerator up to 3 days.

PER SERVING: *Calories 208 (From Fat 75); Fat 8g (Saturated 3g); Cholesterol 0mg; Sodium 4mg; Carbohydrate 36g (Dietary Fiber 4g); Protein 2g.*

NOTE: If you'd like the fruit salad to last longer, use canned fruits and add the banana just before serving. Then you can keep the salad up to 5 days in the refrigerator.

VARY IT! Kiwi, apples, and berries also make for colorful additions.

Miso and Lemon Kale Salad

PREP TIME: ABOUT 10 MIN	COOK TIME: NONE	YIELD: 6 SERVINGS

INGREDIENTS

12 large kale leaves

½ lemon, juiced

2 teaspoons yellow miso

3 tablespoons extra-virgin olive oil

¼ teaspoon garlic powder

⅛ teaspoon onion powder

½ teaspoon freshly ground black pepper

3 tablespoons grated Parmesan cheese

DIRECTIONS

1 Remove the stems from the kale leaves. Place the kale leaves on top of one another, roll them up, and do a thin slice of the kale leaves, creating a chiffonade cut. Place the kale in a serving bowl. Squeeze the lemon over the kale and massage the leaves to tenderize.

2 In a small bowl, whisk together the miso, olive oil, garlic powder, onion powder, and pepper. Pour the dressing over the kale and toss to coat. Sprinkle with Parmesan and serve.

PER SERVING: *Calories 97 (From Fat 71); Fat 8g (Saturated 1g); Cholesterol 2mg; Sodium 126mg; Carbohydrate 5g (Dietary Fiber 1g); Protein 3g.*

NOTE: Lacinato or Tuscan kale is a more tender and flavorful variety. It's a flatter leaf than traditional kale. Kale is a fall and winter crop, but in many parts of the United States, it can be grown year-round.

NOTE: Miso is a fermented soy paste, imparting a salty, umami (meat-like) taste. It gives the greens a creamy coating, as well. There are a variety of colors of miso, but the yellow is the mildest and most common at grocery stores. Look for miso in the refrigerated section of the grocery store. If you can't find miso, this recipe is still great without it.

VARY IT! My family has this salad almost weekly. Some days we add pumpkin seeds or sunflower seeds; other days we add dried cranberries or orange wedges.

Simple Salads for All Four Seasons

| PREP TIME: ABOUT 10 MIN | COOK TIME: NONE | YIELD: 6 SERVINGS |

INGREDIENTS

8 cups torn lettuce (romaine, butter, red leaf, or green leaf)

Spring Salad, Summer Salad, Autumn Salad, or Winter Salad toppings (see the following recipes)

Spring Salad, Summer Salad, Autumn Salad, or Winter Salad dressing (see the following recipes)

DIRECTIONS

1 In a large mixing bowl, place the lettuce.

2 Add the toppings of your chosen salad.

3 Toss with the dressing of your chosen salad before serving.

Spring Salad

1 avocado, diced

½ cup canned mandarin oranges, drained

½ red onion, thinly sliced

¼ cup sunflower seeds

¼ cup poppy seed dressing

DIRECTIONS

1 In a bowl, place the avocado, mandarin oranges, onion, and sunflower seeds. Set aside these toppings.

2 In a measuring cup, put the dressing; set aside.

Summer Salad

1 cup halved cherry tomatoes

6 basil leaves, torn or thinly sliced

1 cup grated mozzarella cheese

1 cup grated carrots

¼ cup Italian dressing

DIRECTIONS

1 In a bowl, place the tomatoes, basil leaves, mozzarella, and carrots. Set aside these toppings.

2 In a measuring cup, put the dressing; set aside.

Autumn Salad

1 apple thinly sliced

½ cup chopped pecans

½ cup dried cherries or cranberries

¼ cup honey mustard vinaigrette

DIRECTIONS

1 In a bowl, place the apple, pecans, and cherries or cranberries. Set aside these toppings.

2 In a measuring cup, put the dressing; set aside.

Winter Salad

½ cup shredded red cabbage

¼ cup dried cranberries

¼ cup pumpkin or sunflower seeds

1 pear, diced

¼ cup crumbled blue cheese or feta cheese

¼ cup red wine vinaigrette

DIRECTIONS

1 In a bowl, place the cabbage, cranberries, pumpkin or sunflower seeds, pear, and blue cheese or feta cheese. Set aside these toppings.

2 In a measuring cup, put the dressing; set aside.

PER SERVING (SPRING SALAD): *Calories 129 (From Fat 95); Fat 11g (Saturated 1g); Cholesterol 0mg; Sodium 55mg; Carbohydrate 8g (Dietary Fiber 3g); Protein 2g.*

(continued)

PER SERVING (SUMMER SALAD): *Calories 102 (From Fat 64); Fat 7g (Saturated 3g); Cholesterol 15mg; Sodium 302mg; Carbohydrate 5g (Dietary Fiber 1g); Protein 5g.*

PER SERVING (AUTUMN SALAD): *Calories 132 (From Fat 71); Fat 8g (Saturated 1g); Cholesterol 0mg; Sodium 70mg; Carbohydrate 16g (Dietary Fiber 2g); Protein 1g.*

PER SERVING (WINTER SALAD): *Calories 121 (From Fat 68); Fat 8g (Saturated 2g); Cholesterol 4mg; Sodium 252mg; Carbohydrate 12g (Dietary Fiber 2g); Protein 3g.*

NOTE: The idea behind these salads is to make use of what's in season. When fruits and vegetables are at the height of their season, they don't have to travel as far to get to your plate, which means their nutritional content is greater.

TIP: Look for pre-torn lettuce mixes and chopped fruits and vegetables. When the season isn't right, opt for canned items like baby corn, roasted peppers, and artichoke hearts to add elegance to any salad.

VARY IT! Have fun with fruits and vegetables that are on sale and in season at your local market, and get inspired by the variety of salads you can make.

» **Making your own energy balls**

» **Swapping out all-purpose flour with whole-wheat pastry flour**

Chapter **18**

Simple Snacks to Make Ahead

RECIPES IN THIS CHAPTER

- ☺ **Whole-Grain Pumpkin Bread**
- ☺ **Peanut Butter–Date Energy Balls**
- ☺ **Perfect-for-the-Trail Mix**
- ☺ **Tart Cherry and Walnut Granola Bars**
- ☺ **Wild Blueberry and Lemon Mini Muffin Bites**
- ☺ **Ham and Cheese Roll-Ups**

Whether you're sending a little one off to school or grabbing a snack on the run, having nourishing snacks on hand is helpful. Snacks provide nourishment, taste great, and fill you up in the mealtime gaps when hunger strikes. If you're planning a hike, grab the Perfect-for-the-Trail Mix. If you're wanting to have something ready when your little one gets home from school, consider the Whole-Grain Pumpkin Bread or Tarty Cherry and Walnut Granola Bars. And if you're hungry for something after a bout of exercise, keep the Peanut Butter–Date Energy Balls on hand.

TIP

Snacks don't have to be complicated or require baking. Here's a quick list of grab-and-go snacks that don't require a recipe:

» Apples dipped in almond butter

» Hummus and pretzels

» Peanut butter and celery sticks

» Carrots and ranch dip

>> Sliced avocado and lime or avocado toast

>> Popcorn (okay, this may require some cooking or the store-bought variety)

>> Dates stuffed with walnuts (my daughter's favorite)

As a mom and a person on the go, I see the value of having both homemade and store-bought snacks on hand. I hope you enjoy my family's favorites in this chapter!

Whole-Grain Pumpkin Bread

PREP TIME: ABOUT 15 MIN	COOK TIME: 1 HR	YIELD: 36 SERVINGS

INGREDIENTS

6 large eggs

3 cups granulated sugar

1⅓ cups canola oil

One 28.5-ounce can pumpkin puree

4¾ cups whole-wheat pastry flour

1 tablespoon baking soda

1 tablespoon cinnamon

2 teaspoons ground nutmeg

2 teaspoons salt

1½ cups chopped walnuts, pecans, or pumpkin seeds (optional)

DIRECTIONS

1 Preheat the oven to 350 degrees. Spray cooking spray in 8 mini loaf pans or 3 standard bread pans. If using a convection oven, reduce the heat to 345 degrees.

2 In a stand mixer or with a handheld mixer on medium speed, blend together the eggs, sugar, and canola oil until light and fluffy, about 4 minutes. Add in the pumpkin to blend.

3 In a separate bowl, whisk together the flour, baking soda, cinnamon, nutmeg, and salt.

4 Slowly incorporate the dry ingredients into the wet ingredients. It's okay if there are lumps of flour. With a spoon, stir in the chopped nuts or seeds.

5 Pour the pumpkin batter into the loaf pans. Bake for 35 to 40 minutes in mini loaf pans or 50 minutes to 1 hour in a standard bread pan. The internal temperature should read 190 to 210 degrees.

PER SERVING: *Calories 209 (From Fat 83); Fat 9g (Saturated 1g); Cholesterol 35mg; Sodium 248mg; Carbohydrate 30g (Dietary Fiber 3g); Protein 3g.*

NOTE: This is my aunt Nancy's recipe and one that our entire family cherishes. I've added in the whole-wheat pastry flour for additional nutrition, but you can use all-purpose flour if you prefer — just increase the amount of flour to 5¼ cups. Muffin pans can also be used to bake the batter if you run out of loaf pans. Bake muffins for 20 to 25 minutes.

TIP: Cool bread and tightly wrap in plastic wrap and then foil to freeze. The bread is quite possibly tastier after being frozen, because it's more moist. Defrost and enjoy! Frozen pumpkin bread can be kept up to 3 months.

VARY IT! Add chocolate chips, chopped pecans, or dried cranberries.

Peanut Butter–Date Energy Balls

PREP TIME: ABOUT 10 MIN	COOK TIME: NONE	YIELD: 12 SERVINGS

INGREDIENTS

1 cup dried dates

¼ cup natural peanut butter

2 tablespoons cocoa powder

1 tablespoon chia seeds

1 cup rolled oats

DIRECTIONS

1 In a food processor, combine all the ingredients. Pulse until combined, about 2 minutes. If the mixture is too dry, add in 1 or 2 tablespoons water.

2 Using a large spoon, scoop out the date mixture and roll into 12 balls. Place the balls onto a parchment-lined plate or airtight container. Store in the refrigerator up to 2 weeks in an airtight container.

PER SERVING: *Calories 125 (From Fat 37); Fat 4g (Saturated 1g); Cholesterol 0mg; Sodium 2mg; Carbohydrate 20g (Dietary Fiber 3g); Protein 4g.*

NOTE: Date balls freeze beautifully. Freeze up to 3 months.

TIP: Dried dates are like sticky sugar bites! Our favorite are Medjool.

VARY IT! Swap out peanut butter with almond butter, if you like. You can also skip the oats and opt for pretzels instead for a salty addition. Flaxseeds work great in place of chia seeds, too.

Perfect-for-the-Trail Mix

PREP TIME: ABOUT 3 MIN	COOK TIME: 0 MIN	YIELD: 10 SERVINGS

INGREDIENTS

1 cup dried fruit (cherries, blueberries, raisins, chopped apricots, or chopped mango)

1 cup honey-roasted peanuts

½ cup roasted unsalted pumpkin seeds

½ cup raw, unsalted sunflower seeds

1 cup dry-roasted, unsalted almonds

1 cup dark chocolate chunks, chocolate chips, or M&M's

DIRECTIONS

In a large mixing bowl, place all the ingredients and stir. Store in glass quart-size jars for up to 1 month in the pantry.

PER SERVING: *Calories 325 (From Fat 202); Fat 22g (Saturated 5g); Cholesterol 0mg; Sodium 44mg; Carbohydrate 29g (Dietary Fiber 6g); Protein 9g.*

NOTE: Trail mix is versatile and easy to make. Preparing your own can be much less expensive than buying a premade mix. Plus, making your own gives you the power to pick and choose which fruits, nuts, and seeds you prefer to snack on.

VARY IT! Many grocery stores have fun candied, spicy, or sweet seed and nut combos. Pack your favorite and keep them on hand in your pantry. Our favorite combo is dried mango, walnuts, almonds, pumpkin seeds, sunflower seeds, and M&M's.

Tart Cherry and Walnut Granola Bars

PREP TIME: ABOUT 5 MIN	COOK TIME: 6 MIN	YIELD: 10 SERVINGS

INGREDIENTS

½ cup unsalted pumpkin seeds

½ cup dried, unsweetened shredded coconut

1 cup chopped walnuts

1 cup rolled oats

1 cup dried tart cherries

⅓ cup honey

2 tablespoons unsalted butter

1 teaspoon salt

½ teaspoon vanilla extract

DIRECTIONS

1 Place a piece of parchment paper in a 9-x-9-inch casserole dish.

2 In a food processor, place the pumpkin seeds, coconut, and walnuts, and blend for 30 seconds. Transfer to a medium bowl, add the oats and dried cherries, and mix.

3 In a small saucepan, heat the honey and butter over medium heat until it comes to a rolling boil; then let simmer for 1 minute. Remove from the heat and stir in the salt and vanilla. Pour the hot honey mixture over the oats and stir. Working quickly, pour into the prepared pan and press down the bars to flatten. Cool the bars in the refrigerator for 2 hours.

4 Cut with a sharp knife and store in the refrigerator for up to 2 weeks or freeze for 6 months.

PER SERVING: *Calories 267 (From Fat 119); Fat 13g (Saturated 5g); Cholesterol 6mg; Sodium 236mg; Carbohydrate 33g (Dietary Fiber 5g); Protein 5g.*

NOTE: Rolled oats are also called old-fashioned oats. Steel-cut oats can't work in this recipe, because they're too tough to bite into.

TIP: If you don't have a food processor, use a sharp knife and roughly chop ingredients. This process helps create a more compact bar and an easier bite.

TIP: An easy way to measure honey is to spray a measuring cup with cooking spray or rub it with oil and then measure. The honey will easily pour out of the measuring cup after!

VARY IT! Try a variety of combinations — dried apricots and peanuts, chopped almonds and dried wild blueberries, or chopped dates and cashews.

Wild Blueberry and Lemon Mini Muffin Bites

PREP TIME: ABOUT 10 MIN	COOK TIME: 18 MIN	YIELD: 12 SERVINGS

INGREDIENTS

½ cup unsalted butter, softened or at room temperature

¾ cup granulated sugar

2 large eggs

½ cup whole milk

1 lemon, zested and juiced

2 cups whole-wheat pastry flour

2 teaspoons baking powder

½ teaspoon salt

2 cups frozen wild blueberries

DIRECTIONS

1 Preheat the oven to 375 degrees. Spray a mini muffin tin with cooking spray.

2 In a stand mixer or large bowl, add the butter and sugar; cream together with a hand mixer until light and fluffy. Then add the eggs, and blend for 1 minute. Add in the milk and lemon juice and blend until combined.

3 In a medium bowl, whisk together the lemon zest, flour, baking powder, and salt. Add the dry ingredients to the wet ingredients and mix for 30 seconds, or until combined.

4 Place the frozen blueberries in a colander and rinse. Shake off the excess water, and with a spoon, stir the blueberries in with the other ingredients.

5 Using a cookie scooper, scoop 1 scoop per mini muffin cup or 2 scoops per regular muffin cups. Bake mini muffins for 15 to 18 minutes or regular muffins for 25 to 30 minutes.

6 Store cooled muffins in an airtight container in the refrigerator for 5 days or freeze for up to 1 month.

PER SERVING: *Calories 215 (From Fat 83); Fat 9g (Saturated 5g); Cholesterol 57mg; Sodium 197mg; Carbohydrate 31g (Dietary Fiber 3g); Protein 4g.*

NOTE: We keep these muffins in our freezer for a quick snack in the morning or after school. Microwave for 20 seconds before serving.

TIP: Most cookie scoops are a heaping tablespoon.

VARY IT! Try replacing the blueberries with 1 cup dried cranberries and use orange and orange zest in place of the lemon.

Ham and Cheese Roll-Ups

PREP TIME: ABOUT 10 MIN | COOK TIME: NONE | YIELD: 6 SERVINGS

INGREDIENTS

Six 8-inch flour tortillas

¾ cup (3¼ ounces) cream cheese

¾ cup shredded cheddar or Monterey Jack cheese

6 slices deli ham

¾ cup chopped baby spinach

DIRECTIONS

1 Lay the tortillas out flat. Using a knife, spread 2 tablespoons of cream cheese across each tortilla. Next, sprinkle 2 tablespoons cheese onto each tortilla. Lay a ham slice down the center of each tortilla. Sprinkle 2 tablespoons of chopped spinach across the top of the ham on each tortilla.

2 Next, roll up each tortilla like a cigar. Place the tortillas in a storage container and chill in the refrigerator until ready to slice and eat. Place a dry paper towel on top of the tortillas to absorb moisture while refrigerating. Tortillas can keep up to 4 days in the refrigerator.

3 To serve, cut tortillas into 6 slices, creating pinwheels.

PER SERVING: *Calories 340 (From Fat 177); Fat 20g (Saturated 10g); Cholesterol 55mg; Sodium 718mg; Carbohydrate 28g (Dietary Fiber 2g); Protein 13g.*

NOTE: Three-quarters cup equals 12 tablespoons, which is useful to know when breaking down into multiple rolls in this recipe.

VARY IT! Add canned pepperoncini, chopped olives, artichoke and spinach dip, Sriracha, or pickle slices. Kale is a great substitute for spinach and can hold up better in storage. Lettuce can't be stored with good results for more than 2 days.

VARY IT! Try a variety of flavored cream cheese spreads or goat cheese. If you want an elegant variety, my family's favorite is goat cheese, fig preserves, and chopped walnuts.

Chapter **19**

Simple Yet Elegant Desserts

Sweet, salty, crunchy, fruity, or smooth — are your taste buds salivating yet? Desserts are a satisfying way to finish a meal, savor something sweet, or skip dinner and just enjoy dessert instead! When you're meal planning, it's easy to forget the importance of dessert. Desserts can feel decadent, but don't forget to factor in a little something to round out the day. It can be a simple as a date stuffed with nuts or a chocolate wedge dipped in peanut butter. In this chapter, I spotlight ways to make fruit the star-studded sweet, visit some classic desserts, and even offer a fun dessert just for one!

Dessert was never a big deal for my family growing up. My mom would make tapioca pudding, vanilla pudding, milk toast, Jell-O, cookies, or rice pudding all year long. I grew up loving these simple desserts, and I'm excited to share my family's favorites with you! If you're craving a showstopper, opt for Strawberries with Mascarpone, Basil, and Balsamic. Want to meal-prep desserts for the week? Consider making the No-Bake Lemon and Cherry Cheesecake or Creamy Vanilla Pudding. If chocolate is your favorite, whip up the Chocolate Avocado Mousse. If you have kids around, get them involved in making Peanut Butter Cereal Bars or the Lemony Mug Cakes.

Strawberries with Mascarpone, Basil, and Balsamic

PREP TIME: ABOUT 5 MIN	COOK TIME: 5 MIN	YIELD: 4 SERVINGS

INGREDIENTS

¼ cup granulated sugar, divided

½ cup balsamic vinegar

4 cups sliced strawberries

¼ cup thinly sliced basil

½ cup mascarpone or cream cheese

DIRECTIONS

1 In a small skillet or saucepan, heat 1 tablespoon of the sugar with the balsamic vinegar over medium heat. When the vinegar begins to simmer, reduce the heat to low and continue cooking until the vinegar thickens into a syrup and reduces in half, about 4 minutes.

2 Meanwhile, in a large bowl, gently stir together the strawberries, 1 tablespoon of the sugar, and the basil.

3 In a food processor or with a hand mixer, whip the remaining 2 tablespoons of sugar with the mascarpone cheese or cream cheese until smooth. Place a dollop of mascarpone cheese into 4 bowls. Top with 1 cup of the strawberry mixture in each bowl.

4 Drizzle the reduced vinegar syrup on top of the strawberries, rendering a sweet and tart dessert.

PER SERVING: *Calories 229 (From Fat 94); Fat 10g (Saturated 6g); Cholesterol 32mg; Sodium 102mg; Carbohydrate 32g (Dietary Fiber 3g); Protein 3g.*

NOTE: You're creating a balsamic reduction in this recipe, which sweetens as it thickens. Use a good-quality balsamic vinegar. If you find a balsamic reduction in a bottle at the supermarket, be sure to look at the ingredients list — they often include many unwanted ingredients, like food coloring. Making your own is simple, as you can see!

TIP: If you're prepping in advance, make the syrup first and store it in the refrigerator. Make the whipped mascarpone up to 5 days in advance. Keep the strawberries washed, patted dry, and stored separate in the refrigerator between paper towels. Slice the strawberries just before preparing the dessert — this dish looks adorable in pint-size Mason jars.

VARY IT! You can use cherries, peaches, plums, or berries in place of the strawberries. Use whatever's in season!

Grilled Peaches with Amaretti Cookies

PREP TIME: ABOUT 5 MIN	COOK TIME: 4 MIN	YIELD: 4 SERVINGS

INGREDIENTS

4 fresh peaches or thawed frozen peaches, pitted and halved

1 tablespoon melted coconut oil or avocado oil

½ cup small curd cottage cheese

2 tablespoons brown sugar

12 amaretti cookies, crushed

DIRECTIONS

1 Heat a grill or grill pan over medium–high heat. Brush the halved peaches with coconut oil or avocado oil. Place the peaches cut side down on the grill and cook for 2 minutes on each side.

2 Meanwhile, in a small bowl, mix together the cottage cheese and brown sugar.

3 Place the peaches onto a serving platter, cut side up. Place 1 tablespoon of sweetened cottage cheese into the center of each peach and top with crushed amaretti cookies. Serve immediately.

PER SERVING: *Calories 159 (From Fat 44); Fat 5g (Saturated 1g); Cholesterol 1mg; Sodium 120mg; Carbohydrate 25g (Dietary Fiber 2g); Protein 5g.*

NOTE: Amaretti cookies are gluten-free cookies made from egg whites, sugar, and almond flour. They're light and crispy, and they have a beautiful almond flavor. If you can't find amaretti cookies, try using biscotti or graham crackers instead.

VARY IT! You can use canned peaches, pineapple, or mango in place of fresh peaches. If you're using sweetened fruit, just leave out the brown sugar.

TIP: This dish makes for a perfect afternoon snack because cottage cheese is packed with protein and balances the sweetness of the fruit.

No-Bake Lemon and Cherry Cheesecake

PREP TIME: ABOUT 10 MIN	COOK TIME: NONE	YIELD: 8 SERVINGS

INGREDIENTS

2 cups crushed gingersnap cookies

Two 8-ounce packages cream cheese

1 can sweetened condensed milk

2 lemons, zested and juiced

24 Bordeaux maraschino cherries or 1 cup cherry pie filling

DIRECTIONS

1 At the bottom of eight 4-ounce or 8-ounce Mason jars, place ¼ cup crushed gingersnap cookies. Use a spoon to pack the cookies into the bottom of the jar.

2 In a food processor, whip together the cream cheese, condensed milk, lemon zest, and lemon juice. Divide this filling among the 8 jars. Top with cherries or cherry pie filling. Serve immediately or chill in the refrigerator up to 5 days before serving.

PER SERVING: *Calories 476 (From Fat 232); Fat 26g (Saturated 14g); Cholesterol 75mg; Sodium 434mg; Carbohydrate 55g (Dietary Fiber 1g); Protein 8g.*

VARY IT! If you don't love ginger, use Amaretti cookies for an almond flavor or graham crackers for something simple.

NOTE: Bordeaux maraschino cherries are an Oregon-based product from Royal Harvest. They're a dark maraschino cherry, much less sweet than the artificially colored variety. You can find them online or at major retail markets. They're heavenly!

TIP: Crush the cookies using a food processor or blender, or place them in a resealable bag and use a rolling pin or skillet to hit them until they're finely crushed.

TIP: Try layering the cream cheese and cookie crumbs for a layered effect.

VARY IT! Lemon, cherries, and ginger go beautifully together, but you can also try these combos, too: orange zest, cranberry compote, and graham crackers; fig preserves, goat cheese (instead of cream cheese), and crushed walnuts (instead of cookies); or strawberry jam, cream cheese, and chopped peanuts with graham crackers.

Instant Pistachio Rice Pudding

PREP TIME: ABOUT 3 MIN	COOK TIME: 23 MIN	YIELD: 6 SERVINGS

INGREDIENTS

2 cups cooked white rice

1 cup chopped pistachios

3 cups whole milk

¼ cup granulated sugar

¼ teaspoon cardamom

1 teaspoon vanilla extract

DIRECTIONS

1 Choose one of the following methods:

    a. *Stovetop:* In a medium saucepan, add the rice, pistachios, milk, and sugar. Heat over medium-high heat for 5 minutes. Reduce the heat to medium and add the cardamom. Heat until thickened, stirring regularly, about 15 minutes. Remove from the heat and stir in the vanilla extract. Serve warm or chill in the refrigerator.

    b. *Instant Pot:* Place the rice, pistachios, milk, sugar, and cardamom into the pot and stir. Select Pressure Cook (High) for 3 minutes. Allow the rice pudding to naturally release the pressure for 20 minutes (do not do a Quick Release of pressure). Stir in the vanilla extract. Serve warm or chill in the refrigerator.

PER SERVING: *Calories 302 (From Fat 120); Fat 13g (Saturated 3g); Cholesterol 12mg; Sodium 53mg; Carbohydrate 38g (Dietary Fiber 2g); Protein 9g.*

NOTE: A multicooker helps this dessert be a hands-off dessert, but it's tasty and successful using either method!

TIP: If you're prepping in advance, store cooked rice puddings in 8-ounce Mason jars. Place plastic wrap over the surface to keep a thin layer from forming on the surface as it cools.

VARY IT! Try chopped pecans and cinnamon or raisins and nutmeg.

Creamy Vanilla Pudding

PREP TIME: ABOUT 5 MIN	COOK TIME: 12 MIN	YIELD: 8 SERVINGS

INGREDIENTS

4 cups whole milk

3 large egg yolks

½ cup granulated sugar

6 tablespoons cornstarch

¼ teaspoon salt

1½ teaspoons vanilla extract

2 tablespoons unsalted butter

DIRECTIONS

1 In a medium saucepan, add the milk, egg yolks, sugar, cornstarch, and salt. Whisk together, and then turn the heat on to medium, stirring occasionally, until thickened, about 10 to 12 minutes. When small bubbles begin to appear on the surface, simmer another 2 minutes. Remove from the heat, and gently stir in the vanilla extract and butter.

2 Serve immediately or transfer to 8 pint-size Mason jars and refrigerate to enjoy later.

PER SERVING: *Calories 189 (From Fat 77); Fat 9g (Saturated 5g); Cholesterol 98mg; Sodium 129mg; Carbohydrate 23g (Dietary Fiber 0g); Protein 5g.*

NOTE: You really can put all the ingredients into the saucepan and cook them at once if you want. Older recipes will tell you to temper the yolks and add cornstarch to cold milk, but guess what — this way works!

VARY IT! Stir in 1 mashed banana for a banana pudding or use ½ teaspoon almond extract for almond yogurt.

Chocolate Avocado Mousse

PREP TIME: ABOUT 4 MIN	COOK TIME: NONE	YIELD: 4 SERVINGS

INGREDIENTS

2 large Hass avocados, peeled and pitted

3 tablespoons cocoa powder

¼ cup sweetened condensed milk

DIRECTIONS

1 Place all the ingredients in a food processor. Process until creamy, about 3 minutes. Chill or serve immediately.

PER SERVING: *Calories 231 (From Fat 153); Fat 17g (Saturated 4g); Cholesterol 7mg; Sodium 32mg; Carbohydrate 21g (Dietary Fiber 8g); Protein 4g.*

NOTE: Chocolate and avocado are meant to be together! If you have sweetened condensed milk around, give it a whirl. No one will know it's packed with this nutrient-dense power fruit!

TIP: Pudding is best made and eaten within 24 hours.

TIP: Make pudding pops by freezing this mixture in popsicle molds.

VARY IT! Skip the cocoa and add lemon zest and 1 tablespoon of lemon juice for a tangy mousse. Want to ditch the sweetened condensed milk? Try adding maple syrup and milk instead.

Caramelized Bananas with Walnuts

PREP TIME: ABOUT 5 MIN	COOK TIME: 6 MIN	YIELD: 4 SERVINGS

INGREDIENTS

1 tablespoon unsalted butter

1 tablespoon vegetable oil

2 medium bananas, sliced in half lengthwise

3 tablespoons brown sugar

½ teaspoon cinnamon

¼ cup chopped walnuts

2 tablespoons water

2 cups vanilla ice cream

DIRECTIONS

1 In a heavy skillet, heat the butter and vegetable oil over medium-high heat. Place the bananas in the pan and brown them, about 1 minute on each side. Remove the bananas onto a plate; set aside.

2 Lower the heat to medium-low and add the brown sugar, cinnamon, walnuts, and water to the pan; stir until the brown sugar begins to melt. Return the bananas back to the pan and flip to coat them with the sugar mixture.

3 To serve, place ½ cup ice cream into 4 bowls each. Top each bowl with 1 banana half and sauce. Serve immediately.

PER SERVING: *Calories 320 (From Fat 169); Fat 19g (Saturated 7g); Cholesterol 37mg; Sodium 56mg; Carbohydrate 37g (Dietary Fiber 2g); Protein 4g.*

NOTE: Firm bananas work best in this dish.

VARY IT! Replace the walnuts with pecans, pistachios, cashews, hazelnuts, or peanuts. Pears and apples also make for a great warmed dessert instead of bananas.

Peanut Butter Cereal Bars

PREP TIME: ABOUT 2 MIN	COOK TIME: 8 MIN	YIELD: 12 SERVINGS

INGREDIENTS

4 tablespoons unsalted butter

4 cups marshmallows

½ cup creamy peanut butter

6 cups rice cereal

½ teaspoon sea salt

DIRECTIONS

1 Spray a 13-x-9-inch baking dish with cooking spray.

2 In a heavy saucepan, heat the butter over medium heat until the butter melts and begins to brown. Stir in the marshmallows and peanut butter until melted. Pour in the rice cereal and sea salt; remove from the heat.

3 Pour into the prepared pan and press gently to even out the bars. Cool for 15 minutes at room temperature; then cut into bars. Store in an airtight container at room temperature up to 5 days.

PER SERVING: *Calories 200 (From Fat 85); Fat 9g (Saturated 4g); Cholesterol 10mg; Sodium 286mg; Carbohydrate 27g (Dietary Fiber 1g); Protein 4g.*

NOTE: Browning the butter really elevates the flavors of these marshmallow cereal bars — don't skip it!

VARY IT! Add chopped nuts, sprinkles, or chocolate chips for a fun spin on these peanut butter bars.

Jam Bars

PREP TIME: ABOUT 5 MIN | COOK TIME: 35 MIN | YIELD: 12 SERVINGS

INGREDIENTS

1¼ cup whole-wheat pastry flour

1¼ cup rolled oats

½ cup packed brown sugar

½ cup unsalted butter, softened

½ teaspoon baking powder

½ teaspoon salt

1 cup strawberry, cherry, or preferred preserves

DIRECTIONS

1 Preheat the oven to 350 degrees. Spray a 9-x-9-inch baking pan with cooking spray.

2 In a medium bowl, mix together the flour, rolled oats, brown sugar, and butter. Measure out 1 cup of this mixture for the topping; set aside.

3 Stir in the baking powder and salt. Press this mixture into the bottom of the prepared baking pan to create the crust. Spread the preserves on top without going all the way to the edge. Then sprinkle the reserved topping on top.

4 Bake until golden brown, about 35 minutes. Cool for 30 minutes before cutting into 12 bars.

PER SERVING: Calories 282 (From Fat 81); Fat 9g (Saturated 5g); Cholesterol 20mg; Sodium 130mg; Carbohydrate 47g (Dietary Fiber 4g); Protein 5g.

NOTE: To soften butter quickly, pour boiling water into a liquid measuring cup or heatproof glass. Empty out the water and place the cup on top of a wrapped butter stick. Let the butter sit for 1 minute. Remove the glass, and your butter should be softened but not melted.

TIP: These bars are perfect for the freezer! To freeze, cut into bars, place onto a plate, and freeze until solid, about 1 hour. Then transfer the bars to a freezer bag and freeze up to 1 month.

VARY IT! If you love nuts, replace ½ cup of the rolled oats with finely chopped pecans, walnuts, or peanuts.

Lemony Mug Cakes

PREP TIME: ABOUT 5 MIN	COOK TIME: 1 MIN	YIELD: 1 SERVING

INGREDIENTS

3 tablespoons all-purpose flour or whole-wheat pastry flour

1 tablespoon granulated sugar

⅛ teaspoon baking soda

¼ teaspoon lemon zest

½ teaspoon lemon juice

2 tablespoons whole milk

1½ teaspoons vegetable oil or coconut oil

1 pinch salt

¼ cup ice cream

DIRECTIONS

1 Mix the flour, sugar, baking soda, lemon zest, lemon juice, milk, oil, and salt in a large coffee mug, stirring to combine. Microwave for 1 minute to 1 minute 15 seconds. Serve warm with ice cream.

PER SERVING: *Calories 252 (From Fat 88); Fat 10g (Saturated 8g); Cholesterol 10mg; Sodium 346mg; Carbohydrate 38g (Dietary Fiber 1g); Protein 4g.*

NOTE: Mug cakes are so fun and a great way to get kids in the kitchen. Help children with measuring ingredients, but allow them to do the stirring and microwaving. It's a rewarding dessert for a young chef!

VARY IT! Serve with lemon curd or strawberry jam as glazed frosting.

6

The Part of Tens

IN THIS PART . . .

Explore ways to dress up a meal with sauces and marinades.

Create meal kits at home.

Discover ways to build a better lunch box for the whole family.

Discover secret shortcuts for quick meal prep.

Chapter **20**

Ten Sauces to Make Meals Pop

Does your weekly meal prep focus on the following formula:

Protein + Starch + Vegetables

Here's your chance to revitalize leftover chicken and give your dish a pop of color, new texture, and a splash of visual appeal. Even if this isn't your meal-prep formula, sauces are a great way to do simple prep work for the week and add a touch of elegance to the plate.

Planning the meat or protein foods to make, and then adding in the vegetables and a simple starch, is often easy, but it can start to feel boring. A simple sauce can transport this dish to the next level. And guess what? Those costly meal-prep services know this — sauces are often a big focus of their meal plans.

In this chapter, I share my top ten sauces and how to pair them and create an all-star meal. Plus, each of these sauces should take you less than five minutes to pull together!

Greek-Inspired Yogurt Cucumber Sauce

Have you heard of tzatziki? It's a popular Mediterranean sauce that is creamy and tart, and instantly makes you feel like you're on the Med! It combines creamy yogurt with grated cucumbers, garlic, and lemon. Every bite makes you feel like it's summer on the Mediterranean!

To make it, follow these steps:

1. **Grate a cucumber, and give it a quick squeeze; discard the liquid.**

2. **Add the cucumber to 1 cup plain Greek yogurt, and give it a stir.**

3. **Add 1 minced garlic clove and the zest of 1 lemon.**

   If you like more lemon, add in a squeeze or two!

4. **Season with salt and pepper.**

You can add in fresh or dried dill, parsley, or oregano, if you like. Yep, it's that simple!

Serve with grilled meats or vegetables; bean patties; raw vegetables or salads; or baked, broiled, or roasted meats or fish.

Creamy and Tangy Butter Sauce

In the restaurant industry, we often keep this sauce on hand to drizzle over blanched or grilled veggies. It's incredibly easy and flavorful and also great on baked or grilled meats. My daughter loves it on shell pasta.

To make it, follow these steps:

1. **Melt 6 tablespoons butter in a small saucepan and let it slightly brown in color.**

2. **Whisk in 2 tablespoons white wine vinegar, 2 tablespoons Dijon mustard, and 1 tablespoon chopped fresh herbs (like parsley, thyme, tarragon, or dill).**

3. **Season with salt and pepper.**

TIP

Make extra and freeze in silicon muffin cups or ice cube trays. Take out of the freezer anytime you need that extra zing!

Serve with seafood (like grilled or baked white fish or shrimp); grilled or baked chicken; grilled, roasted, or blanched carrots, broccoli, cabbage, potatoes, or Brussels sprouts; or noodles.

Honey Sriracha

Crank up the heat a bit with this sweet and spicy Asian–inspired sauce. If you dig hot wings, you'll love this sauce. It's also great as a dipping sauce for a simple sandwich wrap with chicken and lettuce.

To make it, follow these steps:

1. **Melt 3 tablespoons butter.**

2. **Whisk in 2 teaspoons low-sodium soy sauce, the juice of ½ of a lime, ¼ cup honey, and as much Sriracha sauce as your spicy heart desires (start off with a couple tablespoons and work up from there — I use ¼ cup!).**

Serve with cooked eggs; chicken wings; grilled or roasted shrimp; baked, roasted, or grilled chicken; or whitefish.

Lemony Tahini

This is another popular Mediterranean sauce that makes for a winning addition to roasted vegetables or salads or drizzled on sliced chicken breasts. Tahini hails from sesame seeds. This dressing pairs garlic, lemon, and key Mediterranean spices and herbs.

To make it, follow these steps:

1. **Place ⅓ cup well-stirred tahini paste into a blender or food processor (or get ready to stir).**

2. **Add in 2 chopped cloves of garlic, 3 tablespoons lemon juice, ¼ cup chopped parsley, 2 tablespoons extra-virgin olive oil, 2 teaspoons honey, ½ teaspoon cumin powder, and ¼ teaspoon paprika.**

3. **Blend or pulse until smooth.**

4. **Adjust the seasonings with sea salt and pepper.**

Serve with grilled or roasted vegetables, salads, cooked chicken or lamb, grilled beef, meatballs, or pita bread.

REMEMBER

Store leftover tahini in your refrigerator, because it can become rancid. If your tahini has a bitter taste, it's probably best to buy a new jar.

Pan Drippings Gravy

Stop! The pan isn't dirty — it's just ready to be deglazed. *Deglazing* is when you add in liquid and scrape up the delicious browned bits on the pan. You can deglaze a pan with wine, broth, milk, or water, each of which will give you a different flavor profile. For this simple gravy, I stick with broth. This is easy when you do a quick pan-fry or sear of meat or poultry. Add in a little flour and butter to melt and thicken, and then whisk in the liquid to create a sauce. If your meat is marinated, it can create a salty sauce, so this is best with meats that have been simply seasoned.

To make it, follow these steps:

1. **In the skillet in which you just cooked the meat, scrape up the bits of browned meat.**

2. **Add in 2 tablespoons unsalted butter and 3 tablespoons all-purpose flour, and heat over medium heat.**

3. **Whisk gently to mix the browned bits and flour. Let the mixture cook and slightly brown.**

4. **Whisk in 1 cup chicken, turkey, or beef broth (use the broth that matches whichever meat you cooked).**

5. **Continue cooking the thickened sauce, and season with salt and pepper to taste.**

6. **Add in fresh herbs, as desired, for both taste and color. Thyme, sage, parsley, and rosemary pair well with gravy.**

Serve with grilled, roasted, or pan-seared meats and poultry, or over mashed potatoes, noodles, or oven-roasted vegetables.

Zesty Horseradish

Horseradish has a kick and pairs perfectly with roasted beef, lamb, or potatoes. You can make this sauce spicier or less spicy. This sauce is quite popular throughout Eastern Europe.

To make it, stir together ½ cup plain yogurt or sour cream, 1 to 2 tablespoons jarred horseradish, 2 teaspoons Dijon mustard, 2 teaspoons white wine vinegar, and salt and pepper to taste.

Serve with grilled, roasted, or pan-seared steak or roast; drizzled over steamed or roasted vegetables; stirred into mashed potatoes or with roasted potatoes; or as a dollop on your favorite stew!

TIP

Jarred horseradish actually doesn't go bad (unless, of course, it's contaminated), but it can lose its intensity and slowly become less spicy over time.

Asian-Inspired Peanut Sauce

Creamy peanut butter is not just for sandwiches. In this dip, creamy peanut butter is stirred together with ginger, soy sauce, and lime for a zesty combo that's quite popular in Thai cuisine. This sauce may quickly turn into your new favorite dip for carrots and celery!

To make it, follow these steps:

1. **Combine ½ cup peanut butter; 1 tablespoon low-sodium soy sauce; ½ teaspoon ginger powder or 1 teaspoon fresh chopped ginger; and 1 tablespoon lime juice, lemon juice, or white wine vinegar. Stir.**

   If you have a food processor, you can use that instead.

2. **Add in ¼ to ½ cup water, depending on your desired thinness, and stir or process until smooth.**

3. **If you'd like your peanut sauce to have a kick, stir in Sriracha.**

Serve with grilled, roasted, or pan-seared chicken; steamed or roasted vegetables; rice noodles; or raw vegetables; or use as a salad dressing.

Chimichurri

Chimichurri is a traditional Argentinian sauce that combines parsley with red wine vinegar and olive oil. You can make this spicier with cracked red pepper and fresh garlic. If you prefer this sauce to be creamier, put it in a blender.

To make it, follow these steps:

1. Mix together ½ cup finely chopped parsley, ½ cup extra-virgin olive oil, and 1 to 4 finely minced garlic cloves.

2. Season with salt, pepper, and red pepper flakes, to taste.

Serve with grilled meats, poultry, or vegetables; roasted or pan-seared proteins; or blanched vegetables.

Buttery Wine Sauce

Butter and wine are divine together! This sauce is thinner, not thickened by a starch (making it great for those who can't tolerate gluten). This sauce helps elevate steamed veggies, mild whitefish, or shrimp. The sauce also tastes great with pasta!

To make it, follow these steps:

1. In a small skillet or saucepan, heat ¼ cup unsalted butter over medium heat.

2. Add in 2 tablespoons finely chopped onion and sauté for 2 minutes.

3. Add 1 minced garlic clove and 1 teaspoon fresh or dried thyme.

4. Whisk in ¼ cup white wine (Sauvignon Blanc, Chardonnay, or Pinot Gris all work well).

5. Simmer for 2 minutes.

6. Whisk in a splash (about 2 teaspoons) of white wine vinegar or lemon juice, and season with salt and pepper.

Serve with grilled or steamed veggies, mild whitefish, shrimp, or pasta.

Pico de Gallo

Head south of the border with this fresh and chunky-style salsa — *salsa* means sauce! Pico is a combination of sun-ripened tomatoes, onion, cilantro, and jalapeño with a splash of lime. It's simple, but it can take that boring piece of chicken to the next level. If it's not summertime, opt for Roma tomatoes or even canned diced tomatoes!

To make it, follow these steps:

1. **Finely chop ½ of a small onion and add to a medium mixing bowl.**

2. **Chop 2 medium tomatoes and add to the bowl.**

3. **Finely chop ½ of a jalapeño and add to the bowl.**

   If you like it spicy, keep the seeds; if not, take the seeds out.

4. **Finely chop 4 to 8 sprigs of cilantro and add to the bowl.**

5. **Stir to combine.**

6. **Squeeze ½ of a lime (or more based on your liking) over the veggies and season with salt and pepper.**

Serve with grilled meats, firm whitefish, chicken, vegetables, or oven-roasted or pan-fried poultry or steak. It's also great on baked potatoes!

Chapter **21**

Ten Meal-Kit Recipes

Meal-kit services have become wildly popular and are only estimated to grow exponentially in the coming years. But, at $8 to $10 per person per meal, they can quickly drain your food budget. Meal kits are delivered with the notion that they're pre-portioned, requiring very simple prep work to complete the meal in 15 to 45 minutes. As a dietitian and busy working mom, I absolutely understand the appeal. But you can also make these same meal kits with easy-to-find seasonal ingredients (as opposed to the same shelf-stable veggies and fruits they use), and for much less money. Stock your pantry, skip the delivery, and make these meal kits instead!

These kits pull from the recipes in this book. There are three main chapters to consider when making meal kits: Chapter 8, Chapter 14, and Chapter 16. Why? Because these chapters have simple packing elements to help you cut, chop, and prepack meals for the week.

REMEMBER When prepping in advance, store all prepped items in the refrigerator. Spices and seasonings or canned goods can be stored at room temperature, but they can also be stored with the other prepped items. This makes it easy to grab and get cooking the day you plan to have the meal!

TIP If you have narrow storage containers, place each meal prep into the storage container and store in the refrigerator to easily pull, cook, and serve on the day you choose. Or grab a paper bag and place all the ingredients in the bag, label, and refrigerate. Keeping your items all together is key to making the meal kit a success.

Fiesta Taco Salad

I make this recipe on every camping trip because it's simple to prep and easy to serve in just minutes!

TIP

Look for the recipe in Chapter 8, and keep these tips in mind:

>> Either precook the meat with seasonings or just prep the seasonings in advance and cook the meat the day you serve.

>> Prechop the lettuce, cabbage, onions, and cheese, and pack them in individual containers.

>> Prerinse the beans, and store them in a separate container.

>> Wait to chop the tomatoes and avocado until the day you make the meal.

>> Whisk the dressing and store in a small container.

When you're ready to make the meal, follow these steps:

1. **Cook the meat with the seasoning packet.**
2. **Chop the tomatoes and avocado.**
3. **Assemble the salad, and serve.**

Thai Steak Salad

Bright, bold colors make this salad, which is packed with nutrient-dense ingredients. The peanut butter sauce is easy to make, but you can also buy premade peanut dressing if you're really short on time.

TIP

Look for the recipe in Chapter 8, and keep these tips in mind:

>> Make the peanut sauce and store in a small container.

>> Preshred the lettuce, cabbage, and carrot. (If you have a food processor or handheld mandoline, you can do this in minutes.) Store in individual containers.

>> Thinly slice the onion and place in a small container.

>> Prechop the peanuts and store in a small container, either at room temperature or in the fridge.

>> Save the steak to cook the day you serve.

When you're ready to make the meal, follow these steps:

1. **Cook the meat with the seasonings.**

2. **Assemble the salad, and serve.**

Mediterranean Quinoa Bowls

Bowls are popular in meal-prep kits for a reason: They're simple elements that can be pulled together in minimal time. You can substitute rice, couscous, or farro for quinoa in this recipe. *Remember:* A well-stocked pantry is your friend! If you want more substantial protein, add in a rotisserie chicken or from-the-freezer fish sticks!

TIP

Look for the recipe in Chapter 8, and keep these tips in mind:

>> Precook the quinoa.

>> Prechop the olives.

>> Save the tomato, cucumber, and herbs for the day you serve. (Tomatoes and cucumbers do best when cut and served immediately.)

>> Put all the items together in the refrigerator, making it easy to pull out and prepare in less than 5 minutes!

When you're ready to make the meal, follow these steps:

1. **Reheat the quinoa in the microwave for 1 minute.**

2. **Cut the tomatoes, cucumbers, and herbs.**

3. **Assemble the bowls, and serve.**

Sausage and Bell Peppers

Sausage holds up well in the refrigerator, as do potatoes, bell peppers, and onions. This recipe is another favorite camping meal because of the storage stability. Instead of roasting, everything goes into a skillet.

TIP

Look for the recipe in Chapter 14, and keep these tips in mind:

>> Save the potatoes for the day you serve to microwave and add to the pre-sliced items.

>> Preslice the sausage, bell peppers, and onions, and store in individual containers.

>> Premix the paprika, garlic powder, salt, and pepper, and store in a small container.

When you're ready to make the meal, follow these steps:

1. **Heat the potatoes in the microwave.**

2. **Toss together the potatoes and chopped items with the seasoning mix, spread onto a baking sheet, drizzle with olive oil.**

3. **Bake and serve.**

TIP

Save glass honey and jelly jars for seasoning mixes! These small jars save space and are easy to clean.

Moroccan Mini Meat Loaves with Cauliflower

If you were to ask me what my "signature dish" is, I might say this one! It's frequently on request from both my family and friends. Cauliflower is a perfect fall, winter, or spring vegetable that can hang out in the fridge for a couple weeks.

TIP

Look for the recipe in Chapter 14, and keep these tips in mind:

>> Mix together the meat seasonings of panko, curry powder, and sea salt, and store in a small container.

>> Prechop the cauliflower and store in a separate container.

>> Mix together the spices for the cauliflower, curry, sea salt, black pepper, and turmeric. Store in a small container.

>> Premeasure the red wine vinegar and olive oil, and store in a small container.

>> Store all the remaining items (eggs and chutney) with the mixes in the refrigerator.

When you're ready to make the meal, follow these steps:

1. **Mix together the ground meat, eggs, and meat seasoning mix and form the meat loaves.**

2. **Season the cauliflower with the seasoning mix and red wine vinegar and olive oil.**

3. **Place the items on a sheet pan and top the meat loaves with tomato chutney or jam.**

4. **Bake and serve.**

WARNING

Ground meat is best mixed the day you cook it, because it can spoil quicker.

Skewer-Free Chicken Kabobs

Skewering all these items on kabob sticks is what takes so much time, so skipping the skewering saves time, but doesn't sacrifice flavor.

TIP

Look for the recipe in Chapter 14, and keep these tips in mind:

>> Precook the potatoes in the microwave. Then place the potatoes and the chopped vegetables (bell peppers, mushrooms, and onions) into a large container and pour over half a bottle of Italian dressing. Stir to mix and refrigerate.

>> Precube the chicken and store in a container with the remaining Italian dressing.

When you're ready to make the meal, follow these steps:

1. **Drain off the marinade for both the vegetables and the chicken.**

2. **Place all the items onto a baking sheet and bake.**

3. **Serve with crusty French bread or cook rice for 4 minutes in an Instant Pot (1 cup rice to 1¼ cups water).**

Marinated chicken is best cooked within 48 hours, so plan this meal for earlier in the week.

Sheet-Pan Mediterranean Pasta

This pasta dish is so fast to pull together and bake, it'll easily become a favorite! If you crave more protein, add in rotisserie chicken, frozen chicken nuggets (yes, they have their place on the table, too!), or sliced sausage. If goat cheese or feta are too strong for your household, opt for cream cheese.

Look for the recipe in Chapter 14. Place all the ingredients (except the pasta) into a baking dish. Cover the baking dish with plastic wrap and refrigerate until you're ready to bake.

When you're ready to make the meal, follow these steps:

1. **Place the baking dish in the oven.**

2. **Cook the pasta according to package directions (the pasta water will heat and the pasta will cook before the sauce is done).**

3. **Drain the pasta.**

4. **Pull the baking dish out of the oven and give the sauce a hearty stir to mix all the ingredients together.**

5. **Toss in the pasta and serve.**

If goat cheese or feta are too strong for your household, use cream cheese instead.

Zesty Bean and Cheese Tostadas

Tostadas, also called chalupas, are a great way to use up leftover meat or create a meal that can pull together in 15 minutes. If you're craving more protein than beans, add in rotisserie chicken or leftover, sliced steak.

Look for the recipe in Chapter 16, and keep these tips in mind:

>> Drain and rinse the beans and place in a container.

>> Preshred the lettuce and cheese and place in separate containers.

>> Place the salsa and tortilla shells together and store with the meal-prep items in the refrigerator.

When you're ready to make the meal, follow these steps:

1. **Place the fried shells onto a baking sheet.**
2. **Top with beans and cheese and bake.**
3. **Top with lettuce and salsa to serve.**

Loaded Baked Potatoes

Break out the baked potato bar! You can choose to assemble the potatoes or serve as a "fix your own" potato bar. Either way, it just takes a little prep work, and this meal can be ready in minutes.

TIP

Look for the recipe in Chapter 16, and keep these tips in mind:

>> Prep the potatoes the day you serve.

>> Cook the bacon in the microwave and place in a small container.

>> Finely chop the broccoli and place in a small storage container.

>> Preshred the cheese and place in a container.

>> Premeasure the sour cream and place in a container.

>> Place the green onions in a bin with the other ingredients (and any other topping you'd like — see a more extensive list in the recipe).

When you're ready to make the meal, follow these steps:

1. **Cook the potatoes in the microwave.**
2. **Reheat the bacon in the microwave for 30 to 45 seconds.**
3. **Set up the ingredients for a self-service potato bar or fix the potatoes and serve.**

Pan-Fried Burgers with Creamy Feta Green Salad

Burgers are popular options in meal-prep kits. Readying your salad greens, dressing, and seasonings can help pull this recipe together in under ten minutes!

TIP

Look for the recipe in Chapter 16, and keep these tips in mind:

>> Wait to season and cook the patties until the day you serve.

>> Premake the feta dressing and place in a small container.

>> Save the tomatoes to chop the day you serve.

>> Prechop the olives, and place in a small container.

>> Place all the ingredients in a container together in the refrigerator.

When you're ready to make the meal, follow these steps:

1. **Season the meat with salt and pepper and make the burger patties.**

2. **Pan-fry the burgers.**

3. **Chop the tomatoes.**

4. **Prepare the salad and serve with feta dressing.**

Chapter **22**

Ten Ways to Build a Bento Lunch Box

Bento boxes are a popular Japanese-style meal box, with everything neatly placed in small compartments, creating an aesthetically pleasing appearance and flavor palette. This concept has become wildly popular for lunches, whether in the form of premade kits from popular coffee shops or as school lunches for kids. But you can make them for all ages! The concept behind these clever lunch boxes is that they're convenient, packable foods, with a nutrient-dense focus, and they don't need to be reheated. The amounts are up to you! You can choose to make one of each for the week or keep it simple by packing multiple days of the same meal.

There are numerous styles of bento boxes to choose from. For little ones, the Bentgo lunch boxes (https://bentgo.com) are a great size and material. For older children, LunchBots (www.lunchbots.com) makes a great stainless-steel product. For adults, I prefer two- or three-compartment glassware with a fitted lid. Whatever you use, make sure it's leakproof, able to stay cold for hot climates, and nonbreakable for children heading off to school.

REMEMBER

Kids can eat more variety than we think. Ditch the store-bought meat, cheese, and crackers and have them help you make their own boxes. Make them fun, and don't forget to add in something sweet, like chocolate chips, marshmallows, or gummy bears every once in a while.

TIP

Serve a mixture of packaged, canned, and fresh items in each box.

Mediterranean

The Mediterranean diet is full of legumes (beans), seafood, nuts, seeds, whole grains, fruits, and vegetables.

Add the following to your bento box:

>> Walnuts, almonds, or pistachios

>> Pitted dates

>> Olives

>> Hummus

>> Cucumbers, carrot sticks, celery, or broccoli

>> Grapes

TIP

Choose a variety of nuts, because they have different health benefits. Eating a handful or two of nuts daily can yield healthy rewards!

Lentils and Grapes

Lentils are packed with fiber and nutrition, and they cook up in 20 minutes from dried beans! Mix together lentils, grated carrots, parsley, green onions, and a red wine vinaigrette for a quick salad.

Add the following to your bento box:

>> Lentil salad

>> Kiwi

>> Melon balls

>> French bread slices or crackers

Pasta Salad

Keep this pasta salad simple by using a store-bought vinaigrette for the dressing! Mix together cooked pasta (whatever shape you prefer) with tomato halves, broccoli, olives, and cheese cubes.

Add the following to your bento box:

>> Pasta salad

>> Watermelon

>> Pineapple

>> Salami sticks

Southwestern

Bean dips can be homemade or store-bought. Veggies, chips, and crackers taste great with bean dip.

Add the following to your bento box:

>> Bean dip

>> Chips

>> Baby corn

>> Sliced cheese

>> Sliced bell peppers

>> Grapes or berries

TIP

Save glass honey and jelly jars for storing dips, like hummus, ranch dressing, or bean dip! They fit perfectly in most bento boxes.

Almonds and Cheese

Almonds pair beautifully with a variety of cheeses, including smoked Gouda, fresh mozzarella, or sliced Monterey Jack.

Add the following to your bento box:

>> Roasted almonds

>> Cheese slices

>> Whole-grain crackers

>> Cherries or berries

>> Sugar snap peas or edamame

Tuna Salad

Canned tuna can go a long way toward creating a delicious meal! Mix with grated carrots, sliced celery, boiled eggs, mayonnaise or Greek yogurt, salt, and pepper to create a quick, nourishing tuna salad.

Add the following to your bento box:

>> Tuna salad

>> Boiled eggs

>> Crackers

>> Grapes

>> Broccoli, cauliflower, or cucumbers

Smoked Salmon

This box takes me back to Denmark or Norway, with popular Scandinavian elements. Create an open-faced sandwich with the smoked salmon and crackers.

Add the following to your bento box:

>> Smoked salmon

>> Bagel chips or rye crackers

>> Olives

>> Tomatoes, cucumber, and red onion

>> Grapefruit or mandarin oranges

>> Pumpkin seeds

Apples and Peanut Butter

Soaking apples or pears in salted lemon water can help preserve their freshness.

Add the following to your bento box:

>> Apple slices

>> Peanut butter

>> Raisins or dried cranberries

>> Yogurt or yogurt sticks

>> Granola

Quesadillas

Yes, even cold quesadillas are delicious! If this doesn't sound appealing, try a pinwheel sandwich instead, with cream cheese, ham, and tortilla rolled up and sliced into pinwheel sandwiches.

Add the following to your bento box:

>> Ham and cheese quesadilla, cut into quarters

>> Salsa

>> Baby corn

>> Grape tomatoes, cucumbers, or carrots

>> Black beans or bean dip

>> Diced mango

Curried Chicken Salad

Curried chicken salad is always a popular menu item for upscale lunch spots, but you can create the same delicious flavors at home. Mix together grilled, baked, or roasted chopped-up chicken with mayonnaise, curry powder, sliced almonds, raisins or currants, and sliced celery.

Add the following to your bento box:

>> Curried chicken salad, as a sandwich or with crackers

>> Canned mandarin oranges

>> Sea salt and vinegar chips

>> Carrot sticks, celery, radishes, or cherry tomatoes

>> Pumpkin seeds or sunflower seeds

>> Grapes

Chapter **23**

Ten Meal-Prep Shortcuts

We all choose to meal-prep for a reason, whether it's to get back time, eat more fruits and vegetables, simplify our daily schedules, or something else. You have your reasons for prepping your meals ahead of time. If meal prep continues to overwhelm you, make some concessions — meal prep is supposed to make your life *easier*, not more stressful.

In this chapter, I offer a list of my top ten shortcuts to get you on track with meal prep.

Stock Your Kitchen with Meal-Prep Tools

Open your fridge, and scope out your space. Measure your pantry. Find an organization pattern that suits your family. Then shop for the right tools to help you organize and find success in meal prep.

Some folks have more kitchen space and can have a food processor; others may stick with a box grater, and others may opt for preshredded items so they don't need to store a box grater or food processor. Do what works for you!

TIP

Stock up on the following meal-prep tools to make your life easier:

>> Handheld mandoline for fast slicing

>> Mason jars or upcycled glass jars

>> Square glass storage containers for easy, see-through stacking in a refrigerator (if you know what's in it, you know what to grab!)

>> Round glass storage containers for items like sauces, soups, or yogurts

>> Silicone freezing containers for single portions of soups or sauces

TIP

Glass is easy to clean and see through, but if stainless or plastic are easier for travel, look for items that are BPA free. (BPA stands for bisphenol A; it's a chemical used to make some plastics since the '60s, and it's not good for your health.)

Shop for Prepared Foods

In the grocery store, head for the vegetable and deli sections. You can find wonderful prewashed and prechopped vegetables for soups, grilling, or snacking. The deli aisle offers premade salads you can enjoy all week!

TIP

Look for the following prepared items to make your life easier:

>> Spiralized vegetables.

>> Washed and chopped vegetables for roasting (butternut squash, Brussels sprouts, or zucchini).

>> Prechopped *mirepoix* (onion, celery, and carrots — the base for most soups, stocks, and sauces). You can find this in the freezer section, too!

>> Premade grain salads, macaroni salads, potato salads, and veggie salads.

Get Tech Savvy

Technology can be especially useful if you're living a busy life (and who isn't these days?). Have Alexa or Siri help you start a shopping list, set a timer, or tell you a recipe! Use shopping and grocery delivery apps, like Instacart, Amazon Prime, or Shipt — see if your local market has one, too!

TIP

Look for these helpful tech tools:

>> Virtual assistants, like Amazon Alexa, Amazon Echo, or Google Home

>> Grocery delivery apps, like Instacart or Amazon Prime

>> Meal-planning apps, like BigOven, Mealime, MealPrepPro, or Paprika

>> Recipe apps, like Recipe Keeper, Tasty, or Yummly

Break Out the Multicooker

The face of meal prep has evolved with the advancement of traditional slow cookers and pressure cookers. Step into the 21st century with tools that can help you pressure-cook, slow-cook, air-fry, and more!

TIP

Look for these top rated multicookers:

>> Cuisinart 3-in-1 Cook Central

>> Breville Fast Slow Pro Pressure Cooker

>> Instant Pot

>> Magic Chef

>> Ninja Foodi

TIP

Find the tool right for your kitchen. Pay attention to things like how much space you'll need to store and use the multicoooker, the size you need for a small or big family, and the amount of recipes you'd like to make with the tool.

Pick Up Premade Meats

You can find a variety of precooked meats at most supermarkets. From a rotisserie chicken to pulled pork or smoked brisket, all these premade meats are great additions for quick meal prep. You can also scope out the freezer section and discover frozen meats that are quick prep, too.

TIP

Look for these items:

>> Rotisserie chicken

>> Deli meats

>> Frozen fish sticks

>> Breaded or grilled chicken tenders

Grab a Salad in a Bag

Salad mixes are popular and constantly expanding. Salads-in-a-bag are convenient *and* delicious! In this book, I tell you how to make your own, but I also understand how easy these are to pick up and toss together! They're a convenient way to get in more greens, and that's always a win!

TIP

You can use salads-in-a-bag in the following ways:

>> As a side salad or main dish

>> Topped on sandwiches

>> Inside tacos

>> Wrapped up in a pita

>> In a grain bowl

Shop for Store-Made Items

If a store-made product saves you time and energy and keeps your stress in check, it's the right choice, period. Not everything can be homemade when we lead busy lives. You can still choose great, wholesome products from the market. Salad dressings, marinades, sauces, and soups are all great places to look for delicious store-made items. Head over to the deli counter and see which salads and cooked meats your market has on hand, too!

TIP

Look for these items:

>> Salad dressings

>> Meat or poultry marinades

>> Marinara sauce

>> Bean dips, like hummus

>> Sauces (pesto, peanut, or tzatziki)

>> Soups (lentil, tomato, or chicken noodle)

Cook Grains in Bulk

Whole grains and beans are packed with nutrition and taste great. One way to save time and money in meal prep is to make these items in large batches. Then portion them out and freeze them for months to come!

TIP

Here are my favorite grains and legumes for bulk cooking:

>> Beans (black, pinto, kidney, and garbanzo)

>> Farro

>> Quinoa

>> Rice

Prewash and Prep Fruits and Veggies

As soon as you get home from the market, stop and take the time to wash and chop your fruits and vegetables for the week. Break out the food processor or box grater to quickly grate and chop some of your most used vegetables. Wash and have fruits ready to snack on for the week.

TIP

Look for these items:

>> Carrots (grate, dice, cut, and store in water)

>> Celery (cut, dice, and store in water)

>> Onions (chop and store in an airtight container)

>> Berries (store cleaned in a glass jar with a paper towel)

>> Lettuce (wash, dry, and store in a resealable plastic bag with a towel)

>> Herbs (store in a glass of water with a resealable plastic bag over the top)

>> Potatoes (cube and store in water)

>> Grapes (wash and remove stems)

>> Apples and pears (stored sliced in salted lemon water)

Start Simply

Whether you want to prep breakfasts, lunches, or snacks, tackle one at a time and stick with it. Give yourself a couple weeks of being consistent before adding in another element of meal prep.

TIP

Start here:

>> **Breakfast:** Prep overnight oats, yogurt parfaits, or muffins for the week.

>> **Lunch:** Prep salads in a jar and bento lunches for the week.

>> **Dinner:** Prep the ingredients for a salad bar, potato bar, or a pizza bar and have them ready to make for the week.

>> **Snacks:** Make snacks for the week or create a snack tray that's easy to grab from the fridge.

7 Appendixes

Appendix A

Metric Conversion Guide

Note: The recipes in this book weren't developed or tested using metric measurements. There may be some variation in quality when converting to metric units.

Common Abbreviations

Abbreviation(s)	What It Stands For
cm	Centimeter
C., c.	Cup
G, g	Gram
kg	Kilogram
L, l	Liter
lb.	Pound
mL, ml	Milliliter
oz.	Ounce
pt.	Pint
t., tsp.	Teaspoon
T., Tb., Tbsp.	Tablespoon

Volume

U.S. Units	Canadian Metric	Australian Metric
¼ teaspoon	1 milliliter	1 milliliter
½ teaspoon	2 milliliters	2 milliliters
1 teaspoon	5 milliliters	5 milliliters
1 tablespoon	15 milliliters	20 milliliters
¼ cup	50 milliliters	60 milliliters
⅓ cup	75 milliliters	80 milliliters
½ cup	125 milliliters	125 milliliters
⅔ cup	150 milliliters	170 milliliters
¾ cup	175 milliliters	190 milliliters
1 cup	250 milliliters	250 milliliters
1 quart	1 liter	1 liter
1½ quarts	1.5 liters	1.5 liters
2 quarts	2 liters	2 liters
2½ quarts	2.5 liters	2.5 liters
3 quarts	3 liters	3 liters
4 quarts (1 gallon)	4 liters	4 liters

Weight

U.S. Units	Canadian Metric	Australian Metric
1 ounce	30 grams	30 grams
2 ounces	55 grams	60 grams
3 ounces	85 grams	90 grams
4 ounces (¼ pound)	115 grams	125 grams
8 ounces (½ pound)	225 grams	225 grams
16 ounces (1 pound)	455 grams	500 grams (½ kilogram)

Length

Inches	Centimeters
0.5	1.5
1	2.5
2	5.0
3	7.5
4	10.0
5	12.5
6	15.0
7	17.5
8	20.5
9	23.0
10	25.5
11	28.0
12	30.5

Temperature (Degrees)

Fahrenheit	Celsius
32	0
212	100
250	120
275	140
300	150
325	160
350	180
375	190

Fahrenheit	Celsius
400	200
425	220
450	230
475	240
500	260

Appendix B
Sample Grocery List

Before you head out to the grocery store, make a grocery list. Check your pantry, refrigerator, and freezer to make sure you don't have an item before buying more. The following list is a sample of items frequently used in this book for meal prep:

» Fresh produce

- ❏ Apples
- ❏ Avocados
- ❏ Bananas
- ❏ Basil
- ❏ Bell peppers
- ❏ Blackberries
- ❏ Blueberries
- ❏ Broccoli
- ❏ Cabbage
- ❏ Carrots
- ❏ Garlic
- ❏ Dill
- ❏ Grapes
- ❏ Kale
- ❏ Lemons
- ❏ Lettuce

- ❑ Limes
- ❑ Onions
- ❑ Oranges
- ❑ Parsley
- ❑ Raspberries
- ❑ Spinach
- ❑ Strawberries
- ❑ Tomatoes

›› Frozen produce

- ❑ Frozen blueberries
- ❑ Frozen broccoli
- ❑ Frozen butternut squash
- ❑ Frozen cherries
- ❑ Frozen mirepoix (onion, celery, and carrots)
- ❑ Frozen peas
- ❑ Frozen spinach
- ❑ Frozen strawberries

›› Protein

- ❑ Beef (ground, steaks)
- ❑ Chicken (breast, thighs, whole)
- ❑ Eggs
- ❑ Pork (chops, loins, or roasts)
- ❑ Seafood (canned, shrimp, fish)
- ❑ Tofu (extra firm)

›› Dairy

- ❑ Butter
- ❑ Cheese
- ❑ Milk
- ❑ Sour cream
- ❑ Yogurt

>> Pantry staples

- ❑ Baking powder
- ❑ Baking soda
- ❑ Canned artichoke hearts
- ❑ Canned black beans
- ❑ Canned corn
- ❑ Canned garbanzo beans
- ❑ Canned green beans
- ❑ Canned kidney beans
- ❑ Canned pinto beans
- ❑ Canned tomatoes
- ❑ Canned white beans
- ❑ Dried herbs
- ❑ Flour
- ❑ Olives
- ❑ Pickles
- ❑ Roasted red bell peppers
- ❑ Spices
- ❑ Sugar
- ❑ Sundried tomatoes

>> Grains

- ❑ Bread
- ❑ Couscous
- ❑ Farro
- ❑ Flatbreads
- ❑ Oatmeal
- ❑ Pasta
- ❑ Quinoa
- ❑ Rice
- ❑ Tortillas

>> Fats, oils, and condiments

- ❏ Almond butter
- ❏ Almonds
- ❏ Avocado oil
- ❏ Barbecue sauce
- ❏ Cashews
- ❏ Chia seeds
- ❏ Coconut oil
- ❏ Flaxseeds
- ❏ Hemp seeds
- ❏ Honey
- ❏ Mayonnaise
- ❏ Mustard
- ❏ Olive oil (extra-virgin)
- ❏ Peanut butter
- ❏ Peanuts
- ❏ Pine nuts
- ❏ Pistachios
- ❏ Pumpkin seeds
- ❏ Soy sauce or tamari (low-sodium)
- ❏ Sunflower seeds
- ❏ Walnuts

Appendix C
Food Safety Guide

Keeping food safe is an important part of meal prep. Food safety includes everything from food storage to cooking temperatures and understanding ways to stop cross-contamination. Use this appendix as a guide to help you and your family keep foods safe.

Food Storage

During meal prep, you need to consider the shelf stability of foods. Whether they're stored in your pantry, refrigerator, or freezer, all foods have a shelf life. Tables C-1, C-2, and C-3 let you know how long meats, dairy, and produce will keep in the refrigerator and freezer.

TABLE C-1   ### How Long You Can Store Meats

Item	Refrigerator	Freezer
Beef, steak	3–5 days	4–6 months
Beef, ground or stew meat	1–2 days	3–4 months
Deli meats	3–5 days	1–2 months
Fish, cooked	3–4 days	4–6 months
Fish, raw	1–2 days	2–3 months
Ham, fully cooked	3–5 days	2–3 months
Lamb	3–5 days	4–6 months
Leftover cooked meat	3–4 days	2–3 months
Pork chops	3–5 days	1–2 months
Poultry, raw	1–2 days	9–12 months
Sausage, cooked	7 days	1–2 months
Sausage, raw	1–2 days	3–4 months
Shrimp, raw	1–2 days	3–6 months
Veal	3–5 days	4–6 months

TABLE C-2

How Long You Can Store Dairy

Food Item	Refrigerator	Freezer
Butter	1–2 months	6–9 months
Cheese, hard	6–12 weeks	6–12 months
Cheese, soft	1–2 weeks	6 months
Ice cream	N/A	2–4 months
Milk	1 week	3 months
Sour cream	1–2 weeks	N/A
Yogurt	1–2 weeks	1–2 months

TABLE C-3

How Long You Can Store Produce

Food Item	Refrigerator	Freezer
Apples	4–6 weeks	8 months
Asparagus	1 week	5 months
Avocados, cut	3–4 days	6 months
Bananas	3 days	2–3 months
Beans (legumes), cooked	3–4 days	6 months
Berries	1 week	8–12 months
Broccoli	1–2 weeks	10–12 months
Cabbage	1–3 weeks	10–12 months
Carrots	3–4 weeks	10–12 months
Cauliflower	1 week	10–12 months
Celery	2–3 weeks	10–12 months
Citrus fruits	2–3 weeks	4–6 months
Cucumbers	4–6 days	N/A
Green beans	3–4 days	10–12 months
Greens, bagged or boxed	3–5 days	N/A
Melon, cut	2–4 days	N/A
Onions	2 months	10–12 months
Spinach	1 week	10–12 months

Cooking Temperatures

Have a food thermometer on hand to test the inner temperature of the foods you're preparing. Table C-4 is a guide to safe food temperatures for a variety of foods.

TABLE C-4

Cooking Temperatures

Food	Temperature (°F)
Casseroles or leftovers	165
Eggs	145
Pork	145
Poultry	165
Red meat (ground)	160
Red meat (whole)	145
Seafood	145

Storage Temperatures

Dangerous bacteria and toxins can flourish even in cool temperatures. Pay attention to the *danger zone* (40 to 140 degrees), which is the temperature range at which most bacteria thrives. Store foods in the refrigerator at 39 degrees or below and in the freezer below 10 degrees to preserve foods.

Thawing frozen items on the counter isn't safe — different parts of the food will enter the danger zone at different times. Here are the safest ways to defrost food:

>> **In the refrigerator overnight:** This method takes some extra planning, but it's safe and easy.

>> **In water:** Place the food in a leakproof bag and submerge in cold water for 30 minutes. Change the water every 30 minutes until the food is thawed.

>> **In the microwave:** This method requires foods to be cooked immediately. Don't store foods that have been defrosted in the microwave.

Here are a couple additional tips to keeping foods safe:

>> Don't let food sit outside of the refrigerator for more than two hours.

>> To store leftovers, place the food in shallow containers and refrigerate. Remember to store leftovers below 40 degrees within two hours; otherwise, the food may have bacterial growth.

>> To reheat leftovers, make sure foods reach an internal temperature of 165 degrees.

How to Avoid Cross-Contamination

Cross-contamination is another way in which food can be exposed to bacteria and make you sick. If you cut meat and then use that same knife or cutting board to cut anything else, or you forget to wash your hands after cutting meat, you can cross-contaminate anything you cut or touch. Here are key food safety practices to consider when preparing foods:

>> **Wash everything.** Wash your hands before, during, and after food prep. Wash your produce before cutting into it. (Cutting a cantaloupe without washing it first can contaminate the inside of fruit with the bacteria on the outside of the melon.) Wash surfaces, cookware, cutting boards, and utensils used during meal prep.

>> **Store raw meats on a plate or in a bowl or on the lowest possible shelf without anything beneath the meat.** As the meat defrosts, the juices from the meat can contaminate other items in your refrigerator if they drip.

>> **Use separate cutting boards.** Keep your foods safe by having designated cutting boards for different foods. For example, you might use a red cutting board for meat, white for poultry, green for vegetables, blue for fish, and yellow for breads.

>> **Don't wash chicken.** Yes, your grandmother may still do this, but studies have found that washing raw poultry in the sink contaminates more items from the sink to the counter where water splashes. Skip the sink and cook the meat to the proper temperature instead.

Index

C

About the Author

Wendy Jo Peterson, MS RDN, is an award-winning author, speaker, culinary nutritionist, proud military wife, and mom. Whether at work or at the table, Wendy Jo believes in savoring life. Check out her other *For Dummies* titles (all published by Wiley): *Bread Making For Dummies, Mediterranean Diet Cookbook For Dummies, Air Fryer Cookbook For Dummies*, and *Instant Pot Cookbook For Dummies.* When she's not in her kitchen, you can find Wendy Jo strolling a SoCal beach with her Labradors and daughter or exploring the great outdoors in #OlafTheCampervan. You can catch her on social media at @just_wendyjo or check out her website, www.justwendyjo.com.

Dedication

To my mom, Nancy Rice, who managed to work full-time, raise a family, and cook 90 percent of our meals from scratch; she taught me how to shop, chop, and meal-plan before I ever left home. To my dad, Robert Rice, because he is a great cook without a recipe, and there's much to be learned from watching this gift, as well. To my family unit, Brandon and Anya, for allowing me time to test recipes and write in peace and for always being willing to try new foods! Thank you all! I love you.

Author's Acknowledgments

Although I wrote this book alone, my village of friends, family, and colleagues helped along the way. Thanks to Jane Gray Bledsoe for letting me bounce ideas off of you and lending me your expertise; Jasmine Hormati for helping me with the finite details and helping me jump-start the project; Heather Wosoogh for being a friend who shares my love of cooking and always opens her door for playdates so I can keep writing; Robyn Statham, Meghann Scott, Courtney Covert, Rena Armstrong, and Courtney Hansen for testing recipes along the way and giving me feedback; Geri Goodale for helping me capture the right images for this book and for her ever-positive energy along the way. It takes a village, especially during a pandemic!

No book is ever achieved without a great team, and I'm blessed to have worked with this team on many books. To my agent, Matt Wagner, for continually advocating for me, as the writer. I'm forever grateful for Tracy Boggier, Senior Acquisitions Editor at Wiley, who believes in me and my recipes. To my project and copy editor, Elizabeth Kuball, for keeping me on track with deadlines and helping me better express my creative ideas. To Rachel Nix, my recipe tester and nutrition analyst for making sure each recipe surpasses the taste test and is easy to navigate. I thoroughly enjoy the creative process working with each of you. Thank you for your collaboration!

Publisher's Acknowledgments

Senior Acquisitions Editor: Tracy Boggier

Project Editor: Elizabeth Kuball

Copy Editor: Elizabeth Kuball

Recipe Tester: Rachel Nix, RDN

Nutrition Analyst: Rachel Nix, RDN

Production Editor: Mohammed Zafar Ali

Photographers: Wendy Jo Peterson and Geri Goodale

Cover Image: © Wendy Jo Peterson and Geri Goodale

Take dummies with you everywhere you go!

Whether you are excited about e-books, want more from the web, must have your mobile apps, or are swept up in social media, dummies makes everything easier.

Find us online!

dummies.com

dummies
A Wiley Brand

PERSONAL ENRICHMENT

Staying Sharp
9781119187790
USA $26.00
CAN $31.99
UK £19.99

Facebook
9781119179030
USA $21.99
CAN $25.99
UK £16.99

Guitar
9781119293354
USA $24.99
CAN $29.99
UK £17.99

Investing
9781119293347
USA $22.99
CAN $27.99
UK £16.99

Beekeeping
9781119310068
USA $22.99
CAN $27.99
UK £16.99

Digital Photography
9781119235606
USA $24.99
CAN $29.99
UK £17.99

Meditation
9781119251163
USA $24.99
CAN $29.99
UK £17.99

Pregnancy
9781119235491
USA $26.99
CAN $31.99
UK £19.99

Samsung Galaxy S7
9781119279952
USA $24.99
CAN $29.99
UK £17.99

iPhone
9781119283133
USA $24.99
CAN $29.99
UK £17.99

Crocheting
9781119287117
USA $24.99
CAN $29.99
UK £16.99

Nutrition
9781119130246
USA $22.99
CAN $27.99
UK £16.99

PROFESSIONAL DEVELOPMENT

Windows 10
9781119311041
USA $24.99
CAN $29.99
UK £17.99

AutoCAD
9781119255796
USA $39.99
CAN $47.99
UK £27.99

Excel 2016
9781119293439
USA $26.99
CAN $31.99
UK £19.99

QuickBooks 2017
9781119281467
USA $26.99
CAN $31.99
UK £19.99

macOS Sierra
9781119280651
USA $29.99
CAN $35.99
UK £21.99

LinkedIn
9781119251132
USA $24.99
CAN $29.99
UK £17.99

Windows 10 All-in-One
9781119310563
USA $34.00
CAN $41.99
UK £24.99

SharePoint 2016
9781119181705
USA $29.99
CAN $35.99
UK £21.99

Fundamental Analysis
9781119263593
USA $26.99
CAN $31.99
UK £19.99

Networking
9781119257769
USA $29.99
CAN $35.99
UK £21.99

Office 2016
9781119293477
USA $26.99
CAN $31.99
UK £19.99

Office 365
9781119265313
USA $24.99
CAN $29.99
UK £17.99

Salesforce.com
9781119239314
USA $29.99
CAN $35.99
UK £21.99

Coding
9781119293323
USA $29.99
CAN $35.99
UK £21.99

dummies.com

dummies
A Wiley Brand